■■■ Technology & ■■■ Teacher Education

A Guide for Educators and Policymakers

D0780953

Howard D. Mehlinger
Indiana University

Susan M. Powers
Indiana State University

HOUGHTON MIFFLIN COMPANY   Boston   New York

Senior Sponsoring Editor: *Sue Pulvermacher-Alt*
Senior Development Editor: *Lisa Mafrici*
Editorial Development: *Bruce Cantley*
Senior Project Editor: *Christina M. Horn*
Associate Production/Design Coordinator: *Lisa Jelly Smith*
Senior Manufacturing Coordinator: *Marie Barnes*

Credits

Page 48: Figure 2.1 reprinted by permission of Thomas J. Switzer. **Pages 109, 111, 113, 115, 117, 119, 120:** Figures 4.1, 4.2, 4.3, and 4.4 reprinted from *National Educational Technology Standards for Teachers.* NETS Standards, Figure 4.5, and Table 4.1 reprinted from *National Educational Technology Standards for Students.* Copyright © 2000, ISTE (International Society for Technology in Education), 800-336-5191 (U.S. & Canada) or 541-302-3777 (International), iste@iste.org, www.iste.org. All rights reserved. For more information about the NETS Project, contact Lajeane Thomas, Director, NETS Project, 318-257-3923, lthomas@latech.edu. **Page 123:** INTASC Principles reprinted with permission of INTASC. **Page 125, 127:** The Professional Competency Continuum: Professional Skills for the Digital Age Classroom is copyrighted 1999 by the Milken Family Foundation. All rights reserved. The portions of that publication that are included in this book are reprinted by permission. **Pages 192, 196:** Figure 6.1 and 6.2 are copyright © 1998, ISTE (International Society for Technology in Education), 800-336-5191 (U.S. & Canada) or 541-302-3777 (International), iste@iste.org, www.iste.org. All rights reserved. **Pages 202, 206:** Figure 6.3 and ALA Position Statement reprinted with permission of the American Library Association.

Printed in the U.S.A.

Library of Congress Catalog Card Number: 2001131528

ISBN: 0-618-07199-7

1 2 3 4 5 6 7 8 9-FFG-05 04 03 02 01

Contents

Preface

This book is written for educators, policymakers, and others who are passionate about education, who are interested in teacher education, and who believe that good teaching in twenty-first-century schools requires teachers who are competent and comfortable in the use of modern information technology. School systems have committed millions of dollars to hardware and software during the past two decades, but these investments are of little value unless the schools can employ teachers who are capable of making sound judgments about the use of technology and are able to employ it skillfully.

While school systems and other organizations are working hard to meet the training needs of those teachers already in service, teacher education institutions must guarantee schools that all newly employed teachers will be able to use technology well, or the deficiencies in the technology skills of K–12 teachers will be difficult to overcome. Unfortunately, there is a huge gap within the teacher education profession regarding its capability for ensuring technology competence among its graduates. A few teacher education institutions are doing an outstanding job in preparing their students to use technology well; others are doing very little; most are scattered along a continuum between the two extremes.

This book is intended for readers who work in or are concerned about teacher education institutions that are somewhere along the continuum, between the two extremes. Those who teach in schools, colleges, and departments of education where technology is fully integrated into every part of the program are fortunate and will find confirmation for their efforts in this book; those who are associated with teacher education programs that have adopted a wait-and-see attitude toward technology can use the book to see what others are doing and how far they have to travel. This book will be most useful to faculty and administrators who recognize the importance of preparing teachers who can use technology well and are seeking advice for how best to proceed.

This book has been written by two teacher educators who bring very different experiences and training to the task. One of the authors, Howard Mehlinger, is a professor of education and history (emeritus) at Indiana University (IU). From 1981 to 1990 he served as dean of the IU School of Education. Although his training and teaching experience lie outside of technology, during his tenure as dean, he led an effort that resulted in a new state-of-the-art facility for the IU School of Education, enabling it to operate as a showcase for the use of technology in education. The other author, Susan Powers, is an associate professor of education at Indiana State University (ISU). Her doctorate is in instructional technology; an important part of her job is helping teacher educators at ISU integrate technology into their teacher education courses. Together, Powers and Mehlinger provide uncommon perspectives on the problems schools, colleges, and departments of education face as they begin to employ technology in teacher education.

Organization of This Book

This book is structured around nine chapters. Chapter 1 sets forth the problems that schools, colleges, and departments of education (SCDEs) are facing as they seek to employ technology in their teacher education programs. Chapter 2 introduces a self-assessment scheme that SCDEs can employ to evaluate their own progress in using technology for teacher education. This self-assessment scheme, the STaR (School Technology and Readiness) chart, developed by the CEO Forum on Education and Technology, is reprinted both in this chapter and—as a foldout chart—at the end of the book. The chart is a valuable tool that will help SCDEs assess their current status in the integration of technology for teacher preparation, and it will also help guide further development in the use of technology.

Chapter 3 provides alternative approaches for introducing technology to teacher education students. Chapter 4 provides guidelines for integrating technology across the entire teacher education curriculum. Chapter 5 is devoted to the particular technology knowledge and skill requirements expected of special education teachers. Chapter 6 treats the training of lead teachers, technology coordinators, library media specialists, and others who fill technology leadership roles in schools and school systems. Chapter 7 focuses on the technology needs of school administrators and school counselors. Chapter 8 explores how SCDEs can take advantage of distance-learning opportunities for teacher education. And Chapter 9 offers specific suggestions for getting started in transforming the way SCDEs begin to respond to technology across the entire institution.

Each chapter features descriptions of faculty and institutions that are practicing the use of technology in exemplary ways. The examples are drawn from large and small, public and private schools, colleges, and departments of education from all regions of the country. Throughout the book the reader is informed about standards and guidelines that are being employed by accrediting agencies and other organizations that are in the forefront of promoting the use of technology in schools and colleges.

Each chapter opens with a scenario—"Dialogues Within the Academy"—built around lifelike experiences that are faced daily in SCDEs. Each scenario builds upon the preceding one, similar to episodes in a serial. The language throughout the book is informal and nontechnical. The book was written not for "techies" but for people who, although not experts in the use of technology, recognize its importance for teacher education and want to learn what others are doing. Even so, the book contains a glossary of terms that may be unfamiliar to the nontechnology user.

For those readers who are inspired by what they have read and want to go further, we have included an annotated list of resources, containing titles of books, reports, articles, and web sites. In collaboration with Houghton Mifflin, we have also established a web site that will continue to provide up-to-date information relating to technology and teacher education (go to **college.hmco.com** and select **Education**).

Acknowledgments

We wish to express our gratitude to many who have helped us complete this work. We appreciate the dozens of colleagues nationwide who are setting examples for ways that technology can be used productively in teacher education and who allowed us to describe their work. Their names appear throughout the book along with examples of their activities. We were fortunate to secure advice from several remarkable and experienced teacher educators and administrators: Deborah Butler, chair of the Education Department, Wabash College; James Cooper, former dean of the Curry School of Education, University of Virginia; Nancy Farnan, San Diego State University; Allen Glenn, former dean of the College of Education, University of Washington; and Thomas Switzer, dean of the College of Education, University of Northern Iowa, provided suggestions as the project was being planned and reviewed first-draft manuscripts. We are indebted to Professor Christine Bahr for contributing Chapter 5, "Technology for Special Education Teachers." The book is immeasurably better for the special expertise she brought to this topic. We are also grateful for the help we received from Eve Russell, Barbara Frye, and Chris Salmon, who assisted in finding resources and developing the manuscript. And we wish to note the consistently strong support we received from our Houghton Mifflin editors: Bruce Cantley, Christina Horn, Lisa Mafrici, Sue Pulvermacher-Alt, and Loretta Wolozin. They smoothed the path and made the journey seem easy.

And finally, we wish to recognize our spouses—Carolee Mehlinger and Josh Powers—who supported and assisted our efforts in unimaginable ways. We are dedicating the book to our children (Susan's) and grandchildren (Howard's)—Casey, Katlyn, and Koby—who did not contribute a word to the text but who inspire us daily with their love and enthusiasm. They make everything we do worthwhile.

HOWARD D. MEHLINGER
SUSAN M. POWERS

1

The Technology Challenge for Teacher Education

Each chapter in this book opens with a scenario that identifies some of the issues that will be treated in the chapter. The fictitious people who are described in the scenario that follows reappear in subsequent chapters. As a group, the scenarios consist of a series of episodes leading to a conclusion. We call this first episode "Dinner for Eight."

Imagine this scene. The date is October 17, 2000. Eight people, five men and three women, are seated around a table in a popular downtown restaurant in the capital city of a midwestern state. They have just finished dinner.

The eight people could scarcely be called friends; *acquaintances* perhaps is a more accurate description. Each is employed by a college or university within the same state, but they represent eight different institutions—four private and four state supported. It is unlikely that they ever would have dined together if they had not attended the same state education conference earlier in the day and were chosen by those attending the conference to draft an action plan on behalf of the entire group. The dinner was arranged as a first step in deciding what would be done.

The conference had been called jointly by the governor and the commissioner of education. Every teacher education institution in the

1

state—forty-three of them—was invited to send representatives. Nearly all did; some sent three or four.

The purpose of the conference was to allow the governor and the commissioner of education to announce, explain, and justify new legislation that they would be introducing at the forthcoming legislative session beginning in January 2001. Briefly, the legislation would require that every new teacher employed in the public schools of that state demonstrate competence to use computers and other technology sufficient to meet the job requirements of his or her assignment. Those who could not would be denied a teaching license and the opportunity to teach in the state. All current K–12 teachers would be expected to show competence within a three-year period, or their licenses would be revoked and their employment terminated. And, finally, every college professor who was engaged in the preparation of K–12 teachers and administrators would also be required to demonstrate competence in the use of technology appropriate to the courses for students whom they taught. Those who failed to demonstrate technology competence within three years would be denied the opportunity to teach classes taken by those preparing to teach. The college or university could continue to employ the faculty member in some other way, but the person could not teach future teachers.

The governor modeled the proposed legislation after similar legislation enacted a few years earlier in another state. The governor and commissioner justified the importance of the new legislation by arguing that the state had spent millions of dollars to equip school classrooms and had also devoted several million dollars to the in-service education of teachers. While these expenditures were occurring, the teacher education programs continued to graduate new teachers who lacked technology skills appropriate to their assignments. The governor said that this must stop. Although some in-service training would continue to be necessary, the state could no longer afford to retrain those who were insufficiently prepared in their undergraduate programs. He said it was obvious to him, and to a majority of those in the legislature, that new technology could contribute powerfully to helping students learn. The state was willing to do its part; it was now time for teacher educators to accept their responsibility.

Although the new legislation would be introduced in January, the education commissioner said there was still an opportunity to help shape the legislation in order to make it as effective as possible. There was much they did not know about teacher education, and they wanted the advice of the assembled group. Because they wanted the support of the teacher education profession in implementing the legislation, they had called the meeting to seek their advice so that the legislation would be as effective as possible. The governor and commissioner agreed that if the advice were to be of maximum value, it should come in the form of a brief written report and be in their hands by the end of November. The dinner meeting was called to consider how the forty-three teacher education programs in this state ought to respond to the governor's invitation.

Throughout dinner, the group had discussed the proposed legislation. A few were angry. Bill, a professor of educational foundations at a state university who chairs the policy council in his school of education, felt insulted by both the governor and the commissioner of education. He was unsure that the colleges and universities ought even to cooperate with these political leaders. His views were similar to those of Lee, the provost of a small, distinguished liberal arts college that graduates only a few teachers each year. Lee said that state government had no right to dictate policy to a private university. He was not certain that his college would conform to state policy.

Others may have been annoyed but less angered by what they had heard from the governor. Mark, the career placement officer for his private college, said that his college had little choice but to cooperate. Private college or not, the state retained the right to license teachers and accredit teacher education institutions; some students would no longer attend his college if a teaching career were denied to them. Cathy, a professor of instructional technology at one of the state universities, was perhaps the most upbeat among the group. Although she agreed that it was somewhat demeaning to have been put on the spot by the governor and the commissioner of education, she thought the legislation could be turned to the advantage of teacher education programs. Carlos, dean of education at the largest of the state universities, agreed. He pointed out that it was the first time in his memory that he had ever been consulted about pending legislation that could affect teacher education. The others at the dinner—Janatha, chair of the education department of a small liberal arts college; Tom, a technology coordinator for a small private university; and Yunsun, the tech coordinator for a school of education in a midsize state university— were less talkative about their feelings. They did not seem especially angry or annoyed by the afternoon conference, but they had many questions about the best way to respond. Let's join the conversation.

Bill: What makes me angry is that some politician would imply that I am not a good teacher because I do not use technology in my classes!

Cathy: I don't think the governor said you were a bad teacher. He simply stated that computers and other technologies are a fact of life in American society today. We expect students to learn to use computers in school, and this means that their teachers must be competent in their use and that those who teach teachers will have to become role models in the use of technology. We have long said that teachers teach the way they are taught. If we want teachers to use technology well, we must use it in our classes also.

Bill: Look, I am not against teachers' learning to use computers; it's important, perhaps even necessary. We hire people like you, Cathy, to teach them what they need to know. But colleges and universities hire specialists; we don't all do the same things. You teach technology to them; I'll teach them philosophy. What is wrong with that?

Cathy: What is wrong is that they need to use technology tools in their educational philosophy classes in order to make them more powerful learners of philosophy. I can teach them how to use a computer, but they need to use it in the context of the subjects they are studying.

Lee: Well, I am a historian, and when I am not doing my provost duties, I teach American history. Although I don't teach education courses, some of my history students expect to be teachers. If this legislation passes as it is proposed, I will have to stop teaching my courses, or actively use technology in my classes, or our college can drop teacher education altogether. I don't like any of those choices.

Janatha: I am glad that you have raised this point. In our college, only three of us are listed as members of the education faculty. We teach all of the foundation courses, but the content and methods courses are taught by the liberal arts faculty. I am proud of our small program, but I see no easy way to bring on board all of the faculty outside the department of education.

Tom: Don't give up so quickly. As you know, I provide tech support for the entire private college where I work, and I can tell you that many of the humanities and science faculty are well ahead of the education faculty in their use of technology. Sure, there are a few faculty who will have nothing at all to do with computers, but they are a minority and shrinking in number every year. At our college, if you don't use e-mail, you don't know what is going on. Many of the faculty communicate with their students using e-mail, and a few have put their courses on the Web. I don't think the situation is hopeless. It is mainly a matter of resources: faculty will do more if we provide good equipment, prompt tech support, and instruction in new applications when they seek it. I think we should focus on the question of what resources will be needed if we are to fulfill the governor's expectations.

Yunsun: I support Tom's position. I don't provide tech support for an entire university as he does; my job is to support the seventy-five faculty and ninety staff who compose our school of education. I've seen a lot of change over the past five years. True, there are still some faculty fighting the technology, but most want more help and support than we can provide. Furthermore, many of the new faculty we have hired have rather expensive tastes as they relate to technology. Our budget is stretched to the limit to provide the equipment, software, tech support, and training to meet current demand. Who is going to pay for all of this?

Carlos: This is my major concern. I don't doubt the need for solid technology preparation for all of our teacher education graduates, but the cost is enormous. We maintain five hundred computers, support three distance-learning studios, and carry primary responsibility for the operation of data, voice, and video networks within our building. This requires the full attention of six technical experts, and they can't keep up with the demands on their time. We try to upgrade about one-third of the equipment each year; we also offer free training to faculty and staff on new software applications. Fully 10 percent of our budget is devoted to technology, but where are the savings to offset these expenses?

Yunsun: There are no savings, at least to this date. But no teacher training institution can be modern unless it provides the kind of equipment and services you described. It will not be cheap to support a teacher education program that takes full advantage of the available technology, but we have no choice if we want to remain in the business of preparing teachers.

Cathy: I agree with Yunsun that there are no obvious savings yet, but I'm not ready to give up on the productivity issue. For example, technology enables schools and departments of education to provide services we could not otherwise have offered. Last week, for example, I brought a guest lecturer into my class via interactive video. The cost was trivial compared to what it would have been if it had been necessary for me to pay his honorarium, travel, and lodging to bring him physically into my class.

Bill: Okay; that sounds like a good use of the technology, but frankly, I worry that the technology is going to get in the way of good instruction. I am at my best when I am in front of twenty-five students; I can engage in dialogue with them; I can tell when they are having trouble and alter my instruction accordingly. I don't need a machine to help me do what I do best.

Cathy: I presume you are a good teacher, Bill, and perhaps you do not need any technology beyond books and chalkboards. However, today's students are accustomed to obtaining much of their information electronically. Professors who don't take advantage of modern technology may appear out of step with the times. I also imagine that students are expected to produce research papers or projects for your courses. The new technologies are enormously helpful for supporting inquiries and collaboration among students and presenting results. Finally, our students at state universities may be lucky to have classes of twenty-five or so when they become upperclassmen, but in their first two years, they are more likely to be assigned to classes of two hundred or more with discussion sessions led by graduate students. There are many ways to use technology to strengthen instruction in large sections.

Janatha: I don't deny what you have said, Cathy, but I think it misses the main point about technology. Technology can serve as the catalyst for changing the way we teach. For decades, we have claimed an interest in adapting instruction to fit the learning styles of individual learners; technology can help us do this. We know a lot about how adults learn and can use technology to provide the conditions in which people learn better. Unfortunately, we still have too many faculty who equate their "professing" with student learning. Telling is not teaching; listening is not learning. The best college instruction I received was in graduate seminars where the students were expected to carry most of the instructional load and the faculty served as advisers, pointing out resources and challenging our interpretations. We can use the technology to change the way faculty relate to their students. This is what excites me about the new technology.

Bill: I don't think I like what I am hearing. It sounds as though we must adapt our teaching to fit the machines. This is exactly what I fear: dehumanizing the educational process and turning instruction over to machines.

Cathy: I don't think you were listening carefully, Bill. I suppose you can teach as you always have, and the technology may be of assistance. However, every other institution in our society is being affected by computers, video, and other electronic technology. Why do we think that teacher education can remain an island unaffected by the forces transforming society? How we use these technologies is our decision to make—and if I understood the governor and commissioner of education, they are seeking our help in sorting out the details. For example, if we believe that K–12 teachers will need to use technology to make effective presentations, we must use these technologies to make effective presentations of our own. Furthermore, we should ask students to present the results of their studies to us and their classmates by using these technologies. I can teach them to use PowerPoint in my instructional technology course, but if they never see it used by other professors and are never asked to employ it when giving a report, their skill and knowledge will deteriorate.

Tom: And if you accept modern learning theories about collaborative learning, then using electronic networks to support collaborative learning makes a lot of sense.

Lee: I already use the Web when I am conducting my own research, and increasingly my students are using web sources to track down data for their reports. I can't imagine historical research today that ignores these opportunities to tap archives and databases worldwide. I guess I could be more explicit about the use of the Web for research. Is this going to satisfy the governor?

Carlos: I heard the governor and commissioner of education asking us what we think should be done with regard to technology in education. The first step is for us to think about what our students need to know if they are to be effective teachers with technology. We should think broadly about experiences our students should have throughout the teacher education program and not assume that they must have every one of these experiences in every class. Our goal should be for our teacher education faculty to have the technology competence to achieve their instructional goals in their classes, using technology where appropriate.

Tom: It sounds to me as if there is a need for collaboration across the entire faculty; professors are not very good at this. I can't bear the thought of more committee meetings!

Janatha: I know, but there are forces driving us to collaborate on technology. Although my small teacher education program is not approved by NCATE [National Council for the Accreditation of Teacher Education], the same standards for meeting NCATE accreditation are mandated by the state department of education. And the new NCATE standards require that we pay a lot of attention to technology. I fully intend to use the NCATE and state department of education standards and the new legislation as the occasion for our department of education to envision where it wants to be in five years, using technology.

Mark: I think you are right, Janatha. I fear my colleagues are not yet ready to act as you have done, and I worry about the consequences for our teacher education graduates. I have been told by some superintendents that they will no longer hire our graduates if they don't show greater technology proficiency. My worry is that we won't fully accept the message until it is too late, and some of our graduates will be unable to compete for the best jobs and will be forced to choose among less desirable positions.

Carlos: Maybe we have accomplished all we can tonight. Let's return to our campuses and share some of these ideas with our colleagues. Then let's meet in two weeks on my campus, if you are agreeable. Perhaps we can write a report that will advance our interests while helping the governor with his agenda.

INTRODUCTION

This book is about the relationship of technology to teacher education. It is intended for teacher educators and others who care deeply about teacher education. The focus is on the responsibility that American colleges and universities bear for preparing classroom teachers who can use technology effectively for instruction. Unfortunately, not all colleges and universities today are meeting the needs of schools for well-prepared teachers. We shall describe the teacher preparation deficiencies we have found, explain why they exist, and offer examples of schools and colleges that are acting to remedy these problems. Because we shall be using the terms *teacher education* and *technology* throughout the book, it is important to define these terms at the outset.

What Is Teacher Education?

Teacher education may be used to describe the education teachers receive at any time in their careers. Frequently terms such as *preservice teacher education* and *in-service teacher education* (also called *professional development*) are used to distinguish the time in a teacher's career when the training occurs. In general, this book focuses on preservice teacher education: the formal preparation a prospective teacher receives before obtaining a teacher license and beginning service as a full-time teacher. Although we recognize the importance of in-service teacher education and the professional development of teachers, much has already been written about this topic, and much more is being done to address issues of professional development. Better preservice teacher education that meets schools' needs for technology-proficient teachers will reduce the urgency for certain kinds of professional development aimed at remediating technology deficiencies of beginning teachers.

Preservice teacher education is a pluralistic enterprise in the United States. It can be offered mainly to undergraduates, limited to those with baccalaureate degrees, or provided to both. It appears as an academic major in some colleges and an academic minor in others. Approximately thirteen hundred American institutions of higher education prepare teachers. Some are private, others public; some are small, others huge—but they all share a responsibility for preparing teachers for successful service in K–12 classrooms.

There are also differences in how teacher education is organized among various colleges and universities. In some cases, teacher education is the principal business of an entire college or department; in other cases, it is only one activity of a college.

For labeling purposes we shall use the term *schools, colleges, and departments of education* (SCDE) when referring broadly to the range of organizational forms that are responsible for preparing teachers.

What Is Technology?

One widely accepted definition of *technology* is the application of science to industry, but this is not what people are thinking about when they discuss technology in schools. Often *technology* is a term that refers to computers and the peripheral hardware and software that support their use. Others are quick to add other equipment, such as VCRs, overhead projectors, and even textbooks and chalkboards. The Association for Educational Communications and Technology (1996) defines instructional technology as follows: "Instructional Technology is a complex, integrated process involving people, procedures, ideas, devices, and organization for analyzing problems, and devising, implementing, evaluating, and managing solutions to these problems, in situations in which learning is purposive and controlled" (p. 4). Although it is useful to think of technology as a process rather than as an object, unfortunately in the minds of most educators and laypeople, technology consists of *things* rather than ways of using things.

In general, we shall use the term *technology* to stand for relatively new electronic media, such as computers and video and the associated hardware, networks, and software that enable them to function. This is what most people have in mind when they discuss the use of technology in schools. We are also aware that technology can be employed in many different ways, including support of administrative practices, for personal productivity, and to assist teaching and learning. Our primary concern is for the ways that technology can enhance instruction.

We wish to declare at the outset that we are not technology zealots. We do not promote technology simply to see its use expand. We know there is no wisdom in the machine itself. Whether technology is used well or poorly depends on the user. However, we believe that technology can make teaching and learning more available, effective, and interesting; educators need to become competent in the use of technology to gain these advantages.

THREE ASSUMPTIONS
▨ ▨ ▬ ■ THAT GUIDE THIS BOOK ■ ▬ ▨ ▨

In writing this book we have been guided by three assumptions:

1. Technology will have (is having, has had, can have) an impact on how we teach and learn.

2. Technology will change (can change) the ways SCDEs conduct their work.

3. Technology will have (is having) an impact on the role and performance of education professors.

Because we refer to these assumptions at various points throughout the book, we elaborate on them here. Note that in stating these assumptions, we are indecisive about the appropriate verb form. This is because the verb form that fits best varies greatly among and within particular institutions.

Technology Will Have (Is Having, Has Had, Can Have) an Impact on How We Teach and Learn

We provide four choices of verb form here. We believe that whichever form is selected, the statement is true. In some cases, technology has already had an impact on how teachers instruct and students learn; in other cases, the impact lies in the future; in still other cases, the potential is there but only if technology is employed appropriately. Note that we have rejected the opposite assumption: that technology will have *no* impact on teaching and learning.

Our confidence in the impact that technology will have on teaching and learning is not driven by blind faith in it. It is a result of a simple, sociological observation: Computers and other information technologies are transforming nearly every aspect of society. American education may have responded less rapidly to these technologies than have business or some other sectors of society, yet the impact of these technologies on schools and colleges is already obvious and is certain to grow. The question is no longer whether technology will have an impact on teaching and learning; the interesting questions are what that impact will be, how rapidly it will grow, and whether the results will be beneficial to individuals, schools and colleges, and society as a whole.

This topic of how technology will have an impact on teaching and learning may be interesting to many, but for professional educators it is a fundamental issue, lying at the very core of their professional lives. For example, SCDE faculty view themselves as carriers of the education culture. Although their philosophies may differ and they frequently disagree over particular matters ranging from federal education policy to the best method for teaching reading, education faculty believe that they are the principal spokespersons for and the experts on education— more than any other group in society. All efforts to transform the way SCDEs treat technology must begin with this understanding.

A portion of teacher educators' resistance to technology is prompted by their suspicion that technology will alter education in undesirable ways. For example, some fear that technology will dehumanize education by handing over to a machine tasks that should be done by an understanding teacher. We understand this fear and do not dismiss it as foolish or trivial. There are instances in which teachers have turned over control of instruction to machines, confident the machines could do it better. But we approach this fear in the same way we think about technology and medicine. We want caring doctors; we do not wish to be treated by machines. On the other hand, we want caring doctors to use the very latest technology to diagnose our illnesses and to treat us appropriately. In schools and colleges, those preparing to teach must become aware of and skilled in using every technology that can advance each individual's ability to grow intellectually, psychologically, and socially. Not to know what technology is available to assist children educationally and not to use it thoughtfully is evidence of instructional malpractice.

Some educators are cautious about the effects of technology on children. For example, they wonder what effect technology will have on students' willingness to recall information when information is so easily stored electronically. What will be the long-term effect on students' willingness to persist in solving puzzling problems when a computer may quickly provide the necessary calculations? These are reasonable concerns; however, we cannot stop the infusion of technology into everyday life. Socrates once deplored the use of note taking and preserving manuscripts because he felt it would destroy people's ability to recall information. Technology will undoubtedly alter the way schooling is done. Our job as educators is to use these technologies to enhance our human capacities, not preserve a skill that was required in the absence of technology. One of the ways in which humans are different from others in the animal kingdom is our unique capacity to use technology to advance our lives.

Some educators are repelled because they believe that technology will be used to support theories of learning they find objectionable. The first development of computerized classroom applications occurred at the same time that behavioral views of learning were dominant. **Programmed learning**, originally designed for paper products, was easily adapted to computers. It is not surprising that many computer-assisted instruction (CAI) programs are designed to fit behavioral theories. The technical limits on computers at that time also accommodated linear programs. This led to the development of software packages that often stressed drill and practice exercises aimed at helping children learn and recall specific kinds of information and skills.

Constructivists—those who believe that learning is an active process requiring the learner to "construct" his or her own understanding of the topic by fitting new content into the learner's prior experience and knowledge base—are often dismayed by CAI programs. They notice that such programs are frequently used with low-achieving students, who may also be denied opportunities to participate in programs that stress higher-order thinking skills. The critics all too often blame the technology rather than those who prescribe instruction.

We do not believe that technology is limited to those who subscribe to behavioral theories of learning. Many innovative programs today are nonlinear, use metaphors, emphasize graphic organizers, place students into decision-making roles, and are designed with the information landscape and cognitive load in mind. These are some of the building blocks of learning as understood by constructivists.

Technology can be used to fit more than one theory of learning. Unfortunately, critics of technology have assumed that using computers or other information technology presumes a behavioral approach. The technology itself is neutral; it is what the developer and/or the teacher choose to make of it that determines its educational use and value. Throughout this book, you will find instances of technology being used to support a wide range of learning theories.

Technology Will Change (Can Change) the Ways SCDEs Conduct Their Work

In the past, SCDEs have been treated as cash cows for colleges and universities. Very little investment was necessary to start and maintain a teacher education program, whether in a small college or a large university. Most of the courses students needed to meet state certification were already provided by the liberal arts and science faculty; K–12 teachers could be hired to provide the methods and practicum courses; and graduate students could supervise student teachers in the field. The cost-benefit ratio was clearly advantageous.

If teacher education programs were required to integrate technology across the teacher education curriculum in order to be accredited, the economics of teacher education could be affected. And if school superintendents were to reject teacher candidates who lack knowledge and skills with computers and other technology, a college or university may decide that it may be best to abandon teacher education altogether as an academic major rather than make the investments necessary to continue in the field. It is possible that the number of institutions preparing teachers could shrink to half the current number.

On the other hand, technology may provide the opportunity for some institutions to add teacher education to their offerings. Alternative teacher education programs that are delivered mainly in a distance-learning mode exist today. Colleges and universities that have been unable to offer teacher education as an option because they could not attract and retain the specialized faculty they needed can now find these faculty on the Web. One can imagine a "National Pedagogy University" that prepares teachers, just as there is now a National Technological University, preparing engineers at a distance and drawing on professors based at leading engineering universities across the nation. Some studies have shown that videotape and film of classroom practice is as effective as transporting students to classrooms for direct observation to fulfill practicum requirements. Although student teaching would require the collaboration of public schools, some American students now fulfill a semester of student teaching at sites remote from their home campuses—even overseas. It should not be difficult to arrange equally satisfactory, supervised teaching sites for teacher candidates who are earning degrees electronically and place them in classrooms where they can be mentored by master teachers who use technology. Such arrangements could lead to a proliferation of teacher education programs, led by institutions with vision, leadership, and technology.

It is also possible, and perhaps even likely, that technology will be used as a catalyst for wide-ranging changes in teacher education programs. This is what has occurred at the Bank Street Graduate School of Education in New York City. The faculty of this widely respected college, led by Dean Patricia Wasley, decided that the college would have to do more to prepare their students to use technology well. Discussions among the faculty regarding ways to integrate technology into their courses led to far-reaching and vigorous debates about the existing curriculum and how it was delivered to students. The result is a completely revamped teacher education program, modern in approach, calling for much greater collaboration and communication among faculty. The revamped program is *not* about technology; its focus, as before, is on those things teachers must know, believe, and be able to do for success in K–12 classrooms. But now technology is embedded throughout the program, not merely a special course.

What has been done at Bank Street College is very difficult to accomplish in higher education. Change is very slow in higher education. Individual professors may make substantial changes in their courses, but there is little chance that such changes will ripple throughout the entire teacher education program.

SCDEs appear to be operating at one of three levels with regard to technology: literacy, integration, and transformation. The literacy level, where a majority of SCDEs are today, calls for an SCDE to employ one or more experts to provide technology instruction through special courses and in special facilities (computer labs) to ensure that all students preparing to teach have acquired at least a minimal competence in the use of technology. This level does not require changes in any of the other teacher education courses, nor is it necessary for other teacher education faculty to be competent in the use of technology.

The integration level is demonstrated by SCDEs that attempt to employ technology across the entire teacher education program. All teacher education faculty are expected to employ technology appropriately in their courses. While a SCDE may continue to provide a basic introductory technology course, students are expected to add to their technology knowledge and skills as they proceed through the curriculum. At the integration stage, the teacher education program remains fundamentally stable in terms of its content. What has changed is the addition of technology that is pervasive throughout the curriculum.

At the transformation level, SCDEs have begun to use the technology to change the content and delivery of teacher education. Technology is no longer an appendage or a special feature of teacher education. Teacher education itself has been transformed as a result of technology. Few, if any, SCDEs operate at the transformation stage today.

Occasionally a major technological advance occurs in a society that makes it very difficult for previously successful institutions to survive unless they change. Computers and other modern technology may eventually have such an impact on teacher education. Some teacher education programs will be driven out of business, others may appear that did not exist previously, and some may take advantage of the technology to restructure themselves into very different institutions, more in touch with the times in which they are preparing teachers.

Technology Will Have (Is Having) an Impact on the Role and Performance of Education Professors

Traditionally a professor's role has been divided into three parts: teaching, research, and service. The amount of time and effort that is devoted to each of these three activities varies across institutions, within departments, and across the life span of an individual professor. Nevertheless, despite these variations, all professors are likely to spend some portion of their time on each.

Of the three activities, faculty research has been more affected by technology than have the other two. Most education faculty are accustomed to using computer-based web searches, tapping electronic libraries and databases, and calling on computers to tabulate and organize research data. When their research is finished, they send their manuscripts to publishers on disks and present their findings at professional meetings using overhead projectors or PowerPoint slides, and they participate in web-based conferences. Professors who are uncomfortable with technology to support their research know that they are disadvantaged when compared to colleagues who have these skills. Computer-related research skills have become a requirement for graduate study and the training of the next generation's faculty, much as foreign language was in the past.

Most professors do not feel the same urgency regarding the use of technology to support instruction. Many are willing to be judged as "old-fashioned" or "traditional" in their teaching, when they would be embarrassed if such terms were applied to their research. There are several reasons for this anomaly:

- In some cases, especially where teaching loads are heavy, professors lack the time and resources to prepare for their classes, whereas they have more time to prepare for and execute their research.

- The research performance is usually before peers; a teaching performance is given before those who may be more easily impressed by less than an optimum performance.

- Much investment has already been made in existing courses and lectures; investing time in the reinvention of a course in order to employ technology, when the existing course or lecture may be satisfactory for another year, may be difficult to justify in the minds of some professors.

- Faculty who avoid using technology are teaching as they were once taught; this is why it is difficult to break a pattern of instruction that has existed for generations.

- Some faculty have ideological reasons for avoiding technology; for example, they may argue that the technology interferes with the teacher-student relationship or that it may "dehumanize" what should be a very personal relationship.

One can be very suspicious of all of these claims, and especially the last one. We have seen no evidence that faculty who use technology for instruction are judged as less human by their students than are faculty who eschew technology altogether.

We are undoubtedly in a transition period in the transformation of the professor's role with technology. In part, it is a generational issue. As skills in the use of technology develop in K–12 schools and higher education, young faculty will be comfortable with the technology and will use it routinely for personal productivity purposes. But will they use it for instruction without role models of their own? For faculty for whom the learning curve is very steep, they will adapt and use what seems most valuable to them. Few faculty resist the use of e-mail once it is available to them, any more than they would reject the use of telephones or automobiles. As computers become easier to use and more reliable, greater numbers of faculty will embrace them.

What if faculty had complete access to whatever technology they wished and were completely skilled in its use? Would their instructional role change? It is difficult to speak confidently, but information technology has the capacity to entice learners, empower them in the pursuit of knowledge, and support communication among learners and between learners and instructors. There is no reason to believe that faculty would fail to use this power once they were comfortable with it.

In an institution where most, if not all, members of the faculty are using technology for instruction, the role of a faculty member will change. When students are able to consult experts worldwide, faculty will no longer be seen as the only content experts. Although instructors will still bear major responsibility for structuring the course of study, students will gain greater freedom in pursuing topics of their own choice and at a pace that fits their schedules. Professors may have more rather than less contact with students, but increasingly the contact will be mediated rather than face to face. Professors will make greater use of content experts by using distance-learning devices. In turn, they will find themselves in demand to speak to classes at other institutions.

Professors will put their courses on the Web, where not only their own students but others can have access to their instructional ideas, reading lists, and projects. Professors will co-teach courses with professors on other campuses and continue to "meet" their classes while away from the campus. All of these possibilities will be afforded by distance-learning technology.

The fact that students have as much access to sources as do professors will also alter the relationship between professors and students. Information sources are so varied and rich that no professor can be confident that he or she has searched them all. The opportunity will be greater than ever for professors to be learners and students to become teachers.

With regard to their service role, faculty members will find their work as committee members on a campus, as officers in professional associations, as members of editorial boards, and in many other service roles greatly enhanced by computers and other media. They can review dossiers, manuscripts, and proposals that are delivered to them electronically and returned in the same manner without depending on the vagaries of the postal service. They can interview candidates and conduct committee meetings from their own offices. They can make themselves more available to schools, using distance-learning technologies, on-line chats, and other means of communication. In many ways, the professor's service role has already begun to change and will change even more in the future.

HOW SCDES ARE HANDLING THE INCREASED ROLE OF TECHNOLOGY

The dialogue in the scenario that opened this chapter was hypothetical but not fanciful. State governments have passed legislation similar to that described in the scenario; proposals for similar legislation have surfaced in other states and will in some cases become law. Nor were the attitudes of the eight participants farfetched. We have all been in meetings where similar opinions were shared.

What are SCDEs doing to prepare teachers to work in technology-enriched classrooms? This question is not easy to answer. Approximately thirteen hundred institutions of higher education prepare teachers in the United States. They are a diverse group, varying greatly in size, the number of teachers they prepare, their institutional mission, and whether they are public or private institutions. The way each responds to the technology education challenge is affected by their own institutional setting; nevertheless, we can draw some general conclusions.

What the Research Says

In 1996, Jerry W. Willis and I (Howard) published a review of research on the status of educational technology within teacher education that summarized nearly three hundred research articles and reports, most of them published between 1987 and 1995. The review covered a range of research topics relating to the use of technology in teacher education—for example:

- The amount of technology instruction that teacher education students typically receive
- The ways such instruction is provided
- The level of confidence that teacher education graduates have in their technology competence
- Obstacles confronting SCDEs in increasing their own use of technology
- The relationship between preparing teachers to use technology and theories of teaching and learning

Our overarching conclusion, after reviewing all of this research literature, was, "Most preservice teachers know very little about effective use of technology in education and leaders believe there is a pressing need to increase substantially the amount and quality of instruction teachers receive about technology. The idea may be expressed aggressively, assertively, or in more subtle forms, but the virtual universal conclusion is that teacher education, particularly preservice, is not preparing educators to work in a technology-enriched classroom" (Willis and Mehlinger, 1996, p. 978).

Since this review appeared, the purchase of computers and other electronic devices has continued to grow in elementary and secondary schools. The ratio of students to computers was estimated to be 5.7 students for each computer in 1999; in the same year, more than 90 percent of the schools had at least one Internet connection (Technology Counts, 1999, p. 64). Have SCDEs picked up the pace in preparing teachers who are technologically competent for teaching in elementary and secondary schools?

Three National Surveys and a Task Force Report

Three national surveys have been conducted since 1996 to determine what SCDEs are doing to prepare teachers to use technology effectively. These surveys were conducted by the American Association of Colleges of Teacher Education (AACTE), the Regional Technology in Education Consortia (RTEC), and the Milken Exchange on Education Technology. In addition, in 1997, the NCATE published a report by its Task Force on Technology and Teacher Education, *Technology and the New Professional Teacher: Preparing for the 21st Century Classroom*. A brief review of the findings from the three surveys and the task force report provides clues to the present situation.

NCATE Task Force Report. This report is relatively critical of teacher education programs. In answer to the question, "To what degree are higher education institutions meeting their responsibility for preparing tomorrow's classroom teachers?" the report responded:

> Bluntly, a majority of teacher preparation programs are falling far short of what needs to be done. Not using technology much in their own research and teaching, teacher education faculty have insufficient understanding of the demands on classroom teachers to incorporate technology into their teaching. Many do not fully appreciate the impact technology is having on the way work is accomplished. They undervalue the significance of technology and treat it merely as another topic about which teachers should be informed. As a result, colleges and universities are making the same mistake that was made by P–12 schools; they treat "technology" as a special addition to the teacher education curriculum—requiring specially prepared faculty and specially equipped classrooms—but not a topic that

needs to be incorporated across the entire teacher education program. Consequently, teachers-in-training are provided instruction in "computer literacy" and are shown examples of computer software, but they rarely are required to apply technology in their courses and are denied role models of faculty employing technology in their own work. (NCATE, 1997, p. 6)

AACTE Survey. The critique contained in the NCATE report is only partially supported by survey results. For example, a technology survey conducted by the AACTE and NCATE in 1996 found widespread use of technology by faculty in the 466 institutions that responded to the survey. It was reported that nearly half of SCDE faculty (45 percent) used computers, televisions, and VCRs "regularly" as an instructional tool in class; 69 percent of SCDE students demonstrated the use of at least one technology both on campus and during student teaching; and 57 percent of SCDE students had access to the most advanced electronic technologies and software applications (Persichitte, Tharp, & Caffarella, 1997).

Drawing on these and other data from the survey, AACTE published a news brief in November 1997 aimed at destroying three common myths about teacher education and technology: that preservice students are taught only basic uses of technology, which will not have an impact on K–12 classroom instruction; that professors do not use technology but rather just talk with chalk; and that SCDEs have little or no technology due to a lack of resources (AACTE, 1997, pp. 1–4).

However mythical these statements may be, they persist. A belief that many teacher education programs fail to use technology effectively for instructional purposes was the justification for the U.S. Department of Education decision to spend approximately $75 million in fiscal year 1999 to fund 225 proposals submitted by consortia to improve the capacity of teacher education programs to use technology. Of this number, 138 grants, called capacity-building grants, went to institutions that had done little or nothing with technology to that date. Approximately 600 institutions competed for this support. Subsequent competitions were held for fiscal years 2000 and 2001. The interest shown by higher education institutions in this grant competition implies that there is substantial room for progress in the use of technology for teacher education.

RTEC Study. In the mid-1990s, Congress authorized funding for six regional consortia that were to provide help to schools and colleges in their regions seeking to make better use of technology. (In 2000, the number grew from six to ten.) The program is called Regional Technology in Education Consortia (RTEC), and each of the six consortia has its own name. For example, the RTEC whose headquarters is at the North Central Regional Educational Laboratory is called the North Central Regional Technology Education Consortium.

In 1997, five of the six RTECs employed Research Partnerships, an independent marketing research firm, to conduct telephone interviews with SCDE deans and department chairs. This study was directed at obtaining information about the status of computer and technology in teacher education programs and the impact that standards of the NCATE and International Society for Technology in Education (**ISTE**) were having on technology applications in teacher education courses.

The survey found that the vast majority of teacher education institutions (72 percent) offer separate technology courses as well and integrate technology into other courses; only 7 percent reported that they relied solely on separate technology courses. Nevertheless, the results showed that fewer than half of the students (48 percent) among the SCDEs surveyed understood the uses of technology to improve instruction, and only 43 percent were able to integrate technology into teaching. When survey respondents were asked what barriers might exist in efforts to comply with NCATE standards, the need for more and better trained faculty (46 percent) and lack of equipment and funds to purchase hardware and software (42 percent) were most frequently mentioned. Thus, this survey uncovered substantial deficiencies in technology implementation (RTEC Consortia, 1998, pp. 7, 9, 27).

ISTE Survey. In spring 1998, the Milken Exchange on Education Technology commissioned ISTE to survey SCDEs in the United States. ISTE developed a thirty-two-item survey that was sent to 1,326 institutions. By October, ISTE had received completed surveys from 416 institutions, about a third of the institutions preparing teachers.

There were a number of findings:

1. Most institutions report that their technology infrastructure is adequate or better in terms of carrying out their current programs. About a third feel their programs are limited by deficiencies in their IT [instructional technology] facilities.

2. Faculty IT skills tend to be comparable to the IT skills of the students they teach; however, most faculty do not model use of those IT skills in teaching.

3. Distance education and computer-assisted instruction currently affect only a small proportion of students in teacher training institutions.

4. Most programs do not have a written, funded, regularly updated technology plan. The pressure of a technology plan has a positive, but low, correlation with other measures of capacity.

5. Most institutions report that IT is available in the K–12 classrooms where student teachers get their field experience; however, most student teachers do not routinely use technology during field experience and do not work under master teachers and supervisors who can advise them on IT use.

6. The number of hours of IT instruction integrated into the courses has a moderate correlation with other scores on the survey; however, the number of hours of formal IT instruction does not. (Moursund & Bielefeldt, 1998, p. 21)

This list shows that use of technology in the classroom by those preparing to teach is not closely correlated with the number of hours taken in courses devoted to technology. There is some correlation between their use of technology and learning about technology through other teacher education courses they are required to take.

What Is Going on Here? Interpreting the Findings

There appear to be discrepancies in the data. What are we to believe? Are SCDEs providing adequate instruction in the educational use of technology—or not?

The most reasonable answer is that some SCDEs are undoubtedly doing a very good job, a few are shirking their responsibility and are miseducating students to be teachers in modern classrooms, and the majority lie somewhere along the continuum between the two extremes. Whatever the exact number of prospective teachers may be who are gaining a good education in the use of technology, we think it is scandalous that any prospective teacher is being denied the opportunity to gain knowledge and skill to use technology effectively in the classroom.

Those who wish to praise SCDEs point out that nearly 100 percent of those preparing to teach are provided some kind of instruction relating to technology, either in a required course (approximately 80 percent) or by experiencing technology through other teacher education courses. (See Chapters 3 and 4 for a detailed explanation of these two approaches.) We are cautious about the significance to attach to such data. What is the content of the three-credit course? What kinds of experiences are provided to students in their other courses? There is little information from the surveys to answer these questions. In the past, the three-credit-hour, required course was largely devoted to computer fundamentals: word processing, spreadsheets, e-mail, and so forth—the kind of knowledge and computer skill that should be expected of all college graduates, if not high school graduates. Although all teachers need to know how to use these productivity tools, they also need to know how to use the computer as an instructional tool. Where are they acquiring this skill? The survey data are unclear.

In the AACTE survey, respondents were asked to judge the frequency with which technology was used by SCDE faculty. They were given four choices: "The faculty regularly uses computers, television and VCRs as interactive instructional tools during class periods; The faculty occasionally uses some electronic technology to present information during class periods; The faculty does not use electronic technology during class periods; Unknown." The results of the survey were that 45 percent of the institutions reported "regular use" of technology, 53 percent "occasional use," and 1 percent "do not use." The survey was completed by one institutional representative (dean, department chair, faculty member, instructional technology specialist) for the entire institution. Who would report "no use"? What do "regular" and "occasional" mean when applied to the entire faculty? If most faculty use a VCR at some time or another, is this "regular use"? The way in which the survey was completed makes it difficult to know. Here too the data are insufficient to answer these and other questions.

What do we think? From the data and from many visits to SCDEs, we think:

- Almost all SCDE institutions recognize a responsibility to provide instruction in the classroom use of technology.

- Most depend on a required course in the use of a computer to meet their obligation to students and in some cases satisfy state license requirements.

- Most believe that their efforts fall short of what is required.

- Nearly all teacher education faculty use technology but primarily for personal productivity purposes, not as a classroom tool.

- Some faculty are threatened by the demand to use technology for instruction; their concerns inhibit the ability of SCDEs to advance quickly.

- Adequate infrastructure, hardware, and software remain important issues, but they are less significant today than the need for faculty development, faculty support, and curriculum modification.

WHAT OBSTACLES MUST BE OVERCOME IF SCDES ARE TO EMPLOY TECHNOLOGY SUCCESSFULLY?

If the demand for teachers who can incorporate technology into their classroom instruction is great and the advantages to teacher education faculty who can use technology are well known, why are SCDEs not responding to the demand that they integrate technology across the teacher education curriculum?

The answer is that there are obstacles: a lack of vision, absence of planning, insufficient support for experimentation, weak infrastructure, poor access to computers and other technology, lack of incentives, weak technical support, insufficient professional development, and lack of time and money.

Lack of Vision

A vision is a conception of what is possible. A vision statement for technology and teacher education is a description of a teacher education program that is taking full advantage of technology. It is rare to find a teacher education program that includes technology in its vision of what it wants to become and how it wishes to prepare teachers. Technology is merely added to the existing program. A new course on technology is added, equipment is purchased, and some changes are made in graduation requirements. But only rarely does a SCDE imagine how it would do its business differently and what its expectations would be for faculty, staff, and students if everyone had access to all of the equipment they required and possessed the skills and talent to use the technology fully. Rather than dreaming about a future and building toward it, most SCDEs are adding technology bit by bit while holding on to the existing way of doing business.

Absence of Planning

With a lack of vision goes a lack of planning. Many SCDEs have technology plans and faculty committees to oversee these plans, but these plans are usually limited to the purchase, distribution, and amortization of equipment. Plans for training the faculty and staff, recruiting new faculty, modifying the curriculum, and evaluating the results are seldom, if ever, a part of the technology plan. But these elements are required if a SCDE is to incorporate technology into its program fully.

Insufficient Support for Experimentation

Teacher education faculty need to cast themselves as learners and experiment fearlessly in the application of technology. This is not easy. Faculty do not like to appear stupid. Some will be uncomfortable exposing their weaknesses and turning to their students for support. Yet the effort to integrate technology into the teacher education curriculum provides an extraordinary opportunity for faculty to demonstrate to their students what it means to be a lifelong learner.

Faculty are unlikely to take these risks unless they are encouraged to do so by colleagues and administrators. Providing time for faculty to learn new skills, offering assistance from someone who possesses the skill, lending encouragement as faculty test their knowledge and skills in the classroom, and rewarding successful efforts are essential to the integration of technology across the teacher education curriculum.

Weak Infrastructure

Many of the tasks that teacher education faculty wish to undertake require a robust infrastructure. For example, those who wish to connect their teacher education classrooms electronically with K–12 classrooms must have the technical capacity to do so efficiently. Those who wish to invite guest lecturers to present from a distance must be able to avoid technical deficiencies. And those who wish to post their class materials on the Web and communicate electronically with their students should find it easy to do. A few SCDEs have in place infrastructures that can handle these demands. Many do not. We cannot expect teacher education faculty to waste time inventing interesting ways to use technology if their infrastructure will not support it.

Poor Access to Computers and Other Technology

Both faculty and students need access to computers, printers, and other peripheral equipment when they need them. Faculty need up-to-date equipment in their faculty offices, their homes, and the classrooms they use. It is not possible to consider the integration of technology across the curriculum if only computer labs have equipment. Students need access to computers in their dorm rooms or apartments, the library, and open access facilities across the campus. They should have no trouble gaining access to a computer and other required technologies when they need them. Special classrooms, such as science laboratories, require special technology. Few SCDEs are able to make the technology ubiquitous.

Lack of Incentives

Teacher education faculty respond to incentives—for example, time set aside for professional development, summer pay for developing new courses, graduate student help in mastering technology skills and creating course materials, and recognition for success in meeting professional targets in the use of technology. Wise administrators will also set aside funds to send faculty to professional conferences and to visit other SCDEs doing notable work. In the absence of such incentives, few faculty will respond eagerly to the suggestion that they discard what they have been doing successfully for years and begin to employ technology in their instruction.

Weak Technical Support

The best one can expect of faculty is that they learn to use the technology expertly within and outside the classroom. It is not realistic to expect them to become expert in the technology itself. Full-time specialists in technology must be employed to keep networks operating and equipment in good repair. Nothing will kill a technology initiative faster than unreliable networks and equipment prone to failure.

Insufficient Professional Development

We expect faculty to be experts in their fields; whatever ongoing professional development they require is usually considered to be their own responsibility. These normal ways of doing business will not be sufficient in the field of technology education. Many faculty are not at all expert in the use of computers and other information technology, and they need a great deal of support. This need will not be met by offering occasional workshops on one topic or another; faculty require "just-in-time training," that is, direct coaching on what they want to know, on their equipment, when they want to learn it. They need to be coached on new skills and treated individually.

Lack of Money

Lack of money is often the first reason cited by deans and department chairs to justify poor implementation of technology. Money is needed to buy equipment and software, hire the staff to provide technical support services, and supply training for faculty and staff. Furthermore, investments in technology are not one-time events. Equipment must be replaced, new software must be purchased, maintenance is ongoing, and new skills must be learned. Technology expenses must be built into the operating budget just as funds are set aside for telephone, library, and photocopying services. These costs are not trivial, and they have become a part of the cost of doing the business of teacher education. One-time appropriations can help a school or department get started, but one-time investments will not sustain the effort.

In the past, SCDEs were considered to be money-generating units for a university. This may remain true but only if the university is willing to provide the ongoing resources for technology that are required to operate a high-quality program. SCDEs must seek ways to reallocate portions of existing budgets. They must also become more aggressive in seeking external grants and gifts from government, foundations, and corporations.

CONCLUSION

The need for teachers who can employ technology successfully in their classrooms has never been greater than it is today. The public expects SCDEs to prepare teachers that the schools require; the schools are demanding teachers who can use technology. The challenge to teacher education institutions is great; perhaps some teacher education programs will be unable to meet that challenge. But those that do meet the challenge will gain new respect from their colleagues within the college or university and from the schools they serve.

The chapters that follow provide ideas for SCDEs that wish to become proficient in preparing teachers who can use technology well. Each chapter contains descriptions of programs that can serve as models for others.

■■■ REFERENCES ■■■

American Association of Colleges for Teacher Education. (1997). *The use of technology in schools, colleges, and departments of education: Myths and reality.* Washington, D.C.: Author.

Association for Educational Communications and Technology. (1996). The definition of educational technology: A summary. In D. P. Ely & T. Plomp (Eds.), *Classic writings on instructional technology.* Englewood, CO: Libraries Unlimited.

Moursund, D., & Bielefeldt, T. (1998). *Will new teachers be prepared to teach in a digital age?* Santa Monica, CA: Milken Family Foundation.

National Council for the Accreditation of Teacher Education. (1997). *Technology and the New Professional Teacher: Preparing for the 21st Century Classroom.* Washington, D.C.: Author.

Persichitte, K. A., Tharp, D. D., & Caffarella, Edward P. (1997). *The use of technology by schools, colleges, and departments of education 1996: A report to the American Association of Colleges for Teacher Education.* Greeley, CO:University of Northern Colorado.

Regional Technology for Education Consortia. (1998). *Assessment of NCATE/ISTE Standards (awareness of and compliance with) among college/department of education deans and department chairs.* Author.

Technology counts: Building the digital curriculum. (1999). *Education Week,* 19(4).

U.S. Congress. Office of Technology Assessment. (1995, April). *Teachers and technology: Making the connection* (OTA-EHR-616). Washington, D.C.: U.S. Government Printing Office.

Willis, J. W., & Mehlinger, H. D. (1996). Information technology and teacher education. In J. Sikula, T. Buttery, & E. Guyton (Eds.), *Handbook of research on teacher education* (2nd ed., pp. 978–1029). New York: Macmillan.

Establishing Benchmarks for Technology and Teacher Education

▰▰ ■ DIALOGUES WITHIN THE ACADEMY ■ ▰▰
Finding Benchmarks

In Chapter 1, you met eight educators who have accepted responsibility for writing a report for the governor and commissioner of education that will provide advice regarding proposed legislation relating to technology knowledge and skills expected of new teacher education graduates. Janatha, one of the participants and the chairperson of an education department in a small liberal arts college, thought she should share the results of that dinner meeting with her college president on returning to her campus. Let's listen to a portion of their telephone conversation.

President Trumbull: I appreciate your sharing the results of your meeting, Janatha, and I am proud that you have been selected to participate in writing a report to the governor. What can I do to help?

Janatha: I don't think I need any help so far as my work on the report. What worries me most is whether our college will be ready to prepare teachers with appropriate technology skills if the legislation is passed. Frankly, I am worried about the future of teacher education in our college.

President Trumbull: Janatha, you know that I believe teacher education is vital to our mission. So long as I am president, I will do whatever I can to maintain and strengthen our teacher education program. What do you think we must do to be successful? It would help if there were some reliable and credible benchmarks that we could use to determine where we stand when compared to others; we could also use these benchmarks to measure our progress.

Janatha: I don't know if there are such benchmarks, but I will see what I can find. I have learned recently of a document called *Teacher Preparation STaR Chart: A Self-Assessment Tool for Colleges of Education,* published by the CEO Forum on Education and Technology. Perhaps it will serve our purposes. I'll be in touch with you soon.

THE CEO FORUM ON ■ ■ ■ EDUCATION AND TECHNOLOGY ■ ■ ■

President Trumbull has asked Janatha to find a credible source that can be used to assess the ability of the college to meet the governor's expectations for preparing technology-competent teachers. In 2000, only four states (North Carolina, Idaho, Kentucky, and Virginia) had programs in place to assess the technology-related knowledge and skills of teacher candidates. Indeed, creating such regulations is precisely what the governor and the commissioner of education hope will be the result of the proposed legislation described in the vignette. Although the National Council for the Accreditation of Teacher Education (NCATE) has requirements relating to technology as part of its teacher accreditation process, Janatha knows that President Trumbull is unlikely to be persuaded by NCATE standards because her college has never sought NCATE accreditation.

She also knows from experience that when President Trumbull says he wants a document that is "credible," he means that it must be credible to more than teacher educators; it must have the support of political leaders and the business community. Recognition of these facts caused her to propose the CEO Forum on Education and Technology as a source of benchmarks.

The CEO Forum on Education and Technology was founded in 1996 to encourage the appropriate use of technology in elementary and secondary schools. It describes itself as a partnership of business and education leaders; it consists of "chief executive officers" of education organizations, the National Education Association, and the National School Boards Association, and business firms, especially those active in promoting the use of technology, such as AOL, Dell Computer Corporation, Apple Computer, and CompassLearning. The CEO Forum was organized to promote the following principles (The CEO Forum on Education and Technology, 2000):

- All students must graduate with technology skills needed in today's world and workplace.

- All educators must be equipped to use technology as a tool to achieve high academic standards.

- All parents and community members must stay informed of key education technology decisions confronting policy makers, administrators, and educators.

- All students must have equitable access to education technology.

- The nation must invest in education technology research and development.

The mission of the CEO Forum is to publish widely circulated reports on the status of technology and education. Its first report, *The School Technology and Readiness Report: From Pillars to Progress*, published in October 1997, featured a chart that schools could use to measure their progress toward integrating technology to improve education. In February 1999, it published its second report, *Professional Development: A Link to Better Learning*, which provided an update of the original chart and recommendations for professional development as it relates to technology. The goal was to highlight the importance of professional development in the integration of technology in schools. In June 2000, it released *Power of Digital Learning: Integrating Digital Content*.

In January 2000, the CEO Forum published *Teacher Preparation STaR Chart: A Self-Assessment Tool for Colleges of Education*.

("STaR" stands for School Technology and Readiness.) This document contains a chart designed to enable SCDEs to conduct a self-assessment of the status of their use of technology. (See page 36 for a copy of the chart. It also appears as a foldout from the back cover of this book.) (The document is also on a web site, **http://www.ceoforum.org/scde.cfm.**) SCDEs can conduct a self-assessment using the web site. This is the information Janatha will share with President Trumbull.

The Teacher Preparation STaR Chart is intended to provide SCDEs with a tool to assess their status in the integration of technology for teacher preparation and guide further development in the use of technology. The chart has four levels: Early Tech, Developing Tech, Advanced Tech, and Target Tech, the goal that all institutions might attempt to achieve. It is expected that institutions will vary in their level of development and across the various categories for assessment within each institution. Thus, one college might be at the Early Tech level for the category Campus Infrastructure and be at the Advanced Tech level for the SCDE Leadership category. The purpose of the chart is to allow each institution to make its own self-assessment according to each of the categories. The self-assessment will help the institution to judge its strengths and weaknesses and decide where to devote special energy and resources. This kind of analytical tool appears to be exactly what President Trumbull is seeking.

This chapter uses the Teacher Preparation STaR Chart as an organizational device, with sections of the chapter corresponding to each category in the chart. Although probably no SCDE achieves Target Tech across all of the categories, it is undoubtedly true that many SCDEs are doing very well on one or more of the categories. Therefore, SCDEs need not despair. The goals established by the Teacher Preparation STaR Chart are worthy and achievable, albeit difficult to accomplish. Much of this chapter therefore is devoted to descriptions of institutions and practices that serve as examples for each of the categories. The categories are: Campus Leadership, Campus Infrastructure, SCDE Leadership, SCDE Infrastructure, SCDE Curriculum, Faculty Competence and Use, Student Competence and Use, and Alumni Connections.

(Text continues on page 41.)

Teacher Preparation **STaR Chart:**

From the CEO Forum on Educational Technology: School Technology and Readiness (STaR). Reprinted with permission.

	University		
	University Chancellors, College Presidents,		
	Campus Leadership		
	1 Strategic planning incorporating technology	**2** Funding for technology in SCDE	**3** Technology appropriately integrated in courses in all departments
EARLY Tech	Minimal; limited goals	Below most other campus programs	25% of courses
DEVELOPING Tech	Some; clear goals	Equals most campus programs	50% of courses
ADVANCED Tech	Continuous improvement	Equals top 2–3 campus programs	75% of courses
TARGET Tech	Strategic planning around technology for dynamic growth of the institution	SCDE technology funding ranks within the top programs on campus and is given a priority in fundraising efforts	Wherever appropriate, all courses throughout campus integrate technology to support learning

A Self-Assessment Tool for Colleges of Education

		SCDEs	
Provosts and All Deans		**Education Deans and Directors of T.E.**	
Campus Infrastructure		SCDE Leadership	
4	**5**	**6**	**7**
Access to advanced technologies in campus-wide facilities	Campus-wide faculty development and technical support	Strategic planning incorporating technology	Funding for technology internally and via fundraising
25% of facilities	Limited	Minimal; limited goals	No budget line item Limited investments Limited grants and fundraising
50% of facilities	Some	Some; clear goals	Modest budget line item Growing investments Targeted fundraising
75% of facilities	Plentiful and accessible	Continuous improvement	Substantial budget line item Continuous reinvestments Aggressive fundraising .
Advanced technology access provided for all faculty and students	Just-in-time, just-what's-needed training and support for all programs and departments	Vision for meeting expanding goals is built around technology as a catalyst for reform	Adequate funding to support all Target Tech goals

STaR Chart: (continued)

Schools/Colleges/Departments of Education (SCDEs)

Education Deans and Directors of Teacher Education

SCDE Leadership			
8	**9**	**10**	**11**
Hiring, tenure, and promotion of faculty with technology research and teaching expertise	Program guided by NCATE or equivalent technology integration standards	Partnerships with K–12 schools around technology	Access to advanced technologies in SCDE facilities
Not a factor	Standards not met	Limited Few outreach or inservice programs	Less than 25% of facilities Equipment 5+ years old
Rewarded	Meets standards	Some Growing outreach and inservice program	50% of facilities Equipment is 3–5 years old
Priority	Exceeds standards	Two-way flow of expertise Extensive outreach and inservice program	100% of facilities Continuous upgrades
Multiple faculty incentives support technology integration and research	Program is a model for other SCDEs in alignment with and going beyond professional standards for technology integration	Partnerships built around common K–16 vision for technology in education	The right technology is there, when and where it's needed for teaching and research

SCDE Infrastructure		SCDE Curriculum	
12	**13**	**14**	**15**
		Coursework that integrates technology to enhance learning	Use of online resources to support learning opportunities
Faculty development	Technical support		
Few workshops Limited content integration No training incentives	Takes several days	Basic skills course 25% of methods and content courses	Few courses
Many workshops Content focused Training incentives	Takes place next day	Intermediate skills courses 50% of methods and content courses	Many courses
Multiple forms Mentoring, peer or student assistance Integrated with goals Generous training incentives	Takes place same day	Advanced integrated skills courses Most methods and content courses	Most courses
Formal and informal training and mentoring available to all faculty with incentives for application in teaching and research	Tech support available 24/7	All coursework built on research on optimal uses of technology to enhance teaching and learning	Wherever appropriate, courses integrate online resources and collaborative technologies to enhance learning opportunities

STaR Chart: (continued)

Schools/Colleges/Departments of Education (SCDEs)

	Faculty	Students	Alumni
	Competence & Use		Connections
16	**17**	**18**	**19**
Technology in field experiences and student teaching	Understanding and use of technology to enhance teaching and research	Understanding and use of technology to maximize student learning	Connection with the SCDE for continuous growth
25% of field experiences Optional for student teaching	100% at entry or adoption level	50% use technology well in lessons and products 50% meet performance-based competencies 50% enter classroom ready to teach with technology	Occasional, unfocused
50% of field experiences Expected in student teaching	100% at adoption or adaptation level	75% use technology well in lessons and products 75% meet performance-based competencies 75% enter classroom ready to teach with technology	Regular, focused
75% of field experiences Required in student teaching	100% at adaptation or appropriation level	100% use technology well in lessons and products 100% meet performance-based competencies 100% enter classroom ready to teach with technology	Aggressive, targeted
Criteria for field experiences around best practices in teaching with technology; SCDE helps build local capacity to make this possible	All faculty are at the appropriation or invention level in using technology for research, teaching, and meeting professional goals	All graduates meet the highest standard of technology teaching expertise, are sought after for this skill, and become technology leaders in their schools	Targeted program of connections with graduates benefiting SCDE and alumni

■ ■ ■ CAMPUS LEADERSHIP ■ ■ ■

No more than forty years ago, each state had robust institutions called "teacher colleges"—institutions whose primary mission was to prepare teachers. Anyone who wished to become a teacher often chose one of these colleges for preparation. During the 1970s, most teacher colleges reinvented themselves as comprehensive state universities. Thus, Ball State Teachers College became Ball State University, and Indiana State Teachers College became Indiana State University.

Before the 1970s, it was not difficult for the president of a teacher college to give resource priority to the graduate and undergraduate preparation of teachers. But once the college became a comprehensive university, teacher education had to compete for resources with other colleges and departments within it, just as teacher education has long competed for resources within research universities and liberal arts colleges. Today presidents of all higher education institutions are reluctant to trumpet the importance of teacher education against the importance of medicine, engineering, the liberal arts, law, business, and other academic fiefdoms of the university.

Although it is rare for a college or university to emphasize its teacher education program as a campus priority, it has become increasingly more common for a president to stress the importance of technology to advance the overall mission of the college or university, including teacher education. Where teacher education has been able to take leadership for advancing the instructional use of technology on the campus, it has found both honor and resources.

Example of Trustee and Presidential Leadership: Albion College. Albion College is a small, church-related (Methodist), liberal arts institution located in Albion, Michigan, a city of ten thousand residents in the south-central region of the state. Albion has a Department of Education whose mission is to provide courses and experiences that enable Albion students seeking to become elementary or secondary teachers the opportunity to obtain teacher certification. The college has also become an extraordinary site for the use of technology in teacher preparation. Much of the credit is due to William C. Ferguson, a member of the board of trustees and interim president during the 1995–96 academic year.

Ferguson graduated from Albion College in 1952 with a degree in education. Eventually he became CEO of the NYNEX Corporation, a leader in telecommunications. Following his retirement from NYNEX, the Albion College Board of Trustees asked him to fill the presidency on an interim basis for 1995–96. Undoubtedly he was greatly influenced by his early interest in education and his experience as the head of a major telecommunications organization. During his brief tenure as interim president, he proposed the establishment of a center on technology and education that would be linked to the education department. He thought this would make it possible to prepare teachers better to use technology in K–12 classrooms. The board approved his proposal, and the center, named the Ferguson Center for Technology-Aided Teaching, was established.

The center was charged with serving three populations: education faculty and students, teachers in area schools, and others in Albion College, the community, and other higher education institutions. One of the primary indicators of success would be the degree that education faculty took advantage of the center to advance their personal and professional capacity to use technology.

Ferguson also had ideas about the kind of person who should direct the center: someone who was competent in both technology and education and could work easily with Albion faculty and students, as well as teachers in K–12 classrooms.

Reuben Rubio matched the required qualifications and was hired as center director in 1996. Rubio held B.S. and M.S.E. degrees in nuclear engineering and was pursuing his Ph.D. in education at the University of Michigan at the time he was hired. At Michigan, he was engaged in a variety of research projects testing approaches to technology in K–12 schools.

Since Rubio's assuming the post of director of the Ferguson Center, Albion's Department of Education has become a regional leader in preparing preservice teachers to use technology and in providing professional development relating to technology in schools surrounding Albion. (See the Albion College web site: **http://educate.Albion.edu.**)

■ ■ ■ ■ CAMPUS INFRASTRUCTURE ■ ■ ■ ■

The quality of technology infrastructure can strengthen or constrain the educational mission of a college or university. Infrastructure includes access to up-to-date hardware, software, and telecommunications throughout the campus—in dormitories, classrooms and faculty offices, libraries and laboratories, that is, wherever students, faculty, and staff need access to do their work. Infrastructure also includes technical support and training for faculty and staff. A forward-thinking campus needs specialized facilities to support research and development in the use of technology for education. As a result, campus investments in infrastructure have become a significant part of college and university budgets. Without these investments, colleges and universities are finding it increasingly difficult to attract the best faculty and students.

SCDEs generally benefit from substantial investments in technology made by the campus. In a college, most, if not all, of the funds to support infrastructure may come from campus budgets rather than from schools or departments within the college. Even in large universities where each school is expected to pay for many of its own costs, a SCDE may depend on the institutional investment in infrastructure to meet many of its infrastructure needs.

Example of Campus Infrastructure Support: University Information Technology Services, Indiana University. Indiana University is an example of a higher education institution where the greatest portion of technology investment is made by the campus as a whole rather than by individual schools. University Information Technology Services (UITS), headed by Michael

McRobbie, vice president for information technology, is responsible for creating and maintaining a modern information technology environment throughout the university. UITS has offices on the Bloomington and Indianapolis campuses and employs more than five hundred trained professionals to serve these two campuses. UITS staff has expertise that spans the field of information technology. It also has leadership responsibility for technology services on the other six campuses of Indiana University.

UITS is guided by the Indiana University Information Technology Strategic Plan, *Architecture for the 21st Century*. More than one hundred faculty and staff worked on the plan for more than a year. This plan, approved by the board of trustees in 1998, focuses on the design, development, application, and use of information technology in support of teaching, learning, research, service, and the management of university business.

UITS is organized into four divisions and an Advanced Information Technology Laboratory.

The Division of Teaching and Learning Information Technologies provides the support services for faculty, students, staff, and computing support professionals on the Bloomington and Indianapolis campuses. These services include student computing labs, consulting in person as well as by means of an electronic knowledge base, hands-on Student Technology Education Programs (STEP) classes that are free to students, and PROSTEPS (Professional's Technology Education Programs) classes offered to faculty, staff, and students at modest cost. UITS also provides the Technology and Learning Technology Lab (Bloomington) and the Center for Teaching and Learning (Indianapolis), which offer faculty support for the design and development of courses that employ technology.

The Division of Telecommunications is responsible for the development of the university's data, video, and voice communication infrastructure and equipment. It installs, monitors, and maintains all aspects of the computing and telephone networks; oversees the delivery of network and telephone services that provide e-mail, voice mail, and telephone services; and manages the Virtual Indiana Classroom, an interactive video network that connects Indiana University to hundreds of sites within the state and beyond. This division also coordinates the university's participation in major, national high-speed networking resources such as **Abilene, TransPac,** and the **Backbone Network Service (vBNS).** The Division of University Information Systems is responsible for selecting, developing, and managing the software that operates the university's businesses, including student, financial, human resources, information access, library, security, and **decision support systems,** which provide the tools and capabilities to process and present data in a way that assists decision making.

The Division of Research and Academic Computing provides the academic community with computing and **visualization technologies** that enable faculty, graduate students, and staff to conduct leading-edge research in many areas. UITS houses two supercomputers. This division uses these and other computers to support research applications. It is also responsible for creating partnerships with leaders in high-performance computing.

The Advanced Information Technology Laboratory evaluates, tests, and experiments with new and cutting-edge information technologies that may prove useful to the four UITS divisions. Among its efforts is the development of technologies intended to support **virtual reality applications** and to enhance the distribution and access to **digital video.**

UITS also makes no-cost or low-cost software available to faculty, staff, and students through its IUware Online and Softserve service and through agreements with Microsoft, Symantec, Star Division, and Corel. An agreement with NET provides faculty, staff, and students with six hundred on-line instructional technology courses. UITS is also responsible for implementing the university's computer replacement policy that is intended to ensure that no faculty must depend on a computer more than three years old.

UITS thus is not only responsible for building and maintaining voice, video, and data networks for the IU system; it also operates 130 Student Technology Centers with 4000 computers running Windows, Macintosh, and **Unix**; it provides around-the-clock support for computer users, whether they are in classrooms, offices, or residences; and it hosts high-speed computers for those who need such capacity, while providing classes for the novice user. UITS also provides fellowships to faculty and hosts symposia on the role of technology in university instruction. Some portion of these services are used daily by School of Education students, faculty, and staff.

Example of Campus Infrastructure Support: Albion College. If Indiana University stands as an example of campuswide infrastructure support for a large, research university, Albion College illustrates what is needed and can be done at a relatively small liberal arts college. Troy D. VanAken is Albion's vice president for information technology and chief information officer. He heads the Information Technology (IT) Division, with twenty-two employees in addition to himself. The division has four departments: User Services (four staff), Systems and Networking (five staff), Administrative Computing (seven staff), and Instructional Technology (five staff). Telecommunications and video are supported through another division within the college.

The IT division is responsible for one thousand instructional computers, five public computer labs, plus computer labs in every residence hall and several academic departments. Albion also has five special multimedia computer labs and twenty portable, multimedia units (laptop, **DVD players, high-end data video projector, visualizer,** portable cart, and VCR) for use in campus classrooms. In addition to the computer labs in each residence hall, IT provides network ports for each "pillow" in the residence facilities as two-thirds of Albion students bring personal computers to campus. Some off-campus residences are connected to the campus local area network (LAN). Others use high-speed cable modem services to access campus and Internet resources. IT also provides a campus modem pool for dial-up users. All faculty and staff have e-mail and access to computers.

The IT division staffs a Help Desk from 8:00 A.M. to 5:00 P.M. each day except Saturday and Sunday. Student support groups in each residence hall provide student support on the weekends. The division provides training to faculty, staff, students, and the Albion community. It conducts between four and eight sessions each week on software and technology issues.

Approximately 3 to 5 percent of the campus budget is devoted to information technology, depending on the specific budget year. According to VanAken the influx of technology has transformed the way Albion faculty, staff, and students "operate, communicate, and interact both in terms of frequency, and convenience."

■■■ SCDE LEADERSHIP ■■ ■

Strong campus leadership and a robust campus infrastructure are important if SCDEs are to be successful technology users. However, a SCDE may have all of these resources and still be unsuccessful because leadership at the SCDE level is weak or focused on other priorities. For technology to be successful, it requires deans such as James Pellegrino, who had a vision of what technology could do to support cognitive studies at Peabody College of Vanderbilt University in Nashville, Tennessee, and who worked tirelessly to find the funds needed to support research, build facilities, buy equipment, and employ faculty. Patricia Wasley, dean of the Bank Street College of Education in New York City, used the power inherent in technology as a catalyst to encourage faculty to reconsider and revise the teacher education program at Bank Street College. And while many individuals have contributed to the University of Virginia's Curry School of Education's national leadership in technology and education, much of the credit should go to James Cooper, who as dean recognized the opportunities that technology offered the Curry School, encouraged faculty who were interested in technology, and found the funds to support their work.

Across the nation SCDE deans and department chairs are attempting to lead faculty into using technology in ways that strengthen and transform teacher education in their institutions. The successful ones have learned how to advance their agendas in competition with other academic units; they have a vision for what they want their SCDE to become through employing technology and have mobilized faculty and staff behind

Figure 2.1   Technology as Facilitator of Quality Education: A Model

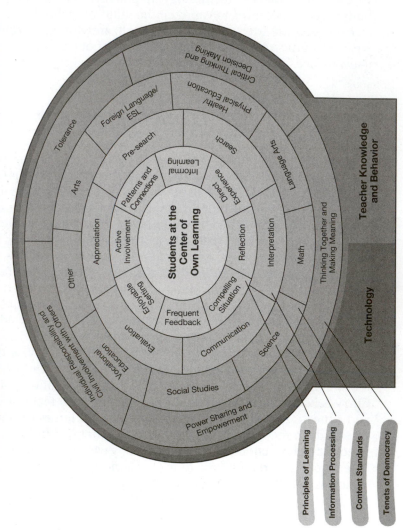

Source: http://www.intime.uni.edu/model/modelimage.html.

their visions and plans. They are quick to take advantage of new and unexpected funding opportunities and seek partners within the college or university, among K–12 schools, and with business corporations when it is clear that these partnerships will advance the SCDE's vision and mission.

Example of SCDE Leadership: College of Education, University of Northern Iowa. One dean who has exhibited effective leadership with regard to technology and teacher education is Thomas J. Switzer, dean of the Cedar Falls, Iowa, College of Education at the University of Northern Iowa (UNI). His leadership has been evident not only at UNI but also nationally among other deans and SCDEs. He has served as chair of the AACTE Committee on Technology and was a member of the NCATE Task Force on Technology.

At UNI, Switzer has been a leader in helping to conceptualize technology as a "facilitator for quality education" (Switzer, Callahan, & Quinn, 1999). Some teacher educators have expressed concerns that technology might degrade the quality of teacher education that preservice teachers have received in the past. Switzer argues a contrary view: that rather than undermining a high-quality education, technology can ensure a quality education in keeping with current requirements.

In order to ensure that teacher education persists in meeting traditional concerns of teacher educators while addressing the need for technology competence, Switzer and his colleagues have created a schema that provides a comprehensive perspective on what K–12 students need to know and be able to do today (see Figure 2.1). The schema also identifies what teachers should be able to do to serve students well and, by implication, what teacher education must accomplish if teachers are to fulfill their roles.

The diagram consists of four concentric circles surrounding a core that places students at the center of their own learning. Each of the circles surrounding the core represents knowledge, skills, and beliefs students should have to be successful in the United States today. The sphere—the core and its four concentric circles—rests on a base of Technology and Teacher Knowledge and Behavior. The base—what teachers bring to the schooling task—will be solid if the teacher education program is sound.

Switzer and his colleagues have drawn heavily on the work of others in shaping their perspective, but they have assembled the pieces to form an original conception. For example, placing the student at the center of learning is a very old idea in education, largely unquestioned by educators. The first circle surrounding "students" represents principles of learning, which are based on publications by Peter Ewell. The circle reminds us of the optimal conditions needed for learning, whatever the task. The next circle, "information processing," draws on the pathways to knowledge model advocated by Marjorie T. Pappas and Ann E. Tepe. The third circle draws attention to the content standards that have been developed for nearly every subject field and for which students are increasingly held accountable. And the outer circle highlights the knowledge, skills, and beliefs students need to acquire if they are to be successful as citizens in a democratic society.

The knowledge, attitudes, and skills that students need will be achieved best when they and their teachers use modern information technology to bring the various components of the model into alignment with each other to produce an integrated curriculum. It can be argued that only through the use of technology can such alignment be achieved. Students will also be fortunate to work with teachers who possess in-depth content knowledge, understand students, can manage classrooms, and are skilled in pedagogy. These two elements—Technology and Teacher Knowledge and Behavior—provide the base for successful schooling.

The ideas represented by the diagram are changing the way teacher education is conducted at UNI. These ideas are also being explored by other teacher education institutions. UNI is the lead institution for a federally funded project, InTime (Integrating New Technologies into the Methods of Education), with the colleges of education of Eastern Michigan University, Emporia State University, Longwood College, and Southeast Missouri State University as partners (**www.intime.uni.edu/**). The project is expected to change teacher education programs in their institutions in three ways:

1. The project will create web-based resources to support new teaching and learning processes in education methods courses. The new learning resources will include video scenarios of pre-K–12 teachers using technology effectively at various grade levels and across subject areas.

2. Methods instructors will revise their courses to model the use of technology, using the video scenarios and an on-line discussion forum, and implementing technology competencies as exit criteria for their courses.

3. Methods faculty will share their work with others in the profession through print and web publications, presentations at national conferences, and participation in the Faculty Online Discussion Forum.

Through leadership in his own College of Education and by helping to organize other colleges of education behind a common effort to strengthen the use of technology in teacher education, Switzer is demonstrating his leadership locally and nationally.

Other Tasks of SCDE Leaders

In addition to providing a vision of how technology can be employed to advance education, SCDE leaders must attend to such day-to-day tasks as constructing budgets that provide adequate funds to support technology, recruiting new faculty, and making certain that new faculty have appropriate skills and interest that will enable them to model the use of technology with their students. From time to time, the SCDE leader will have to attend to the task of teacher education accreditation, by either NCATE or the state department of education. Increasingly accreditation standards include expectations for the use of technology in teacher education. (See Chapter 4 for more details on this topic.)

Another aspect of teacher education that has become increasingly important is the linkage between K–12 schools and SCDEs. Some SCDEs have professional development schools, where a significant portion of teacher education occurs. But even where such formal relationships do not exist, technology has made available new opportunities as well as necessities for collaboration. Because superintendents expect to employ new teachers who have at least a basic capacity in the use of instructional technology, they are often willing to work with SCDEs that are the source of new teacher candidates. SCDEs are finding that the K–12 schools' interest in technology can be harnessed to their advantage. For example, some of the technology training of preservice teachers can be done at school sites. By using interactive video, teacher education programs can arrange virtual field experiences in schools that may be distant from the campus and serve students of diverse backgrounds. Some SCDEs, such as the UNI, are building video cases of classroom practice in schools and using these in their teacher education classrooms.

There is another good reason to promote linkage between K–12 schools and SCDEs in relationship to technology: Some schools are better equipped than SCDEs, and some K–12 teachers are using technology with their classes in ways that go beyond the experience of some professors. Technology is an arena in which classroom teachers often have much to teach college professors.

Example of SCDE Leadership Linking K–12 Schools to Campus: San Diego State University. San Diego State University (SDSU) has launched a program designed to improve the technology preparation of its preservice teachers while serving three urban school districts in its region (SDSU, 1999). The program has the following goals:

- Placing its student teachers with master teachers who are skilled in the use of technology
- Integrating the required technology course with other preservice teacher education courses
- Helping teachers who are skilled in the use of technology but lack time to make their ideas operational in their classrooms
- Providing a broader range of experience for its preservice teachers

- Providing authenticity to materials and lessons created by preservice teachers during one or more methods courses
- Modeling good teaching practice to preservice teachers

The solution SDSU found to these problems was a program it developed: the Learning Through Cyber-Apprenticeship (LTCA) project. The idea was to go beyond the existing three-credit course that introduced preservice teachers to technology and build a community of practice around a common base of resources developed by preservice teachers working collaboratively with teachers in K–12 schools and with SDSU professors. The project has the following elements:

- An apprenticeship model that links teams of preservice teachers with experienced, technology-employing K–12 teachers.
- A management system that tracks hundreds of student-designed projects each year so that anyone can follow the progress of each lesson's development.
- An on-line library of useful technology-based teaching materials developed by preservice teachers working on projects proposed by technology-using K–12 teachers. These materials are used by K–12 teachers, preservice teachers, and college professors.
- Semiannual colloquia that bring together technology-using teachers, university faculty methods instructors, and faculty from sciences and the liberal arts for the purpose of deciding the attributes of good lessons that draw on technology to teach content in powerful ways.
- Semiannual showcases of instructional materials developed by preservice teachers. The showcase is conducted in one of the cooperating school districts.
- Use of Curriculum Assistant, an Internet-based productivity tool for educators that allows users to create their own documents on-line, print reports, and save their documents in a database. Curriculum Assistant is an instructional planning and curriculum management tool that offers automated

alignment to local, state, and national standards. The tool analyzes the concepts contained in a lesson draft and links them to the curriculum standards for which the teacher and the lesson are accountable.

- Use of Curriculum Assistant as a resource for methods classes taken by preservice teachers. Students in methods classes are typically expected to design lessons. When they use the Online Library and Curriculum Assistant, their lessons are designed better than before these resources were available. The use of these resources has also contributed to the infusion of technology into methods courses.

- In the introductory technology course for teachers, every student is a member of a team working on lessons to assist a K–12 teacher. The technology instructor acts more like a coach or facilitator, whereas in the past, this person mainly used lectures and demonstrations to teach about technology.

Each cohort of teachers experiences a similar semester schedule. Two weeks prior to the beginning of a semester, SDSU hosts a colloquium that brings together the technology instructors, methods instructors, faculty from content courses, and master teachers. The purpose of the colloquium is to create a dialogue about what is important to teach and how technology can assist the instructional process. Decisions made during the colloquium set the criteria for the kinds of projects to be undertaken in the semester ahead. The dialogue begun during the colloquium is maintained electronically on a weekly basis throughout the semester.

During the first two weeks of the semester, the K–12 teachers submit proposed projects to the project management team to decide which projects will be undertaken by students in the technology class during that semester. During Week 3, students form into teams and select projects; then they meet the K–12 teacher who has proposed the project. Throughout the semester, preservice teachers work on the lessons and post them using Curriculum Assistant. Methods classes use the lessons as examples; methods instructors, K–12 teachers, and arts and sciences faculty tap into the lessons as they are being developed and offer advice. During the final two weeks of the semester, the preservice students' work is showcased at a school site. The best examples are stored in the on-line library.

Programs like this one not only contribute to improving the use of technology by preservice teachers; they also contribute to building stronger ties between the SCDEs and the school systems they serve.

■■■ ■ SCDE INFRASTRUCTURE ■ ■■ ■

Strong, visionary leadership is essential but not sufficient. To provide an appropriate education in the use of technology, a SCDE must also have an adequate technology infrastructure. It is difficult to know what the minimum requirements for that infrastructure may be. What seemed adequate in 1990 is no longer adequate; what seems optimum today will surely be considered primitive in a decade. While it is difficult to specify exactly what equipment may be required, it is much easier to describe functions that should be provided.

For example, every SCDE requires a networked voice, data, and video system that provides connectivity to all classrooms and offices within the SCDE building and to other locations throughout the world. The building's **technical infrastructure** should be sufficient to meet current requirements and capable of responding to future needs. The **system architecture** must be built according to industry standards and compatible with the products of many vendors so that new tools can be added as they become available. An individual user should have as much control as possible, with limits imposed only for purposes of security and cost of particular services.

Faculty offices should be equipped to send and receive voice and data. Each faculty member should have a personal computer; each member of the faculty and staff requires access to e-mail and voice mail. Each department or administrative unit should have fax and networked laser printing capabilities. Under ideal circumstances, teacher education students should have their own computers, but the SCDE should also make clusters of computers and printers readily available to students to support their work. In addition, the education library should provide computer clusters as well as network connections that enable students to connect laptop computers.

All classrooms need projection systems that support a variety of applications, including the capacity to deliver interactive video from remote locations and computer-based presentation systems that contain data, **graphic slides,** streaming video, and CD-ROM. These systems need to be easy to manage so that faculty members need only to plug their laptops into the classroom connector, access their files off a centralized computer server, and find that all of their presentation needs are met. Future classrooms will require **wireless communication** and be expected to accommodate students and faculty within the classroom and provide connectivity to those beyond the classroom.

SCDEs need computer laboratories for course and lesson development, where high-end equipment and **authoring tools** are available for faculty and students to design their own instructional materials. The building should have studios to support distance learning in a variety of modes, including full-motion, two-way video. It should have micro-teaching rooms capable of video-recording students' work. Many of the content areas, such as science, mathematics, and music, require specially equipped classrooms.

The education library should model electronic search tools that provide access to information and data sources worldwide. There should be an electronic library that stores materials produced by students and faculty. The library should also be the place to find high-quality commercial courseware designed for use in K–12 and college classrooms.

Administrative services should take full advantage of available technology. Academic counselors should employ counseling software that informs students of license and graduation requirements. Students and faculty should be able to gain up-to-date information on employment opportunities and dispatch applications electronically to prospective employers. A SCDE should have a web presence, providing information to students and prospective applicants at their homes. Students and faculty should be able to conduct library searches and gain access to on-line data sources from their dormitory rooms or apartments or from their homes, respectively.

These are the capabilities that seem essential to all SCDEs. Many have them; many others do not, and both students and faculty suffer because of their absence. Some SCDEs are not equipped so well as the elementary and secondary schools they serve.

Example of a SCDE Infrastructure: Towson University, College of Education. Towson University is the largest comprehensive university in the greater Baltimore (Maryland) metropolitan region. From its beginnings as a state teacher college through its evolution as a comprehensive university, Towson has retained its commitment to teacher preparation. The College of Education, with seventy full-time faculty, provides multiple programs at the undergraduate and graduate levels and annually prepares more than seven hundred teacher candidates for initial certification.

Like many other comprehensive state colleges and universities, Towson University has had to be creative and aggressive in planning and implementing an infrastructure to support technology integration. Dennis Hinkle, dean of the college, Paul Jones, department chair, and David Wizer, professor, have led this effort. The development of the infrastructure has advanced in step with professional development for education faculty and with the establishment of a standards-based instructional technology curriculum.

The College of Education developed its first technology plan in 1993. At that time, there was virtually no technology infrastructure, little faculty development, and no technology curriculum for teacher candidates. Since 1994, the college has made substantial progress. It acquired four computer-enhanced classrooms/laboratories: two are Macintosh based and two are PC based (there are thirty workstations and an instructor workstation in each). The student workstations are networked to a server that contains major software packages, provides high-speed access to the Internet, and provides access to printers. The instructor workstations are also networked to the server and the Internet with projection capabilities for enhanced video, audio, and computer-generated presentations.

In addition to the four computer-enhanced classrooms and laboratories, the college also owns the Educational Technology

Center (ETC), the Multimedia Production Center (MPC), and the Assistive Technology Center (ATC). The ETC, which serves as a virtual library and work area for all college students, has workspace for small groups of students, a circulation desk, and twenty to twenty-five workstations with **ethernet** access to campus resources as well as remote databases. All workstations have software corresponding to that in the four classrooms and laboratories so that students have the resources they need to complete classroom assignments. The MPC, which provides advanced multimedia production capabilities, has the latest hardware and software (e.g., digital photography, CBI authoring, video editing) for producing computer-enhanced instruction. The ATC serves as a preview site for a leading producer of computer-based assistive technologies.

In addition to the classrooms and laboratories and the centers, the College of Education has begun to upgrade every classroom in its building with new video and audio displays and active connections to the campus network and the on-line resources available in the ETC, MPC, and ATC. Each classroom contains teaching stations with ethernet access, enhanced audio and video projection, as well as computer pods for small group collaboration.

The College of Education has access to two different distance-learning resources on the campus. The first is the University System of Maryland Interactive Video Network (IVN), an interactive conference and distance-learning system based on digital video compression technology and distributed via a **T-1 line.** IVN sites have been installed at twenty-one University System of Maryland campuses and program locations to provide access to the network. All IVN sites are equipped with a basic V-TEL videoconference system. Network hubs provide major contact points for carriers for access to out-of-state locations. The second resource is the Maryland Interactive Video Distance Learning Network (MIDLIN), a full-motion, two-way interactive video distance-learning system based on digital fiber-optic technology. Bell Atlantic has installed MIDLIN classrooms in approximately 130 sites throughout Maryland, primarily in high schools, community colleges, and four-year colleges and universities. The network and distance-learning classroom equipment have been provided as part of a grant program to extend the network throughout the state. Both of these classrooms have been used in preparing teacher candidates and experienced teachers to use and integrate technology.

As the college has acquired and updated its technological and information resources, it has made a commitment to providing professional development activities for College of Education faculty (Hinkle, Wizer, & Jones, 1999). In addition, Towson requires its teacher candidates to complete a two-course sequence (six semester hours) in instructional technology. Courses have been designed for both teacher candidates and experienced teachers in order for them to gain the knowledge, skills, and experience in the integration of technology in the teaching-learning process.

The College of Education has begun to plan for the future. In addition to maintaining and upgrading the existing classrooms and laboratories, the various centers, and the remaining classrooms, planners are identifying zones within the education building for wireless technology that will support faculty and students who have access to laptop and hand-held computers. Eventually resources will be shifted from maintaining and enhancing traditional computer classrooms and laboratories to supporting "smart classrooms" that contain enhanced teaching stations with wire and wireless high-speed access to technology and information resources and to the Internet.

Faculty Development

The infrastructure that SCDEs need is more than hardware, cables, and software. It also includes professional development and technical support.

Technology has forced SCDEs to respond to the professional development needs of their faculty and staff more than in the past. Traditionally, when higher education employs a faculty member, those who make the hiring decision judge the applicant as being completely trained and an expert in his or her field. Further education, through sabbaticals, conferences, seminars, and so forth, are by choice and usually at the expense of the faculty member. Technology has challenged the traditional system. Many faculty received their undergraduate and graduate training before computers and other electronic technologies were widely available. If a SCDE wants its faculty to use technology for productivity, research, and instructional purposes, it must be ready to provide the training necessary for the faculty member to perform his or her work.

Higher education faculty are not accustomed to attending workshops and training sessions to acquire new skills. Some are reluctant even to admit they lack the necessary skills. Either they claim to possess the expected skills, or they deny their value to their particular work. As a result, SCDEs have devised a variety of ways of providing the technology training faculty need without threatening their egos.

Example of Professional Development by a SCDE: College of Education, Iowa State University. In 1991, the College of Education at Iowa State University in Ames launched a student-faculty mentoring program that continues to this day. This program depends on the use of graduate and undergraduate student technology mentors who work one-on-one with teacher education faculty. These programs allow individualized instruction that appears to meet faculty needs.

Iowa State faculty have reacted favorably to the mentoring program. It has increased their confidence in their ability to use technology and their willingness to try technology applications with their students. They especially value the opportunity to learn about technology "in private," where they are not required to expose their lack of skills to others. The typical mentoring process involves one hour per week on a topic that the faculty member chooses. This allows each faculty member to go as fast or as slow as he chooses; it also permits him to focus on topics of greatest importance to him.

Ann Thompson (1999), chair of the Department of Curriculum and Instruction, identified the following factors as largely responsible for Iowa State's success in the mentoring program:

- The mentor and mentee establish regular meeting times.
- The mentor and mentee collaborate in establishing goals for the relationship.

- The faculty member has easy access to the required technology.
- The program is flexible and can change to meet emerging needs as the semester progresses.
- The mentor assists the faculty member in learning about the technology but does not do technology work for the faculty member.
- The mentor knows the faculty member well and understands his or her approach to teaching and learning.

If the relationship is successful, it can be continued beyond the initial semester.

Technical Support

Technical support is critical if technology is to be used successfully by faculty and staff. Faculty have little patience when networks are down, equipment is broken, software is incompatible, and other hitches. If faculty are willing to invest the time necessary to learn how to use computers and other tools to do their jobs, the equipment must work when they need it, or they will quickly abandon the effort to use it.

Technical support is often provided by a central office for an entire campus; at large universities, some services may be centralized, while others remain the responsibility of the SCDE. Who takes responsibility for technical support is less important than that someone does it, and does it well. Faculty, staff, and students should be able to count on technical support twenty-four hours a day, seven days a week.

Example of SCDE Technical Support: Education Technology Services, School of Education, Indiana University. Indiana University's School of Education devotes approximately $1.5 million, or 9 percent of its budget, to supporting technology each year. Of that total, more than $400,000 is an assessment paid to the central campus for technology support; another $840,000 is budgeted for the Office of Educational Technology Services (ETS) within the School of Education.

ETS provides technology support for faculty, staff, and students located in the Wendell W. Wright School of Education building, the Henry Lester Smith Center for Research in Education, which houses special projects, centers, and institutes, and other remote sites. Taken together, ETS provides service to approximately 100 faculty, 150 full-time and part-time staff, and 1,200 students.

ETS has 10 full-time staff and 4 part-time graduate student employees. The primary role of one staff member is to maintain telephone services (the School of Education operates its own telephone switch), a second full-time employee maintains and repairs the data network, and a third, responsible for the video technology infrastructure, supports the faculty in its use of video. Others are responsible for technology planning and overseeing equipment and software purchases; still others provide training to faculty and staff on the use of new software applications. ETS exists to make certain that no faculty member is discouraged from using technology because of lack of experience. ETS also inspires and leads faculty to experiment with new technology applications.

ETS is responsible for the following tasks:

- *Keeping the networks, equipment, and software operational:* Maintaining the data, voice, and video networks; performing scheduled maintenance; and responding to on-site day-to-day operational difficulties encountered by faculty and staff.

- *Upgrading equipment and software:* Replacing and upgrading equipment and network features on a scheduled basis; soliciting faculty, staff, and student input for technology upgrades; recommending needs for new technology to various School of Education committees; and coordinating ETS efforts with external university units and outside agencies.

- *Training and supporting personnel:* Providing training and support for those who use technology and those who upgrade, install, maintain, and repair these technologies; determining training requirements based on usage and needs data; helping to develop awareness of new technology; conducting or sponsoring workshops for faculty and staff; assisting in the development and support of information systems; and providing technical specifications to faculty developing proposals for funding.

- *Managing technology-rich facilities (computer laboratories, classrooms, auditorium, and distance education studios):* Developing a three-year plan for the unit and updating the plan annually; scheduling the users of computer laboratories and distance-learning facilities; evaluating the performance of new hardware and software; exploring new or alternative technologies; maintaining a tracking system of requests for assistance; working with an advisory committee to develop resource allocation plan; and maintaining hardware and software inventory, and budget.

ETS is headed by Gary Ingersoll, a professor in educational psychology. He is assisted by an advisory committee consisting principally of faculty who are technology users. They review technology plans and set priorities for technology purchases and distributions. The culture is a user-friendly service oriented to the instructional needs of the faculty and administrative support and service requirements.

SCDE CURRICULUM

Thus far, we have discussed the roles played by campus leadership, campus infrastructure, SCDE leadership, and SCDE infrastructure in helping SCDEs meet their responsibility to prepare technology-proficient teachers. These roles are important, but the best leadership and the best technology infrastructure in the world will be worthless if there is no impact on the teacher education curriculum. Leadership and infrastructure are part of the means to an end: a robust teacher education curriculum offered by skilled faculty who provide the technology skills and knowledge that future K–12 teachers need to function effectively in modern, well-equipped classrooms.

The teacher education curriculum includes more than the courses provided for prospective teachers within the SCDE. It also includes courses in the arts and sciences and other academic divisions of the college and university that provide general education as well as the content knowledge that teachers will use in their classrooms. It also encompasses student teaching, a portion of the program conducted in the schools under the supervision of master teachers. All of these aspects of the teacher education program should contribute to helping preservice teachers learn to use technology effectively.

Chapters 3 and 4 deal extensively with courses and procedures for incorporating technology into the teacher education curriculum. Chapter 5 discusses technologies of particular interest to those who teach children with special needs. Therefore, most of our suggestions regarding technology in the teacher education curriculum are contained in those chapters.

Nevertheless, as part of an exploration of the STaR Chart here, it is important to make some points about technology in the teacher education curriculum:

- All those preparing to teach, whatever subjects or graduate levels, must be taught how to use technology for instruction. This must become a teacher education requirement for graduation, if not for licensure.

- All teachers require some of the same technology skills. A portion of these skills are the same as those we might legitimately expect of any college graduate—mainly productivity skills, such as word processing documents, employing databases, using the Internet to obtain information, and communicating by e-mail. Other skills are linked to the teaching profession. Knowing how to use grade book applications, finding educational materials electronically, and designing multimedia presentations are three competencies one may expect of all teachers but not necessarily all college graduates. Other skills and knowledge may be special to particular subject areas or grade levels.

- The most difficult task for teachers with regard to technology is learning how to use the tools for instruction. Most teachers learn to use the productivity tools quickly. They have problems when they try to imagine ways to use technology with their students.

- The best way to teach preservice teachers how to use technology for instructional purposes is to show them—day after day, course after course, year after year. Prospective teachers need role models among the faculty who teach them in colleges and universities. Preservice teachers need to encounter a wide range of technology utilization; they need to be required to use technology as part of performing their work as students.

The goal for the SCDE curriculum is to make every faculty member a role model for the use of technology for instruction. This is an ambitious goal that will not be achieved swiftly.

Example of the Use of Technology in the General Curriculum: Peabody College of Vanderbilt University. Perhaps no SCDE currently can satisfy the goal of having every faculty member use technology effectively for instruction. However, Peabody College of Vanderbilt is far along in achieving that goal (Pellegrino & Altman, 1997). Peabody has been employing technology to support teaching and learning since the mid-1980s. This work in teacher education grew out of the projects underway in the Learning Technology Center, an enterprise that attracts cognitive psychologists, educators, special educators, content specialists, and instructional design and technology specialists, who pool their intellectual resources to conduct research and development on learning, teaching, curriculum, and assessment. This mix of experts has produced innovative programs and products for use in K–12 schools. These projects have also inspired efforts aimed at the redesign of the teacher education curriculum. Although the efforts at Peabody cut across the entire teacher education program, we shall use only one idea as an illustration of what is underway.

A common problem in teacher education is helping prospective teachers master content subjects that may or may not be directly related to the content they will later teach in K–12 classrooms. A goal of many teacher education programs is for students not only to undertake the course as a student but begin to analyze the instruction from a pedagogical perspective. It is part of the socialization process of becoming a teacher.

At Vanderbilt, one of the introductory courses that preservice teachers must take is introductory chemistry. Chemistry is an example of courses that frequently present problems to nonscience majors. They see little purpose in taking a course they will never teach and view it principally as a hurdle they must jump because the institution requires it. Vanderbilt's introductory course is like that of many other universities: lectures to large classes, coupled with textbook reading and laboratory experiments. To help students gain more from their chemistry course, Vanderbilt instructional designers have created ChemWorld, a multimedia program aimed at adding a real-life component to the laboratory experience in the course taken by elementary education majors and many other nonscience majors.

ChemWorld is divided into two sections: Pre-Lab and Post-Lab. The Pre-Lab materials help students to prepare for the laboratory experience. They see a QuickTime movie that helps to make them aware of safety precautions, procedures, and the equipment they will use in the lab. The second section, Post-Lab, features applications of the principles from chemistry learned during the lab experiment. One of the video segments shows elementary school students engaged in activities that are exemplifications of the laboratory exercise just completed by the preservice teachers. Students are given opportunities to judge not only the science displayed in the video segment, but how well the elementary teacher taught the science materials to her students.

This example indicates not only how technology is used to affect instruction, but how students become used to employing technology from their first courses at Vanderbilt. They observe their teachers using technology, and they must use technology to complete their assignments.

Apprentice Teaching

Just as teacher education is not limited to the courses within a SCDE, it is not limited to the campus. Perhaps the most powerful portion of a teacher's preparation program is the student experience that normally comes at the end of the program. Some SCDEs have begun to use the student teaching experience as a special opportunity to teach preservice teachers how to use technology in the classroom.

Example of Student Teaching and Technology: School of Education, University of Michigan. The Master of Arts and Certification (MAC) program at the University of Michigan's School of Education in Ann Arbor has taken steps to ensure that the student teaching experience and preparation to use educational technology influence each other. The MAC program also seeks to strengthen technology use in cooperating K–12 school systems.

Jon Margerum-Leys is a member of the staff and a doctoral student in the School of Education. Working as part of a team, he teaches a course in educational technology, leads seminars, and helps preservice students develop educational inquiry projects. He also spends one day each week working in K–12 schools with student teachers and their mentor teachers. During his visits to the schools, Margerum-Leys talks with teachers about their use of technology for teaching, solves equipment problems, suggests sources of software and lesson plans, interacts with school administrators, and observes the student teachers. He thus serves as a bridge between the University of Michigan and K–12 schools regarding technology issues.

A number of benefits result from this approach. First, he makes certain that the equipment that student teachers are expected to use is working. Second, he gains a deep understanding of how technology is employed in cooperating schools; this knowledge influences his instruction on campus. Third, he is able to be a consultant to both student teachers and mentor teachers on applications that fit their curricular goals. And, fourth, the relationship he has built with classroom teachers allows him to provide subtle, ongoing professional development to them.

The result of this arrangement has great benefits for both student teachers and mentor teachers, as each learns from the other. Student teachers arrive in classrooms fresh from courses that have given them up-to-date knowledge about technology with little practical experience regarding how to employ their knowledge and skills in classroom settings. Mentor teachers provide pedagogical knowledge regarding effective classroom practice when using technology. Margerum-Leys serves as a broker between the two groups to ensure the learning process occurs. The process also has a cyclical effect as each cohort of teachers benefits from applications brought to the site by previous student teachers that are burnished by wise classroom practice.

■■■ FACULTY COMPETENCE AND USE ■■■

In order for faculty to serve as role models in the use of technology, they will need to acquire technology knowledge and skills that will allow them to perform as good role models. Most SCDE faculty already use technology for productivity purposes, and they use it in their research. Few have incorporated it into their instruction.

Research conducted by Apple Classrooms of Tomorrow (ACOT) nearly a decade ago found that classroom teachers pass through five stages as they gain skill and confidence in the instructional use of technology:

Entry stage	The teacher struggles with the basics in using technology.
Adoption stage	The teacher moves from the initial struggle to comfort and skill in the basic uses of technology.
Adaptation stage	The teacher moves beyond basic skills and begins to use technology for productivity purposes.
Appropriation stage	The teacher uses technology fearlessly and effortlessly as a tool to do a variety of tasks.
Invention stage	The teacher is able to create entirely new learning environments with the help of technology. The teacher thinks about the value and use of technology when creating new instructional problems.

It is likely that college professors pass through similar stages in their use of technology. The value of the STaR Chart is that it helps them to appraise their status and what might be required to move to higher stages.

Example of a Program to Build Faculty Competence: Center for Advancement of Teaching and Division of Education, Xavier University of Louisiana. There are 102 historically black colleges and 253 Catholic colleges in the United States. Only one is both black and Catholic: Xavier University of Louisiana, located in New Orleans.

Xavier's history began in 1915 when Mother Katharine Drexel and the Sisters of the Blessed Sacrament founded a coeducational secondary school to serve black people and Native Americans. Two years later she opened a normal school to prepare black students for teaching, one of the few careers open to African Americans at that time. In 1925, with the opening of the College of Liberal Arts and Sciences, Xavier became a university. Two years later, it established the College of Pharmacy.

Xavier University enrolls approximately four thousand students each year, nearly three thousand of them undergraduates. Although the student body is overwhelmingly African American (90 percent), the university is open to all students. Xavier ranks first nationally in the number of African American students earning undergraduate degrees in biology, physics, and the physical sciences overall. Its College of Pharmacy produces more African American pharmacists than any other institution in the nation. Xavier is also first in the nation in placing African American students into medical colleges.

Xavier is not a wealthy institution; nevertheless, its faculty and administration have worked hard to ensure that their students receive an education comparable to any other institution in the United States. Thus, Xavier has made a special effort over the past decade to place itself on the forefront in the use of technology for instruction. In the early 1990s, it received a Kellogg Foundation grant to modernize its technology infrastructure and prepare faculty who could serve as leaders in the use of technology for instruction. Also as a result of the Kellogg grant, President Norman C. Francis established the Center for the

Advancement of Teaching (CAT) to provide leadership for the campus. CAT is a university-wide facility dedicated to strengthening instruction across all of the academic programs, including the Division of Education. Although CAT programs are not limited to technology, many of its seminars, workshops, and projects have a technology focus because this is where the faculty has wanted the emphasis to be.

The university, through CAT, has been aggressive in seeking external funds to support faculty development programs. The Andrew W. Mellon Foundation, the Bush Foundation, and the William and Flora Hewlett Foundation have together contributed approximately $1 million to support faculty development efforts at Xavier, which include workshops to acquire knowledge and skills that will lead to the integration of technology into the curriculum. For example, many of the faculty have been interested in using the Web to post their courses and maintain on-line communication with their students.

The Division of Education has gained from CAT and other campus-wide investments, but it has also pursued activities of its own. In 1999, it was successful in winning one of the federally funded Preparing Tomorrow's Teachers to Use Technology (PT3) implementation grants. This grant includes a partnership with the Louisiana Department of Education, the New Orleans Public Schools, and NASA/Stennis Space Center. The grant is being used:

- To develop further the capacity of the division to serve its students
- To implement the Louisiana Intech model in the teacher education program and in New Orleans schools
- To create the capacity for Xavier to serve as a technology clearinghouse for the thirty-nine colleges that make up the United Negro College Fund

Partly as a result of the PT3 grant, virtually every faculty member in the division possesses state-of-the-art equipment. Every student teacher has access to a laptop computer, an 8-mm video camcorder, a digital camera, and a digital projector that can be borrowed to use in the schools where they are doing student teaching. In addition to efforts to strengthen its own faculty and undergraduate students, the Division of Education and CAT are hosting in-service programs on technology for teachers from the New Orleans school system.

Xavier University is an example of a private college, serving mainly minority students in an urban location, that is committed to helping its faculty become role models in the use of technology while also assisting with the in-service training of teachers for local school systems. Xavier also demonstrates how a university can strengthen its teacher education program through investments in a campuswide teaching center and in the SCDE itself. These efforts can be mutually reinforcing, as is shown at Xavier.

■■ ■ STUDENT COMPETENCE AND USE ■ ■■

The purpose for emphasizing technology in teacher education is to ensure that all of the graduates in a teacher education program enter classrooms ready to teach with technology. Where a state has passed technology skill requirements, a SCDE wants to ensure that all of its graduates can meet the state requirements.

One task for a SCDE is to monitor its preservice teachers to ensure that they are acquiring the needed skills throughout the program. It will be too late if seniors in their last semester are found to be deficient in the required technology skills and standards. Therefore, some way must be found to monitor each student's progress.

Example of Evaluating Student Technology Competence: School of Education, Purdue University. Purdue University is one of the twenty-five largest universities in the nation. A land grant institution, it has approximately thirty-seven thousand students on its West Lafayette campus alone. Approximately fourteen hundred students are enrolled as undergraduate majors in elementary education, special education, and social studies education in the School of Education; a similar number are enrolled as secondary education majors in the Schools of

Science and Liberal Arts. About 25 percent of the School of Education's full-time faculty hold joint appointments with the School of Science or the School of Liberal Arts.

In the 1990s, Purdue University undertook planning to redesign its teacher education program in parallel with the adoption of performance-based standards established by Indiana's Professional Standards Board. These standards specify performances, knowledge, and dispositions that must be assessed by the faculty and staff who are preparing teachers. The new teacher education program also included technology as one of four themes to be given emphasis throughout the program. Although the state of Indiana does not have a technology competence requirement as a condition for licensure, the Purdue faculty placed themselves in a position that they are required to judge each preservice teacher education student as competent in technology prior to graduation.

The faculty made the decision to use electronic portfolios as the mechanism for determining competence. Each student must develop a professional portfolio that is used for self-reflection on learning, to document professional growth, and to provide the foundation for performance-based licensure.

The process of developing a portfolio begins with the first professional courses that teacher education students take. The required course in technology teaches students how to build a portfolio electronically. In the beginning of the program, preservice students construct an entrance portfolio that focuses on themselves as teachers and learners. As they proceed through the program, they add artifacts about schools and learners and about their ability to transform content knowledge into classroom practice. At the end of the program, the teacher candidates create exit portfolios that synthesize their professional development.

Each student's portfolio consists of a variety of multimedia materials, including materials designed by students, videos of classroom experience, lesson plans and written reflections, photographs, instructor comments, classroom observations, research projects, and written or oral commentaries. Electronic portfolios are also a means for documenting the learning processes and outcomes of the K–12 students taught by Purdue preservice teachers, thus linking outcomes of teacher preparation to student learning. In the process of developing their portfolios, teacher education students must develop the skills (e.g., scanning, digitizing, digital video and audio production, web page development) necessary to create it. Faculty advisers monitor the progress of each student's portfolio as he or she progresses through the program. Representatives of the faculty must approve the end product before a student can graduate.

The electronic portfolio keeps the focus on what students need to know and be able to do to be successful as teachers. Making the portfolio electronic ensures that all students acquire the technology skills they need to succeed as classroom teachers.

ALUMNI CONNECTIONS

The final section of the CEO Forum STaR Chart deals with alumni connections. Technology provides a way for SCDEs to maintain a connection to their alumni in ways that would have been more difficult before the arrival of modern technology. Alumni connections to SCDEs can be used for various advantages. SCDEs need to maintain close contact with practitioners in the field in order to ensure that their programs continue to be relevant and up-to-date. Alumni should be able to take advantage of research and developments with higher education, especially through their alma mater. Close collaboration can also lead to new and shared resources that can build programs. In some cases, a SCDE may attempt to serve alumni while serving an even larger constituency.

Example of SCDE Partnership with K–12 Schools Around Technology: Towson University, College of Education and Johns Hopkins University, Division of Education. The Maryland Technology Academy (MTA) was established in the Maryland State Department of Education (MSDE) by the Maryland General Assembly during the 1998 legislative session. Towson University (College of Education) and Johns Hopkins University (Division of Education) have collaborated as partners with MSDE in developing and implementing the Technology Academy program. The Technology Academy is funded in part by the State of Maryland and is also a component of the Maryland Technology Consortium, a five-year, professional development effort funded through a Federal Innovation Challenge Grant from the U.S. Department of Education.

The Maryland Technology Academy is developing a network of teachers, from primary grades through university level, who work together as colleagues in a collaborative program to ensure effective use of instructional and information technology in classrooms within schools and universities. This network provides trainers, mentors, and consultants for other teachers and schools; contributes to research on best practices for using these technologies for student learning and school improvement; disseminates best practices through products, projects, in-service sessions, workshops, and publications; and acts as a change agent in schools.

The first Maryland Technology Academy was conducted during the summer of 1999. Educators from twenty-three of the twenty-four Maryland school districts were selected for participation as academy fellows. The MTA consisted of a three-week summer institute for approximately 120 teachers, library media specialists, and other educators, who met four days per week from 9:00 to 3:30. During the school year, academy activities have included five face-to-face follow-up sessions and continuous communication among the academy fellows through on-line learning communities (**cte.jhu.edu/techacademy**).

The second Maryland Technology Academy was held in summer 2000. In addition to the three-week summer institute and two-day administrator symposium, twenty satellite sites were established across the state. Programs at the various sites were based on specific needs identified through need assessments within the regions in which the sites were established. Among the programs were these:

- Integration of Technology into Mathematics, Language Arts, and Information Resources Classrooms
- Integrating Research and Communications Tools into the Content Areas

- Integrating Technology in the Development of Problem Solving and Critical Thinking Skills
- Technology for Middle and High School Teachers of Algebra and Geometry
- Using Technology to Teach Reading and Writing in the Middle School Curriculum

Evaluations of the first two summer institutes and the satellite sites have been positive. Academy fellows indicate they have increased their abilities to use instructional and information technologies effectively in curriculum development and instructional delivery and in their leadership and mentoring roles in the respective school districts.

CONCLUSION

SCDEs that wish to prepare their students to be competent in the use of technology for instruction need benchmarks for determining their current status and establishing goals. The CEO Forum STaR Chart can serve that function. No current SCDE is likely to have achieved Target Tech across all of the categories used by the chart. Yet many SCDEs have made substantial progress in one or more categories and seem ready to advance in the others. The STaR Chart presents a great challenge to many SCDEs. However, if teacher education programs can reach Target Tech across all of the categories, we may be confident that SCDEs are doing their job well to prepare new K–12 teachers to use technology effectively in their classrooms.

REFERENCES

Hinkle, D. E., Wizer, D. R., & Jones, P. E. (1999). Preparing teachers to match environmental needs: Application of merging technologies. In *Conference Proceedings: Professional Education in an Increasingly Connected World, Teacher Education Council of State Colleges and Universities* (pp. 133–141). University of Northern Iowa, Cedar Rapids, Iowa.

Pellegrino, J. W., & Altman, J. E. (1997). Information technology and teacher preparation: Some critical issues and illustrative solutions. *Peabody Journal of Education, 72*(1).

Professional Development: A link to better learning. (1999). Washington, D.C.: The CEO Forum on Education and Technology.

San Diego State University. (1999). *Learning through cyber-apprenticeship.* Proposal to U.S. Department of Education.

Switzer, T. J., Callahan, W. P., & Quinn, L. (1999). *Technology as a facilitator of quality education: A model.* Unpublished manuscript, University of Northern Iowa.

Teacher Preparation STaR Chart: A Self Assessment Tool. (2000). Washington, D.C.: The CEO Forum on Education and Technology.

Thompson, A. D. (1999). *The faculty professional development challenge: New approaches and structure for teacher educators.* Unpublished manuscript, Iowa State University.

3

Approaches to Technology Instruction in Teacher Education

Do You Think Technology Might Affect Accreditation?

We first met Carlos, dean of a school of education at a large state university, in the first chapter. Several days after that dinner conversation, he found himself preparing to meet with the school accreditation planning committee following the exit interview with the visiting team. The committee will be gathering to discuss the findings of the accreditation team and to prepare a report to share with the rest of the teacher education program. As he puts together his opening comments to the group, he recalls the conversation he had with his colleagues from across the state regarding instructional technology. Although the current accreditation standards did not include technology, he remembers the number of questions that the visiting team had about the type of technology instruction the students received. He decides that this is an opportune time to raise the issue of how the teacher education program should address technology in its program.

Carlos serves as an ex officio member of the committee. The committee members are Lorna, a foundations instructor; Patricia, an elementary education methods instructor; Frank, a secondary education methods instructor; Pradeep, a life sciences instructor who also teaches science methods; Wynne, a music methods instructor; George, an instructional technology instructor; and Katherine, the associate dean for teacher education. We join the meeting just as Carlos has finished a recap of the exit interview and related the issues the governor had raised about technology and teacher education.

Carlos: We did well with our accreditation visit, but given the questions the team asked about our technology and the moves that the governor is considering, I think we need to take a careful look at what we are doing with technology and consider if we are addressing technology instruction in the best way possible for our graduates and their future students. Because I have another meeting, I will leave you now to your discussions.

Lorna: [Pause] Now that the dean is gone, I want to say that I don't know what he is talking about. We already have a technology course that all our students are required to take. If that course isn't doing what needs to be done, then it needs to be beefed up.

George: You are right. The Introduction to Technology course currently isn't adequate, but we are doing all that we can do for one credit hour. A three-credit-hour course would give us a great deal more flexibility, and we could cover all of the technology standards developed by ISTE.

Wynne: What technology standards? And what is ISTE?

George: "ISTE" stands for the International Society for Technology in Education. It has developed standards for what beginning teachers should be able to do with technology. Right now we are not covering very many of them at all.

Katherine: I understand what you are saying about the class, George, but the faculty will not approve additional required credit hours. What if we made the course optional?

Pradeep: I don't know if students will take the course if it is optional. I heard about the ISTE technology standards at a conference, but I don't think a high school science teacher will ever use most of them. Our life sciences students are very capable with the technology that they need in our field, and they don't learn any of it in the technology class.

Wynne: I agree. The students in the arts won't need to use much technology in the schools, and what they do need to know we do in our own classes. I know in particular that our music students work extensively with music composition and orchestration software in a class. Why not just eliminate the course altogether and let the majors handle the technology skills?

Katherine: But aren't there technology skills that are applicable to all teachers? Isn't that what the technology course is supposed to do?

Patricia: I think it would be a mistake to let each major do its own thing. I also don't like hearing that our students are not learning everything they need to know in the technology class, but I don't know that we can add more credit hours to the technology class. There are no credits that we can give up in elementary education. Everything we do is far too important.

Lorna: I have a colleague at another institution who told me they are trying to put technology into a number of their courses. Their faculty has identified three courses that all students take, and a short technology component was added to each. It seems to be working for them.

Katherine: That option seems to make some basic sense, and we do have a handful of courses that all teacher education students take. Your course is one example, Lorna.

Lorna: I was thinking more of the methods courses. We barely have enough time during the semester to cover our material as it is now. I can't imagine giving up several class periods for adding instruction on technology as well.

George: Integrating the technology into existing courses is one option, and it might work. But I think we need to spend more time looking at this issue and our different options.

■ ■ ■ ■ SORTING OUT THE OPTIONS ■ ■ ■ ■

Chapter 1 presented a scenario in which representatives of a variety of colleges and universities debated the value of and need for instruction in technology in a teacher education program. That conversation is probably familiar to many academicians. The territoriality expressed by the various representative SCDEs in the face of the will of a governing body—in this case, the state governor—is common in colleges and universities throughout the country.

Another type of turf protection, one even more familiar to those in higher education, is the conversation that will take place when these different SCDE representatives return to their institutions and attempt to engage colleagues in a discussion on how they instruct preservice teachers on the use of technology. The scenario presented at the beginning of this chapter is illustrative of the type of territoriality that faculty from different disciplines might express when faced with the request to increase the instruction of technology.

This chapter presents a range of options for preparing future teachers to use technology in their classrooms. These options range from technology instruction through a dedicated, or stand-alone, technology class to the delivery of technology instruction through the integration of technology into teacher education courses. The different options are necessary to meet the differing needs of every teacher education program. The unique features of a teacher education program can be a source of pride to SCDE faculty. If they perceive that the addition of technology instruction will threaten those features, the effort to include technology will become contentious. For example, some of the options that will be presented might require the addition of credit hours to a student's program. A program that prides itself on affordability might be extremely reluctant to adopt such an approach. Equally contentious might be a decision to eliminate other courses in favor of a technology course because few faculty may be willing to give up a particular course. To be fair, there are tremendous demands on teacher education programs to present a great deal of information, and the reality is there are not enough hours in the program to do all of these topics justice. Technology instruction must compete for curricular space and time with multicultural education, classroom management, assessment, content areas, and a number of other important topics. Nevertheless, through the careful selection of a particular approach or modification of an approach, it is also possible that technology instruction can enhance elements of pride that already exist in a teacher education program. For example, a teacher education program might deliver instruction on assessment in a way that sets it apart from similar programs. The integration of technology into the instruction of assessment might further provide a point of pride for the SCDE.

In the pages that follow, we provide information about six different approaches that SCDEs use to provide instruction on technology for teacher education students: the stand-alone technology course, the college/university technology requirement, the integrated technology component, integrated technology in field experiences, technology integrated through computer-assisted instruction and distance learning, and technology fully integrated throughout the program. None is mutually exclusive; a SCDE may employ only one of these strategies to prepare students to be as effective with technology as possible, or it may use more than one strategy in order to take full advantage of its available resources.

We describe each approach, with its advantages and drawbacks, and provide examples from SCDEs that employ a particular approach. Table 3.1 gives an overview of the discussion of this chapter and provides a guide for decision making.

STAND-ALONE TECHNOLOGY COURSE

The stand-alone course is devoted entirely to instruction about technology. The majority of teacher education programs that have these courses offer them early in the teacher education program, and the courses range from one to six credit hours each (ISTE, 1999). The focus of these courses is often not only on computer technology, but also on video, audio, and production technology. Whether the focus is solely on computer technology or includes other instructional technologies, the main point of the course is generally an introduction to the tools. Students are taught how to manipulate and create items with these technologies, such as newsletters through desktop publishing and perhaps grade books through spreadsheet and database software.

Table 3.1 Comparing the Technology Instruction Options

Options	Demand on SCDE Faculty	Demand on All Faculty	Demand on Cooperating Schools and Teachers	Demand on Computer Lab Space and Time	Overall Level of Course Transformation
Stand-Alone Technology Course	Low	None	None	High	None
College/University Technology Requirement	Low	None	None	High	None
Integrated Technology Component	High	None	None	High	Medium
Technology in the Field	Low	None	High	Low	Medium
Technology Fully Integrated Throughout the Program	High	High	High	Low	High
Computer-Assisted Instruction and Distance Learning as a Technology Component	Medium	None	None	Medium	Medium

In some instances, the student might be requested to use the technology as part of the instruction she or he delivers, but this practice is not common because the stand-alone courses are often taught early in the sequence of teacher education courses.

It might seem that as students graduate from high schools with more skills in the use of technology, the need for stand-alone courses might disappear. First, SCDE's are only now beginning to see computer-literate students enter their programs. Second, these increased student skills can be viewed as an additional benefit for courses dedicated to technology instruction as opposed to a call for their elimination. As students entering stand-alone technology courses have more basic computer technology skills, the instructor can devote more attention to software and technologies that are specific to the education profession, such as grading software, assessment packages, and special needs technology. Having skilled students in a stand-alone technology course also allows for peer instruction and for mentoring to take place between skilled students and students needing more assistance. Finally, despite how knowledgeable students might feel in terms of information technologies, they may not (and probably do not) know all the capabilities of the technologies, the potential educational applications of the technologies, or even the correct uses of some applications. Direct instruction on the use of the technologies will fill those gaps and provide a model of how to teach about these technologies that students can draw on when they must teach these technologies to their future students.

Computer literacy is not yet universal among all college students. Returning adult students, for example, compose an increasingly larger portion of the student population, and they may not have the same skills as their younger classmates. The older students might be the ones who will benefit the most from peer mentoring. A student population that represents highly computer-literate, preservice teachers and teacher education students who have little or no experience with technology can present a challenge for a course dedicated to instruction on technology, but the needs of all teacher education students can still be served by a stand-alone technology course.

Course Content

The content of stand-alone technology courses varies depending on the technologies available at each institution, but there are some basic applications that are generally covered, depending on the skill level of the students. First, regardless of whether the PC or the Mac is used, students must be familiar with a computer's operating system and understand basic trouble-shooting techniques. In an ideal world, future teachers should have access to a technology specialist who is able to fix all technology problems encountered in the classroom. (It would be equally ideal to have such service at SCDEs.) But reality requires teachers to be able to fix and trouble-shoot all but the most major computer glitches. In addition, full familiarity with the computer operating system enables the preservice teacher to be better able to understand basic functions, such as navigation of software, saving information, copying data, and retrieving data.

Students also need to learn basic productivity applications. These include word processing, spreadsheets, databases, and electronic communications. The instruction of electronic communication skills (e-mail, Internet searching, web page development) illustrates why courses must remain flexible. Only a decade ago, with the possible exception of e-mail, electronic communications would not have been considered an essential productivity tool. All of these tools help students understand other applications they will use throughout their teacher education program and professional careers. The SCDE needs to teach and use software applications that are representative of software used in school systems. The software does not need to be an exact match because students should be learning skills that are transferable to multiple applications. Nevertheless, because of the wide range of software applications that are available, it is impossible to provide instruction on all applications that teachers ultimately will use.

The technology course should also provide instruction on the operation of equipment that students will encounter in schools and any software used with this equipment—for example, scanners, digital cameras, video cameras, digital video cameras, CD recorders, and video projection devices. A stand-alone technology course that prepares teachers for a diverse school environment should also include assistive technologies if the SCDE has access to these technologies and has instructors who know how to use this software effectively.

Another key element of this course is multimedia applications, which range from the simple to the complex. In the context of a single course that provides instruction on all the topics discussed here, it is impossible to teach students how to develop sophisticated multimedia programs. SCDEs therefore address multimedia in a variety of ways. Some classes may choose to enhance the instruction of web page development to emphasize interactive media. Other classes may choose to teach students about user-friendly multimedia programs such as HyperCard or HyperStudio or presentation software that includes different forms of media (images, text, sound, video). Some teacher education programs may have a second technology course, either required or optional, and use it to teach more complex multimedia development programs.

A number of applications and technologies are specific to educators, such as grading and educational software. Stand-alone technology courses should introduce these tools to students and explain the relevance of the software and technology to education. As with electronic communications, these applications may not have been included in stand-alone courses in the past. In the case of grading software, there was little or no software available; it was not used in the schools, or the software was not easy to use. Grading software has now become common, with a variety of packages available to help teachers manage this essential element of their job. The software has become versatile with the functions that it performs and easier to use. Educational software titles have also improved. Although a single course can only begin to introduce teacher education students to the vast number of titles they might encounter in the schools, they can review some of the more popular titles and learn how to evaluate educational software.

Finally, stand-alone technology courses need to spend time on issues related to technology implementation. Teacher education students need to understand the ethical and legal uses of technology. When they enter the school system, they will regularly be faced with copyright issues, for both software that has been purchased and materials that teachers and students produce. In addition, access to technology, particularly Internet technology, continues to be a controversial topic. Preservice teachers must understand the implications of acceptable-use policies and general principles of student safety on the Internet. Again, like so many other parts of technology instruction, legal and ethical technology use continues to change, and the course must be regularly updated.

Advantages of the Stand-Alone Technology Course

The amount of information that needs to be covered in terms of technology instruction is overwhelming. Stand-alone technology courses can provide teacher education students an overview of the technologies they need to know. The courses can also provide students with an opportunity to practice technology skills. For students who are not comfortable with technology, structured practice time with technology is valuable. It can even be valuable for students who believe they already have the necessary skills and knowledge. Another advantage of the course is that when a student successfully completes it, faculty in subsequent teacher education courses can generally assume that students have acquired certain skills. For example, they can expect students to use on-line discussions, conduct web searches for information, and create multimedia presentations.

Drawbacks to the Use of a Stand-Alone Course

The stand-alone technology course can be a ready solution to SCDEs that seek to include technology instruction in their programs. A dedicated technology course can be quite effective, and these courses are being conducted in interesting ways, as the examples we present will show. At the same time, there are some drawbacks that must be considered.

Foremost, the effectiveness of the course is wholly dependent on the course instructor. The ability of the course instructor can be felt in the following ways:

- Knowledge about computers and technology does not necessarily translate into being able to deliver good technology instruction.

- Stand-alone courses must always be evolving, and there must be a commitment of faculty time (probably not as prevalent among adjuncts and graduate students) to make these revisions. Revisions need to reflect new technologies, or new versions of already used technologies, that are available and the changing technology skills of teacher education students.

- The effective instructor must continually assess the abilities of the students during the delivery of the course and increase the material covered if overall student skills are high (or simplify requirements if overall student skills are those of a novice). An even more challenging aspect is when course enrollment is split between very strong students and extremely inexperienced, fearful students. Responding to diversity in student skills requires that instructors modify the course on the fly.

Some drawbacks are related to the existence of a stand-alone course in general. It can be politically difficult to add a course to a program without either increasing credit hours or eliminating an existing course. To do either of these, the entire SCDE, if not the entire institution, must support technology instruction. In the absence of support, it might be easier to implement one of the other options or at least take advantage of one of the other permutations offered in this chapter.

Furthermore, additional resources are necessary to ensure the success of a stand-alone technology course. A course devoted to the instruction of technology should be conducted within a computer lab where all the students have access to computers for practice. Merely observing an instructor manipulate the technology tools will not empower preservice teachers to use and understand the tools themselves.

Finally, the stand-alone technology course typically provides an overview of a number of technology tools. A course that serves this role does not necessarily help teacher education students learn how to employ the technologies in their future classrooms. To help them make the connection to technology integration, they must use the skills they acquire in the technology course over and over again in other courses and in their field experiences.

Permutations of the Stand-Alone Course

A SCDE can make the stand-alone technology fit its needs by offering a stand-alone course in conjunction with integrating technology skills into subsequent teacher education courses (thereby addressing one of the drawbacks). In this situation, students learn the basic, necessary technology skills in the course and then use these skills again in selected courses. For example, a preservice teacher developing a curriculum unit in a methods course might be expected to perform a web search for curriculum resources, word-process the final product, develop a multimedia presentation of the materials, and create a sample **electronic grade book** to support the curriculum unit.

A SCDE does not necessarily need to tackle this technology mountain alone. The resources and curricular requirements of the entire institution can also help with technology instruction. Another permutation is that the stand-alone course can be a university requirement for all students. In this instance, a SCDE does not need to offer a course devoted to technology and does not need to add credit hours to its program because the course is mandated by the university.

Examples of Stand-Alone Courses. The University of Utah in Salt Lake City devised an introductory technology course that seeks to provide basic instruction on technology and a model of good instruction for technology and other topics (Niederhauser, Salem, & Fields, 1999). Following an initial discussion of learning theories, students are directed through two different activities related to web design. Both activities require the students to create the web page with HyperText Markup Language (HTML). **HTML** code was selected instead of easier web editors because it represented a technology that was unfamiliar to students. Students first complete a web page through **didactic instruction.** They are given a handout with the HTML code for a web page on it and quickly learn they can complete the page by copying the material. Although they can complete the web page successfully, a subsequent quiz often reveals that they have little understanding of the activity they completed.

To gain this understanding, students then use HTML to complete a web page through a constructivist approach. The emphasis in this activity is on student understanding of HTML; not as much emphasis is placed on completion of the web page. Students select the topic of their page and find their own resources through web searches. Admittedly, student frustration is higher when they must take more responsibility for their own learning, but they also realize that they have a greater understanding of web page development and feel more confident in their ability to teach others to use technology.

This activity forces students to rely heavily on classmates. The constructivist focus continues as students engage in on-line reflective journals with their peers. University of Utah students learn about classroom technology use by observing classrooms that integrate technology, interviewing teachers and students in the field, and critically evaluating their observations. Teacher education students conduct software evaluations in terms of how the software can be used for didactic or constructivist instruction. Overall, the course encourages the students "to develop a theoretical orientation toward learning that can help guide decisions about effective ways to incorporate technology into their instruction" (Niederhauser et al., 1999, p. 169).

Auburn University in Alabama (Brush, 1998) opted to revise an existing course, Technology Applications in Education, which taught historical aspects of educational technology, programming languages like BASIC and Logo, and basic technology for classroom management. New course objectives were developed based on technology expectations of the teacher education faculty and the ISTE technology standards (ISTE, 1999). Five themes of activities were developed around the new objectives: data collection and analysis, classroom integration of technology, classroom management, multimedia development, and information synthesis. Throughout these themes, the instructors emphasize the pedagogical aspect of technology. That aspect is stressed for the students because all activities completed are relevant to their content area. Finally, Auburn University recognized that this revision would not be the last for this course. The long-term plan of Auburn administrators is that as teacher education faculty become more comfortable with these technologies, they will incorporate the themes and activities into their other teacher education courses.

COLLEGE/UNIVERSITY
▆▆▆ TECHNOLOGY REQUIREMENT ▆▆▆

An increasing number of colleges and universities have recognized that they must ensure that their graduates have technology skills. To meet this need, they are adopting a technology requirement that all students must complete prior to graduation. These courses are required early in the college career and emphasize basic technology literacy.

Course Content

Generally courses that fulfill a technology requirement deal with most of the same topics as the stand-alone education course. Course content includes productivity tools (word processing, spreadsheets, database, electronic communications), information technology skills (Internet navigation and searching), multimedia development (presentation software and web page development), and ethical and legal uses of technology. The course content often does not include technology specific to education. The exception is if the college or university elects to allow a variety of courses to fulfill the requirement. In this case, a SCDE technology course may also fulfill the graduation requirement.

Advantages of the College/University Requirement

The most obvious advantage to this option is that the SCDE is relieved of the need to increase required credit hours by adding a technology course of its own or eliminate another course in order to make room for a technology requirement. Although education-specific applications may not be addressed in a university-sponsored technology course, the other topics covered in the course will prepare teacher education students to use these technologies in subsequent courses. The SCDE has an additional advantage if one of its existing courses can count as the institutional requirement. In this instance, the technology course described in the previous section provides all the necessary technology instruction, and the credit hours count in the general education portion of the degree program instead of in the credits toward the major.

Drawbacks to the Use of a College/University Requirement

The same drawbacks to the stand-alone technology course also apply to this option. There is an additional drawback specific to a technology course required of all students: course control. If the SCDE is able to offer its own course that fulfills the institutional requirement, the teacher education program is then able to maintain control over course content, ensure quality instruction, and include education-related material. However, when the requirement is that all students, regardless of major, participate in the same course, it is likely that the SCDE will have little input into who provides the course instruction or course content. The effectiveness of the instructor and the content of the course can have a significant impact on how students perceive technology and their ability to use technology in the future.

Examples of the College/University Requirement. When Utah State University in Logan adopted a new university studies curriculum, the faculty committee elected to add a requirement that all students be computer and information literate. This requirement is not fulfilled through a course or credit hours. Instead, all students complete a set of basic skills. Students might also have a set of more advanced modules required by their major. The knowledge modules include e-mail, computer basics, operating systems basics, ethics and access of computer and information use, information resources, document preparation, and data visualization and spreadsheets. The modules are self-paced, computer-assisted courseware. Within the courseware, students receive instruction and are tested on their competency. The courseware provides a preview of the software, a demonstration of the software, and practice through a simulation. Recently Utah State University added a direct instruction course for students who needed more instruction than the modules provide.

The teacher education program at Utah State uses this university requirement to its advantage. In secondary education, students must successfully complete the computer literacy requirement for admission. Because the students are expected to have basic computer literacy skills, they take a required advanced technology course prior to student teaching. The elementary education program also requires students pass the computer literacy requirement prior to admission.

INTEGRATED TECHNOLOGY COMPONENT

The intent of the integrated technology component is to deliver technology instruction without the addition of a course and to divide the technology instruction across a number of teacher education courses. The technology skills that students must learn are matched with a series of courses. Ideally, the technology skills that students are developing complement the content of the course, and the skills build on each other. For example, if faculty determine that students should be able to communicate electronically, as well as navigate and search the Internet, then electronic communication skills would be addressed in an early course and put to use in subsequent courses. To help students complete their technology assignments, students receive some direct technology instruction, for instance, on doing **Boolean web searches** (that is, defining the search parameters). Either the course instructor or possibly a special technology instructor who participates in the course as necessary does the direct instruction.

After the technology instruction is completed, students use those skills through the remainder of the course, and possibly in subsequent courses. In such a manner, the content of the stand-alone course can be covered as integrated components within five or six teacher education courses. Each component would probably need, on average, the equivalent of two weeks of direct technology instruction. Time does not need to be allocated to the completion of the technology assignments that demonstrate competence and understanding because the assignments become a part of the course in which the technology is embedded. The course assignments and expectations are not increased in order to accommodate technology expectations. Rather, the previous course expectations evolve to reflect the technology skills covered in that course.

Advantages of the Integrated Technology Component

Some of the drawbacks of the stand-alone technology course are resolved when the decision is made to create an integrated technology component. When the technology is placed in a series of courses, the pressure on required credit hours issue disappears. Furthermore, when technology is integrated into a number of teacher education courses, preservice teachers have technology addressed multiple times and by several instructors, thereby reinforcing the pedagogical importance of technology.

The integrated technology component also brings the technology into mainstream assignments. Because teachers tend to teach the way that they were taught, when teacher education instructors integrate technology into their teaching and in the way they structure course expectations, students achieve a greater understanding of how to use technology. They no longer complete technology assignments that are separate from their other course work. Instead, they use the technology as a tool to complete their "real" education assignments, and all course work becomes indivisible.

Drawbacks to the Integrated Technology Component

This option is not without its own drawbacks. Some of these concerns are not unlike those expressed earlier, but have their own nuances that come with the use of the integrated technology component. Resource issues such as computer lab space and availability, as well as faculty resources, must be considered.

Although long stretches of time in the computer lab are not needed, as would a stand-alone course, the short technology components themselves should still be conducted in a lab where students have access to equipment to follow along with the instructor. While scheduling computer lab time might be helped by allocating shorter time periods for technology to a number of courses, the logistics of scheduling technology components for several sections of several different courses can quickly overwhelm lab availability. Because many of these courses may be offered at the same time and instructors may want to complete the technology component early in their courses, the computer lab schedule can quickly become a scheduling problem that is resolved only when instructors and computer lab managers work together cooperatively.

The issue of quality instruction remains important for the technology component. SCDEs can use one of two approaches to provide a technology component within a regular teacher education course. One is to have the course instructor conduct the technology instruction. This option is particularly appealing because the instructor will be embedding the technology expectations into course assignments and assessing that work. However, if the course instructor is not capable of providing quality, effective technology instruction, the SCDE might choose to have an experienced technology instructor provide the technology instruction portion of the course. The technology instructor can also consult with the course instructors and help them modify their instruction and the course expectations to reflect the technology component. Over time, the regular course instructors may become more empowered and technology literate and be able to take over the technology instruction.

Although credit hours are not an issue in the integrated technology component, whether faculty are willing to surrender several weeks of their courses to technology remains an issue. Moreover, this component requires faculty to modify the way that they teach these courses, which might require a change in the way an instructor has taught a course for years. A sufficient number of faculty in a sufficient number of courses must cooperate and participate in the integrated technology to cover the required technology content. We have estimated that an integrated technology component could cover the content of a stand-alone course when placed within five or six courses. If the component is integrated into fewer courses, SCDEs may need to choose which technology skills are covered.

One of the advantages of this option is that the course instructors model the use of technology. However, having technology modeled in only a handful of courses is not as effective as having technology integrated throughout the program. Students might believe that technology is important only in courses with the technology component, again sending the message that technology can be separated from the everyday educational mission. Although there are advantages to integrating technology across several courses, it is easy to implement this option inappropriately through thoughtless errors at initial efforts or a lack of follow-through by participating faculty. When this integrated technology component is not truly integrated, the result is a "stand-alone integrated technology component."

The stand-alone, integrated technology component emerges when the decision is made to place a technology component in a specific set of teacher education courses. However, course expectations and assignments are never modified to reflect the technology instruction. Essentially, the technology instruction is conducted in the class, as is intended. However, the integration falls apart when nothing else occurs in the courses related to technology. For example, in the integrated technology component, students learn about the development of web pages and multimedia presentations during the first two weeks of the course. The integrated component would expect that students use the technology for in-class presentations throughout the semester and that they might spend much of the semester developing a web-based portfolio. In the stand-alone integrated technology component, the students spend the first two weeks of class learning how to use the particular technology tools, but they never again use the technology during the course.

The stand-alone integrated technology component sends a message to students that technology is separate and apart from all other instruction. They will complete any technology expectations, if there are any, so that they can move ahead to the "real" part of the course. This failure is most likely to happen if someone other than the course instructor, most likely a technology instructor, delivers the technology component. The technology instructor teaches the students how to use the tools and then leaves the course. The course instructor then carries on with the course as it has always been taught, minus the two weeks spent in the lab.

The problem of the stand-alone, integrated technology component can appear during the early stages of implementation. As willing as faculty might be to modify their course expectations and make the technology component work, it may take time for these modifications to occur. If a technology specialist is delivering the technology component, it is possible that the course instructor is also learning more about the technology. As everyone involved becomes more comfortable with the technology and the concept of integrating technology, the stand-alone component may evolve into an integrated component.

For that evolution to occur, it is important that complacency does not take root within the technology component. The SCDE must evaluate and assess the effectiveness it is having with technology integration. Careful assessment will indicate whether the technology is truly being integrated or if only technology instruction is taking place. If the assessment reveals that a stand-alone technology component is occurring, the SCDE must work with the faculty who play a role in the technology integration to ensure that all participants fully understand what it means to integrate technology into course work.

It is also possible that the integrated technology component is not working because the faculty who must make the option succeed have little or no interest in technology or may believe that technology has no role in education. It can be a big battle to convince individual faculty to change their viewpoints. The best way to avoid this snare is to involve teacher education faculty from the initial planning stage. If there are reluctant faculty or instructors who do not feel capable of implementing the technology, the SCDE must provide support and training and possibly even a separate technology specialist for the direct technology instruction in order to help the instructors modify the courses. Again, the stand-alone integrated technology component can appear all too easily. Caution in the implementation process can help to ensure that SCDEs avoid this pitfall.

Example of the Integrated Technology Component. Wabash College is a small, independent, liberal arts college for men located in Crawfordsville, Indiana. During the late 1990s, the teacher education program at Wabash recognized the need for and importance of building the technology competencies of students. Through a series of five teaching courses and the student teaching seminars, preservice teachers are introduced to a variety of technologies and then use the technologies for projects. The teacher education program first takes advantage of a technology workshop that all freshmen attend during orientation. During the workshop, students learn e-mail and word processing basics, as well as how to access networked **course accounts.** The first teaching course focuses on field observations. Students in the course are then expected to demonstrate their competencies with course accounts, word processing, and e-mail by communicating with instructors and posting observation notes to the course accounts. The second teaching course then involves preservice teachers in a workshop on effective electronic database search techniques. These skills are then incorporated into research papers. A similar process flows through remaining teaching courses as students have workshops related to a technology and then incorporate the technologies into class projects (such as presentation software, multimedia, electronic grade books, and web publishing).

During the student teaching semester, the instructor informally assesses student technology ability and needs and incorporates whatever technology is necessary to further their learning. For example, one group was fairly advanced in technology ability and knowledge and therefore explored **streaming video and audio** and the incorporation of the media into multimedia.

A handful of elements highlight this integrated technology component. First, the technology component has never been identical from one semester to the next. As faculty and student skills change and the technology changes, adjustments are made to instruction and projects. In order to increase the technology instruction, the instructor is in the process of developing on-line, self-paced tutorials for students to complete. Also, as a small teacher education program, there is no instructional technologist on staff. However, whenever necessary, Wabash College hires instructional technology consultants to provide the workshops and consult with the teacher education program on the direction of its technology.

TECHNOLOGY IN THE FIELD

Another form of the integrated technology component is to place the technology component in the field, that is, in specific field experiences instead of in selected courses. The technology instruction itself can take place on campus, at the field experience sites, or both. The key element is that preservice teachers demonstrate their competency with technology by using it in the field—in real classrooms, with real children.

Advantages of Integrating Technology in the Field

Ultimately, using these various instructional technology tools in the field is the objective of technology implementation. Therefore, one of the chief advantages of this integrated technology component is that the emphasis of the component is on the use of the technology in the field. If the modeling of technology integration can have a positive impact on future teachers, then who better to model the use of technology than practicing teachers?

A SCDE that is able to work with K–12 schools that have good access to technology can share the cost of computer labs and facilities with the cooperating schools with this form of technology component. One of the challenges of a teacher education program that integrates technology is to stay current with the technology tools being used in the schools, as well as the innovative ways in which these tools are being used. To stay current, higher education faculty should stay in contact with teachers and media specialists in the field and attend conferences where K–12 educators present their work. An even better way to keep the technology program current is to have preservice teachers out in the field, learning about and observing teachers using the technology to enhance their pedagogy.

Drawbacks to Integrating Technology in the Field

If all the essential elements are in place, not much can derail this type of technology component. However, all of the essential elements must be present. Teachers and media specialists in the cooperating schools must be an integral part of the planning process. Representatives of the schools can make it clear what they are able to offer the teacher education students in terms of technology instruction and their limitations.

One of the advantages is that the SCDE can share responsibility for the resources necessary to make an effective integrated technology component. However, if the partners are in fact resource poor in terms of instructional technologies, the preservice teachers will not have the experiences that they need to be fully prepared to teach with technology. Another resource that must be available is the people who provide technology instruction. By taking the technology component to the field, the SCDE expects to have its students see master teachers using technology in effective, innovative ways. These K–12 teachers become role models for the teacher education students. Role models should be good role models, that is, master teachers seamlessly bringing technology into all aspects of the curriculum. Few SCDEs can identify a significant number of teachers who are available and willing to work with preservice teachers and help deliver the SCDE's technology component.

Examples of Programs That Integrate Technology in the Field. The K–8 program at the University of Southern Maine (USM) in Gorham integrates its technology into student field experiences through the TEAMS (Technology in Elementary and Middle Schools) program. In this program, students gain all of their technology experience and demonstrate their competence in the cooperating schools. The technology instruction itself is delivered by school media specialists and, in special cases, by middle school students who are part of the school computer club. Once the teacher education students have acquired the technology skills, they work with cooperating teachers who are using technology in their classrooms. The preservice teachers also create instructional materials that use the tools they have learned and can be incorporated into the classrooms. The school media specialists work with the USM faculty to assess the projects.

This program is possible because USM is working with cooperating teachers, media specialists, and students who are already using technology to strengthen the instructional mission of the schools. A team of individuals representing teachers from the field, undergraduate students, and higher education faculty developed the technology integration program. What helped this entire process come together is that the teachers in the field were asked what would be the best way to provide teacher education students the necessary instruction and experience with technology. The university was also fortunate to be working with schools that had sufficient technology in place to make such a program possible.

Lehigh University, Bethlehem, Pennsylvania, has established the Technology-Based Teacher Education (TBTE) program, which first integrates technology throughout the course work and experiences of their teacher education students. A key element of TBTE is a partnership between Lehigh and Moravian Academy, a K–12 independent school. Field experience students are placed in technology-rich environments. Not only do the teacher education students observe and reflect on the use of technology for teaching and learning, but they also have the opportunity to collaborate with teachers to determine how to integrate technology effectively into the curriculum. In turn, the preservice teachers also have the opportunity to teach these experienced teachers about the newest technologies. This relationship continues throughout the semester. At the end of the semester, the teacher education students must develop and deliver a technology-rich lesson to the students in the K–12 class and then receive feedback from the cooperating teacher (Hornung & Bronack, 2000).

COMPUTER-ASSISTED INSTRUCTION AND DISTANCE LEARNING AS A TECHNOLOGY COMPONENT

Technology can work as a component in the curriculum without directly being part of a course. These instructional methods include the use of computer-assisted instruction (CAI) and distance learning. CAI can be used to create an integrated technology component, but not in the typical way the other technology components operate. It does not serve as a tool to deliver technology instruction but rather is employed to deliver instruction related to teaching in general. In the process of using the program, students become comfortable with technology and its instructional uses. For instance, teacher education students may use CAI to learn about alternative forms of assessment and practice with assessment tools. The program has not taught them how to create their own interactive multimedia program, but perhaps the students now have a clearer idea how CAI can be a tool for their own students and have become so comfortable with manipulating an interactive multimedia program relating to assessment that similar technologies hold little fear for them. Distance learning operates in a similar fashion as an alternative approach to the technology component and is discussed in greater detail in Chapter 8.

Advantages of CAI as a Technology Component

CAI can be an effective tool for an integrated technology component. The course instructor integrates technology into instruction by presenting information in the most effective way possible, so that students learn not only important educational materials from these interactive computer programs but also how to effectively integrate CAI. There are other laudable features of using CAI. As we have noted throughout this chapter, technology is not the only topic that may get short shrift in the teacher education program. CAI can deliver instruction and conduct assessment for teacher education students, and the students can receive all of this information outside the bounds of traditional class time. Furthermore, there are thousands of CAI software titles that teachers can use in the schools. In many instances, teachers may use these programs to keep students busy or to reward students who have completed their work early. Many educational software titles have more capabilities than are being explored by teachers. For example, problem-solving programs and simulations can be used for cooperative learning activities. If the SCDE has modeled a variety of techniques for pedagogical applications of CAI, the teacher education students can draw on those experiences when they use software in their own classrooms.

Drawbacks to the Use of CAI as a Technology Component

CAI is just one tool that can be part of an integration approach. CAI alone cannot be the integration approach adopted. Although there are some innovative programs that can teach students some of the "how-to" principles of a variety of applications, many students need the assistance of instructors to learn how to manipulate technology. Therefore, once students have learned the technology basics, CAI is easier for them to manipulate. Because CAI is not the center of the learning activity but merely a transparent tool that provides new experiences and learning, student comfort with technology usually increases.

Example of Using CAI as a Technology Component. The Peabody College of Vanderbilt University has employed CAI in a number of education classes. One of these tools is a program that walks teacher education students through a number of classroom management issues. One simple activity in the program asks students to arrange the furniture and seating in a classroom. Students click and drag desks, tables, bookcases, and other furniture onto the classroom floor plan. Given the features that are fixed in the room such as lights, whiteboard, doors, and windows, students seek to create a conducive physical learning environment. When the preservice teachers have completed the activity, they save the program on the schoolwide computer server. During class, each student can open the saved activity and present it to the instructor and class. The CAI also provides video vignettes of classroom behavior issues. These case studies are a tool to help students practice classroom decision-making skills. The topic of classroom management can often become lost in the teacher education curriculum but is often of the greatest concern for preservice teachers. CAI presentation of this information and practice activities therefore perform several functions. First, students are presented with valuable information. Second, since much of the work on this topic can be done outside the scheduled class time, valuable class hours are saved. Finally, students are using and manipulating software while completing the activities, thereby increasing their familiarity and comfort with the technology.

TECHNOLOGY FULLY INTEGRATED THROUGHOUT THE PROGRAM

Chapter 4 is devoted to the topic of how to make a program of full technology integration work, with innovative examples and ideas for the range of technologies recommended for inclusion in a teacher education program by ISTE (1999). However, within the context of how all of these other options have been discussed, it is also beneficial to discuss the advantages and drawbacks regarding a plan to integrate technology fully into all parts of a teacher education program.

The difference between a fully integrated technology approach and an integrated technology component is the breadth of when and where technology is integrated. A technology component can be integrated into a handful of select, planned courses. With the fully integrated approach, teacher education students experience different technologies everywhere in their programs. Some courses might use technology extensively, and others might use it in more subtle ways. Similar to the integrated technology component, it is important that technology is incorporated into all aspects of the course. It cannot simply be an add-on to a course or an additional, separate assignment that is completed so that students can be credited for a competency. Instead, the technology should transform the way the course is taught, the manner in which the instructor and students interact, the work the students complete, and the way the students are assessed. Chapter 4 examines how this transformation can be completed.

Advantages of Integrated Technology Throughout the Program

The most advantageous feature of fully integrated technology is within the successful integration itself. Throughout the chapter, we have extolled the importance of faculty modeling the use of technology. The modeling of pedagogical applications of technology is more likely to have an impact on students the more often they witness it. Therefore, if every instructor whom a teacher education student encountered modeled some aspect of technology instruction and integration, the student would be more likely to accept and adopt that form of teaching.

A teacher education program that is fully integrated may not need to devote additional credit hours to technology instruction. When technology instruction and the pedagogical use of technology are used seamlessly in all teacher education courses, the SCDE may find that a stand-alone course is not necessary. However, when a SCDE combines a stand-alone technology course with a fully integrated technology approach, the additional technology exposure can only benefit the teacher education students.

Drawbacks to Integrating Technology Throughout the Program

A full integrated approach can be very demanding on a number of resources. First, a variety of demands will be made on faculty. Faculty must be willing to participate in a program of full integration, must have or be willing to develop the necessary technology skills to model the pedagogical applications of technology to students, and must be willing and knowledge-able about how to modify their courses to reflect the integrated technology.

A full integration program means exactly what it says: the program is integrated throughout the entire teacher education program, including field experiences and student teaching. For technology integration to be effective in the cooperating schools, the SCDE must be able to work with cooperating teach-ers who are competent with technology and integrate technol-ogy into their teaching. In turn, the cooperating schools must have technology in place in the classrooms and have it available for teacher education students to use when in the field.

In addition to the participation of the cooperating schools and teachers, a full integration program also must include the participation of instructors who are not part of the SCDE. Full technology integration extends beyond the walls of the SCDE. The teacher education student must experience technology in-tegration throughout all aspects of the degree program. That level of integration requires the participation and cooperation of all faculty at the college or university.

Finally, a program of full technology integration will draw on the SCDE's store of patience. A great deal of development time and effort will be required to create a technology integration program that includes all college and university faculty, trans-forms all courses that teacher education students take, and in-cludes the cooperating K–12 schools. The fruits of these efforts will not be realized overnight; the transformation will take time and be gradual. There will be a number of bumps along the way, and the SCDE will need to remind all those involved of the im-portance of their efforts.

CONCLUSION

This chapter provided a number of approaches to technology instruction for teacher education students. Through careful planning and curriculum development (discussed in Chapter 9), a SCDE must select the option that is the best match for its fac-ulty and students. A teacher education program might combine two or more of the approaches in order to custom-fit technology instruction for the students.

Chapter 4 is dedicated to a discussion on how to integrate technology fully into all classes that teacher education students take. However, we have also noted in this chapter the obstacles that must be surmounted to launch a fully integrated technology program. The SCDE must carefully evaluate what it is capable of at this time and determine if full integration is possible.

We believe that full integration is the best approach for technology instruction for teacher education. SCDEs are preparing teachers who will be technology leaders in the schools. To accomplish this task, we need to rethink not only the way we provide technology instruction but also the way that all pedagogy is delivered. SCDEs that adopt the philosophy that technology instruction must be a dominant element in their teacher education program will need to select whatever approach allows them to begin a process of technology integration. Over time, the technology instruction is likely to begin the slow, transformative process to full technology integration.

■■■ REFERENCES ■■■

Brush, T. A. (1998). Teaching preservice teachers to use technology in the classroom. *Journal of Technology and Teacher Education*, 6(4), 243–258.

Hornung, C. S., & Bronack, S. (2000). Preparing technology-based teachers: Professional lessons from a K–12/university collaboration. *TechTrends*, 44(4), 17–20.

International Society for Technology in Education. (1999). *Will new teachers be prepared to teach in a digital age?* Santa Monica, CA: Milken Family Foundation.

Niederhauser, D. S., Salem, D. J., & Fields, M. (1999). Exploring teaching, learning, and instructional reform in an introductory technology course. *Journal of Technology and Teacher Education*, 7(2), 153–172.

4

Integration of Technology Across the Teacher Education Curriculum

DIALOGUES WITHIN THE ACADEMY
From Dinner for Eight to Lunch for Three

Tom, the technology director for a small, private university, has returned from the State Teacher Education Conference and the dinner meeting with his colleagues encouraged by the directions the state is moving in with regard to technology and teacher education. Because of the number of liberal arts faculty members at his school who already use technology, Tom is not overwhelmed by the possibility of integrating technology throughout the teacher education program. We join him and two faculty colleagues as they discuss technology integration over lunch.

Tom: I still have concerns about how the university will be able to gather enough resources to make full integration possible, but I believe that our best way to graduate future teachers who are competent with technology is to integrate technology throughout the teacher education program.

Vanessa: With the secondary education program, we really don't have all that many teacher education courses. Are there enough courses to give students the technology exposure they need?

Pam: If you consider just the teacher education courses, probably not. However, Tom is talking about the teacher education program, and that includes all the courses that teacher education students must take to graduate, including general studies.

Vanessa: That does make more sense. But wow! How can we make that happen? There are a lot of courses and faculty to involve. It sounds as if it could be a big mess. And don't forget that we also have to integrate the state-mandated teaching standards.

Tom: What we need is a framework. I thought we should present a plan at the next Teacher Education Committee meeting, but we need a model or framework first so everyone will understand what we are talking about. I think the idea of technology integration will make much more sense to everyone on the committee if there is an example to follow and modify that brings all of these pieces together.

Pam: A model makes sense. Do you have one in mind? Does such a model even exist?

FINDING A MODEL FOR ■■■ ■ TECHNOLOGY INTEGRATION ■ ■■ ■

Does such a model exist? Wouldn't it be nice if there were a tool that outlined everything that a SCDE should do to integrate technology successfully? We need something to show us not only what technology to use and when to use it, but also how to make technology experiences meaningful to students and how those skills and experiences relate back to the variety of standards a SCDE must fulfill.

The International Society for Technology in Education (ISTE) has provided one piece of our puzzle. Through an initiative funded by the U.S. Department of Education, ISTE, in concert with numerous educational organizations, developed the National Educational Technology Standards (NETS) for Teachers (ISTE, 2000a). These standards are in alignment with the NETS for K–12 students (described later in this chapter). The 2000 NETS for Teachers are part of an evolutionary process that began in 1993 with the first edition of the ISTE Technology Standards for All Teachers and then moved to the second edition of these standards (adopted by NCATE and discussed previously in the book). The standards are presented in Figure 4.1.

Figure 4.1 ISTE National Educational Technology Standards and Performance Indicators

I. **TECHNOLOGY OPERATIONS AND CONCEPTS.** Teachers demonstrate a sound understanding of technology operations and concepts. Teachers:
- demonstrate introductory knowledge, skills, and understanding of concepts related to technology (as described in the ISTE National Education Technology Standards for Students).
- demonstrate continual growth in technology knowledge and skills to stay abreast of current and emerging technologies.

II. **PLANNING AND DESIGNING LEARNING ENVIRONMENTS AND EXPERIENCES.** Teachers plan and design effective learning environments and experiences supported by technology. Teachers:
- design developmentally appropriate learning opportunities that apply technology-enhanced instructional strategies to support the diverse needs of learners.
- apply current research on teaching and learning with technology when planning learning environments and experiences.
- identify and locate technology resources and evaluate them for accuracy and suitability.
- plan for the management of technology resources within the context of learning activities.
- plan strategies to manage student learning in a technology-enhanced environment.

III. **TEACHING, LEARNING, AND THE CURRICULUM.** Teachers implement curriculum plans that include methods and strategies for applying technology to maximize student learning. Teachers:
- facilitate technology-enhanced experiences that address content standards and student technology standards.
- use technology to support learner-centered strategies that address the diverse needs of students.

(continued)

- apply technology to develop students' higher order skills and creativity.
- manage student learning activities in a technology-enhanced environment.

IV. **ASSESSMENT AND EVALUATION.** Teachers apply technology to facilitate a variety of effective assessment and evaluation strategies. Teachers:
- apply technology in assessing student learning of subject matter using a variety of assessment techniques.
- use technology resources to collect and analyze data, interpret results, and communicate findings to improve instructional practice and maximize student learning.
- apply multiple methods of evaluation to determine students' appropriate use of technology resources for learning, communication, and productivity.

V. **PRODUCTIVITY AND PROFESSIONAL PRACTICE.** Teachers use technology to enhance their productivity and professional practice. Teachers:
- use technology resources to engage in ongoing professional development and lifelong learning.
- continually evaluate and reflect on professional practice to make informed decisions regarding the use of technology in support of student learning.
- apply technology to increase productivity.
- use technology to communicate and collaborate with peers, parents, and the larger community in order to nurture student learning.

VI. **SOCIAL, ETHICAL, LEGAL, AND HUMAN ISSUES.** Teachers understand the social, ethical, legal, and human issues surrounding the use of technology in PK–12 schools and apply those principles in practice. Teachers:
- model and teach legal and ethical practice related to technology use.
- apply technology resources to enable and empower learners with diverse backgrounds, characteristics, and abilities.
- identify and use technology resources that affirm diversity.
- promote safe and healthy use of technology resources.
- facilitate equitable access to technology resources for all students.

Source: ISTE, 2000a.

NETS for Teachers have four performance profiles for teacher preparation:

- General Preparation (lower division class, typically part of the arts and sciences curriculum)
- Professional Education (teacher preparation classes typically taught in the SCDE)
- Student Teaching Internship
- First-Year Teacher

Each performance profile has its own set of indicators that relate to the standards and pinpoint the developmental stage of the teacher education student. The profiles for the first three are detailed in Figures 4.2 through 4.4.

Figure 4.2 General Preparation Performance Profile

The roman numerals in parentheses relate to the standards presented in Figure 4.1.

1. Demonstrate a sound understanding of the nature and operation of technology systems. (I)

2. Demonstrate proficiency in the use of common input and output devices; solve routine hardware and software problems; and make informed choices about technology systems, resources, and services. (I)

3. Use technology tools and information resources to increase productivity, promote creativity, and facilitate academic learning. (I, III, IV, V)

4. Use content-specific tools (e.g., software, simulation, environmental robes, graphing calculators, exploratory environments, Web tools) to support learning and research. (I, III, V)

5. Use technology resources to facilitate higher order and complex thinking skills, including problem solving, critical thinking, informed decision making, knowledge construction, and creativity. (I, III, V)

(continued)

6. Collaborate in constructing technology-enhanced models, preparing publications, and producing other creative works using productivity tools. (I, V)

7. Use technology to locate, evaluate, and collect information from a variety of sources. (I, IV, V)

8. Use technology tools to process data and report results. (I, III, IV, V)

9. Use technology in the development of strategies for solving problems in the real world. (I, III, V)

10. Observe and experience the use of technology in their [students'] major field of study. (III, V)

11. Use technology tools and resources for managing and communicating information (e.g., finances, schedules, addresses, purchases, correspondence). (I, V)

12. Evaluate and select new information resources and technological innovations based on their appropriateness to specific tasks. (I, III, IV, V)

13. Use a variety of media and formats, including telecommunications, to collaborate, publish, and interact with peers, experts, and other audiences. (I, V)

14. Demonstrate an understanding of the legal, ethical, cultural, and societal issues related to technology. (VI)

15. Exhibit positive attitudes toward technology uses that support lifelong learning, collaboration, personal pursuits, and productivity. (V, VI)

16. Discuss diversity issues related to electronic media. (I, VI)

17. Discuss the health and safety issues related to technology use. (VI)

Source: ISTE, 2000a.

Figure 4.3 Preparation Performance Profile

The roman numerals in parentheses relate to the standards presented in Figure 4.1.

1. Identify the benefits of technology to maximize student learning and facilitate higher order thinking skills. (I, III)

2. Differentiate between appropriate and inappropriate uses of technology for teaching and learning while using electronic resources to design and implement learning activities. (II, III, V, VI)

3. Identify technology resources available in schools and analyze how accessibility to those resources affects planning for instruction. (I, II)

4. Identify, select, and use hardware and software technology resources specially designed for use by PK–12 students to meet specific teaching and learning objectives. (I, II)

5. Plan for the management of electronic instructional resources within a lesson design by identifying potential problems and planning for solutions. (II)

6. Identify specific technology applications and resources that maximize student learning, address learner needs, and affirm diversity. (III, VI)

7. Design and teach technology-enriched learning activities that connect content standards with student technology standards and meet the diverse needs of students. (II, III, IV, VI)

8. Design and peer teach a lesson that meets content area standards and reflects the current best practices in teaching and learning with technology. (II, III)

9. Plan and teach student-centered learning activities and lessons in which students apply technology tools and resources. (II, III)

10. Research and evaluate the accuracy, relevance, appropriateness, comprehensiveness, and bias of electronic information resources to be used by students. (II, IV, V, VI)

(continued)

11. Discuss technology-based assessment and evaluation strategies. (IV)

12. Examine multiple strategies for evaluating technology-based student products and the processes used to create those products. (IV)

13. Examine technology tools used to collect, analyze, interpret, represent, and communicate student performance data. (I, IV)

14. Integrate technology-based assessment strategies and tools into plans for evaluating specific learning activities. (IV)

15. Develop a portfolio of technology-based products from course work, including the related assessment tools. (IV, V)

16. Identify and engage in technology-based opportunities for professional education and lifelong learning, including the use of distance education. (V)

17. Apply online and other technology resources to support problem solving and related decision making for maximizing student learning. (III, V)

18. Participate in online professional collaborations with peers and experts. (III, V)

19. Use technology productivity tools to complete required professional tasks. (V)

20. Identify technology-related legal and ethical issues, including copyright, privacy, and security of technology systems, data, and information. (VI)

21. Examine acceptable use policies for the use of technology in schools, including for addressing threats to security of technology systems, data, information. (VI)

22. Identify issues related to equitable access to technology in school, community, and home environments. (VI)

23. Identify safety and health issues related to technology use in schools. (VI)

24. Identify and use assistive technologies to meet the special physical needs of students. (VI)

Source: ISTE, 2000a.

Figure 4.4 Student Teaching Internship Profile

The roman numerals in parentheses relate to the standards presented in Figure 4.1.

1. Apply troubleshooting strategies for solving routine hardware and software problems that occur in the classroom. (I)

2. Identify, evaluate, and select specific technology resources available at the school site and district level to support a coherent lesson sequence. (II, III)

3. Design, manage, and facilitate learning experiences using technology that affirm diversity and provide equitable access to resources. (II, VI)

4. Create and implement a well-organized plan to manage available technology resources, provide equitable access for all students, and enhance learning outcomes. (II, III)

5. Design and facilitate learning experiences that use assistive technologies to meet the special physical needs of students. (II, III)

6. Design and teach a coherent sequence of learning activities that integrates appropriate use of technology resources to enhance student academic achievement and technology proficiency by connecting district, state, and national curriculum standards with student technology standards (as defined in the ISTE National Educational Technology Standards for Students). (II, III)

7. Design, implement, and assess learner-centered lessons that are based on the current best practices on teaching and learning with technology and that engage, motivate, and encourage self-directed student learning. (II, III, IV, V)

8. Guide collaborative learning activities in which students use technology resources to solve authentic problems in the subject area(s). (III)

9. Develop and use criteria for ongoing assessment of technology-based student products and the processes used to create those products. (IV)

(continued)

10. Design an evaluation plan that applies multiple measures and flexible assessment strategies to determine students' technology proficiency and content area learning. (IV)

11. Use multiple measures to analyze instructional practices that employ technology to improve planning, instruction, and management. (II, III, IV)

12. Apply technology productivity tools and resources to collect, analyze, and interpret data and to report results to parents and students. (III, IV)

13. Select and apply suitable productivity tools to complete educational and professional tasks. (II, III, V)

14. Model safe and responsible use of technology and develop classroom procedures to implement school and district technology acceptable use policies and data security plans. (V, VI)

15. Participate in online professional collaboration with peers and experts as part of a personally designed plan, based on self-assessment, for professional growth in technology. (V)

Source: ISTE, 2000a.

The NETS for Teachers document also provides scenarios of the types of integrated, developmental, technology activity that would take place in the higher education setting to address the standards (see the Resources section of this book for information on how to find the full NETS document). These scenarios can be a good start for faculty wanting to integrate technology. However, the opening discussion between Tom, Vanessa, and Pam also mentioned the need for a model that brings together technology standards, other teaching standards, and the teacher education program.

A tool similar to what we want does exist for the K–12 teaching environment: the National Educational Technology Standards. The NETS Project brought together numerous stakeholders in P–12 education to develop technology standards and expectations (ISTE, 2000b), with the emphasis on integration and the transformation of student learning. Six technology foundation standards for students were developed:

1. Basic operations and concepts
   - Students demonstrate a sound understanding of the nature and operation of technology systems.
   - Students are proficient in the use of technology.
2. Social, ethical, and human issues
   - Students understand the ethical, cultural, and societal issues related to technology.
   - Students practice responsible use of technology systems, information, and software.
   - Students develop positive attitudes toward technology uses that support lifelong learning, collaboration, personal pursuits, and productivity.
3. Technology productivity tools
   - Students use technology tools to enhance learning, increase productivity, and promote creativity.
   - Students use productivity tools to collaborate in constructing technology-enhanced models, prepare publications, and produce other creative works.
4. Technology communications tools
   - Students use telecommunications to collaborate, publish, and interact with peers, experts, and other audiences.
   - Students use a variety of media and formats to communicate information and ideas effectively to multiple audiences.
5. Technology research tools
   - Students use technology to locate, evaluate, and collect information from a variety of sources.
   - Students use technology tools to process data and report results.
   - Students evaluate and select new information resources and technological innovations based on the appropriateness for specific tasks.
6. Technology problem-solving and decision-making tools
   - Students use technology resources for solving problems and making informed decisions.
   - Students employ technology in the development of strategies for solving problems in the real world. (ISTE, 2000b, p. 14)

Like NETS for Teachers, NETS for Students are broken down into performance indicators at various developmental levels throughout P–12, with performance indicators of the standards that are appropriate at each developmental level. A sample of these performance indicators across developmental levels is shown in Table 4.1.

Like the teacher standards, the performance indicators are different at various developmental levels. The expectations evolve and grow as the students develop. In early childhood (P–2), students are accessing and retrieving information and learning the basics of computer technology. They begin the process of using technology to produce their own knowledge. By the end of the twelfth grade, the emphasis of the technology standards and performance indicators is on the use of technology for knowledge production.

The NETS for Students Project brought together writing teams comprising teachers from different grade levels and content areas to create curricular activities that integrate technology. The technology integration activities are composed around the content-area curriculum standards of English language arts, foreign language, mathematics, science, and social studies. For example, in English language arts, the activities relate to the technology standards for students by NETS and the Standards for English Language Arts developed by the National Council of Teachers of English and the International Reading Association. The curriculum integration activities are a tool to provide direction on how to transform the teacher and student—and therefore the entire course. The NETS document maps the curriculum activities to the curriculum standards and the NETS performance indicators. A social studies example that maps learning activities to NETS and the National Council for the Social Studies thematic standards is provided in Figure 4.5.

The NETS document brings together all of these elements—standards, performance indicators by developmental level, and curriculum activities—to create a complete package for technology integration:

> Curriculum integration with the use of technology involves the infusion of technology as a tool to enhance the learning in a content area of multidisciplinary setting. Technology enables students to learn in

Table 4.1 Example of NETS Performance Indicators

Grades P–2	Grades 3–5	Grades 6–8	Grades 9–12
	Performance Indicators		

Standard 1: Basic Operations and Concepts

Grades P–2	Grades 3–5	Grades 6–8	Grades 9–12
Use input devices to successfully operate computers, VCRs, audiotapes, and other technologies.	Apply strategies for identifying and solving routine hardware and software problems that occur during everyday use.	Apply strategies for identifying and solving routine hardware and software problems that occur during everyday use.	Make informed choices among technology systems, resources, and services.
Use a variety of media and technology resources for directed and independent learning activities.	Demonstrate an understanding of concepts underlying hardware, software, and connectivity, and of practical applications to learning and problem solving.	Demonstrate an understanding of concepts underlying hardware, software, and connectivity, and of practical applications to learning and problem solving.	
Communicate about technology using developmentally appropriate and accurate terminology.			
Use developmentally appropriate multimedia resources to support learning.			

Source: ISTE, 2000b.

ways not previously possible. Effective integration of technology is achieved when students are able to select technology tools to help them obtain information in a timely manner, analyze and synthesize the information, and present it professionally. The technology should become an integral part of how the classroom functions—as accessible as all other classroom tools. (ISTE, 2000b, p. 6)

Figure 4.5   Example of NETS Mapping Process of Activities to Curriculum Standards and Technology Performance Indicators

The Gettysburg Address (Grades 9–12)

Students use a multimedia project, *The Valley of the Shadow: Two American Communities in the Civil War,* which has been cited by the National Endowment for the Humanities as an example of the "best of the humanities on the Web" to create a presentation about the significance of the Gettysburg Address. Students work on expert teams to explore the interactive history materials.

Activities	Social Studies Standards	NETS Performance Indicators
Divide students into four expert teams. Each team synthesizes its findings about the Battle of Gettysburg using newspapers, letters, photographs, or maps.	II	7–10
Use the newspaper database search engine to locate newspaper articles about the Battle of Gettysburg.		10
Use the Civil War letters database search engine to locate letters about the Battle of Gettysburg.	II, X	3, 5, 6, 7, 8, 9, 10

Source: ISTE, 2000b.

BUILDING A FRAMEWORK
SPECIFIC TO THE SCDE

A document similar to the NETS for Students would be handy for the SCDE. Wouldn't it be nice if faculty could pull a book from the shelf and find proven techniques for integrating technology into, for example, a child development course? However, a document like the NETS for Students would assume a certain degree of uniformity among teacher education programs. In fact, as both a source of pride and economic survival, SCDEs work hard to differentiate themselves from each other. Teacher education programs must subscribe to varying sets of standards depending on their accreditation organizations and state licensure requirements. Teacher education programs also vary in the general structure of the program: four-year, five-year, graduate, and so forth. Finally, although course topics may be similar across programs, the individual faculty members who teach these courses approach the topics in unique and differing ways. Therefore, any framework or tool for integration would need to be flexible to allow the flavor of a program to emerge.

What is needed is a framework that teacher education programs can understand, use, and adapt to their own unique needs. The framework must be flexible while simultaneously pointing SCDEs in the direction of successful technology integration. We suggest a model that uses elements similar to the NETS for Students (standards, developmental levels, technology activities, and course and student transformation) and also the developmental aspects of the NETS for Teachers. To that end, we offer Figure 4.6 as a model for the full integration of technology.

The model presented here combines the Principles of the Interstate New Teacher Assessment and Support Consortium (INTASC), the Professional Skills for the Digital Age Classroom developed by the Milken Exchange on Education Technology (1999), and three developmental levels of the teacher education program. Each of these elements is described in greater detail.

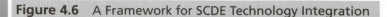

Figure 4.6   A Framework for SCDE Technology Integration

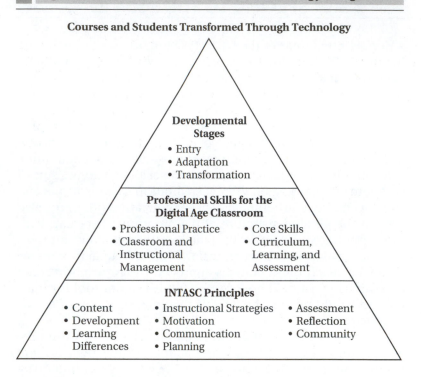

Courses and Students Transformed Through Technology

Developmental Stages
- Entry
- Adaptation
- Transformation

Professional Skills for the Digital Age Classroom
- Professional Practice
- Classroom and Instructional Management
- Core Skills
- Curriculum, Learning, and Assessment

INTASC Principles
- Content
- Development
- Learning Differences
- Instructional Strategies
- Motivation
- Communication
- Planning
- Assessment
- Reflection
- Community

INTASC and the Framework

INTASC originated with the Council of Chief State School Officers in 1987, which sought to bring collaboration among states to promote reform in education, licensing, and professional development of teachers. INTASC used the framework of the National Board for Professional Teaching Standards to develop a core set of performance standards to evaluate new teachers. Numerous states have adopted these standards as tools to evaluate and certify new teachers. For example, the Indiana Professional Standards Board (IPSB) and the state of Indiana were cited in *Quality Counts 2000* as being a forerunner in teacher assessment and licensure (Education Week, 2000). The IPSB adopted the INTASC Standards and used these principles as a basis for its own performance-based standards developed according to student developmental age and content area. Ten principles constitute the core INTASC standards:

1. The teacher understands the central concepts, tools of inquiry, and structures of the discipline(s) he or she teaches and can create learning experiences that make these aspects of subject matter meaningful for students.

2. The teacher understands how children learn and develop, and can provide learning opportunities that support their intellectual, social and personal development.

3. The teacher understands how students differ in their approaches to learning and creates instructional opportunities that are adapted to diverse learners.

4. The teacher understands and uses a variety of instructional strategies to encourage students' development of critical thinking, problem solving, and performance skills.

5. The teacher uses an understanding of individual and group motivation and behavior to create a learning environment that encourages positive social interaction, active engagement in learning, and self-motivation.

6. The teacher uses knowledge of effective verbal, nonverbal, and media communication techniques to foster active inquiry, collaboration, and supportive interaction in the classroom.

7. The teacher plans instruction based upon knowledge of subject matter, students, the community, and curriculum goals.

8. The teacher understands and uses formal and informal assessment strategies to evaluate and ensure the continuous intellectual, social and physical development of the learner.

9. The teacher is a reflective practitioner who continually evaluates the effects of his/her choices and actions on others (students, parents, and other professionals in the learning community) and who actively seeks out opportunities to grow professionally.

10. The teacher fosters relationships with school colleagues, parents, and agencies in the larger community to support students' learning and well-being. (http://www.cssso.org/intascst.html)

The INTASC standards are in the framework as a representative of teaching standards that SCDEs must consider in their program. As we described in Chapter 3, a fully integrated technology approach must be used throughout the entire teacher education program. Therefore, if an SCDE uses a set of accreditation standards, those standards must form the base of its integrated technology approach. We have included INTASC as the base of our framework, on which the other elements are built. However, a SCDE can substitute another set of teaching standards if INTASC is not applicable.

The Professional Skills for the Digital Age Classroom and the Framework

As written, the INTASC standards have little direct connection to technology, but there are a number of linkages with technology standards. Just as the INTASC standards emphasize teacher performance, the Professional Skills for the Digital Age Classroom also emphasize the ability of the teacher to perform in the classroom with technology.

The Milken Exchange on Education Technology, an initiative of the Milken Family Foundation, developed the Professional Competency Continuum: Professional Skills for the Digital Age Classroom (1999). Recognizing that technology has had little measurable impact on classroom practice, the Milken Exchange engaged in a process to develop a tool that school systems could use to gauge their technology use. For this element of the framework, technology standards, we could also have used the ISTE Technology Standards for Teachers (ISTE, 1998), which have been adopted by NCATE for use in accreditation and were discussed earlier in the book, or the NETS for Teachers presented in this chapter. Both sets of standards cover similar competency skills, and it is important for SCDEs to be familiar with the standards developed by ISTE. However, we selected the Professional Skills for the Digital Age Classroom for our framework because, like the INTASC Principles, they focus on what teachers should be able to do in the classroom. In addition, we want to present a range of technology standards options that help SCDEs select the most appropriate ones for their needs.

There are five standards in the Professional Skills for the Digital Age Classroom document. Four of these five standards are used in the technology integration framework; the last standard applies to administration and is not discussed here. The four areas covered in the framework are core technology skills, curriculum learning assessment, professional practice, and classroom and instructional management. Additional specific skills fall under each of these broad categories:

1. Core Technology Skills

   1.1 The educator has a firm understanding of the principles of operation of the computer system and peripherals. This understanding has translated into the ability to adapt quickly to new technologies as they become available.

   1.2 The educator is familiar with technologies specific to the discipline she teaches and is able to use these technologies successfully to support student learning.

   1.3 The educator has mastered the use of basic software applications and is able to generalize these skills quickly to learn new applications.

   1.4 The educator has sufficient skill and experience to make efficient and effective use of complex electronic information resources.

   1.5 The educator understands the power of computer networks and is able to use those networks to facilitate communications, professional growth and student learning.

   1.6 The educator is familiar with multimedia and presentation technologies and is able to guide students in the application of these technologies to create knowledge products.

2. Curriculum, Learning and Assessment

   2.1 The educator is skilled at identifying opportunities within the curriculum for improved student learning through technology and is capable of designing technology-enriched learning activities that support the curriculum.

   2.2 The educator has a variety of instructional strategies for teaching and learning with technology and is able to match specific strategies with the learning needs of individual students.

   2.3 The educator understands the possibilities for new roles for educators that might better support learning in the technology-rich classroom and has mastered specific strategies for adopting these roles.

   2.4 The educator understands the possibilities for new roles for students in the technology-rich classroom and has explicit strategies for supporting students as they adopt these roles.

2.5 The educator has skill in the design and implementation of a variety of assessment strategies, including performance and product-based assessments that are often more relevant in the technology-rich classroom.

3. Professional Practice

3.1 Technology has had a significant impact on the personal and professional productivity of the educator.

3.2 The educator is able to use technology to participate in increased levels of professional collaboration.

3.3 The educator is able to use technology to communicate with students, parents, educators and the wider community more effectively.

3.4 The educator is skilled in the use of technology to access a wide variety of professional resources.

3.5 The educator is sufficiently knowledgeable to play a significant role in the identification and acquisition of technology resources in support of learning.

4. Classroom and Instructional Management

4.1 The educator is skilled in the organization of classroom technology resources and orchestration of activity within that environment.

4.2 The educator is aware of how to locate and access technology resources that will support instructional strategies.

4.3 The educator is skilled in the use of technology to track student progress through curriculum and manage curriculum resources. (Milken Exchange, 1999, pp. 19–31)

These specific skills should be familiar in that they reflect the content that is generally found in the stand-alone technology course, as discussed in Chapter 3. There is an additional link between the technology skills and the INTASC principles that is less apparent. Both sets of standards in fact describe the same performances, that is, the standards are naturally integrated together in the performances—for example:

- INTASC Principle 8 is reflected in the following performance indicator of Professional Skill 2: "The educator has skill in the design and implementation of a variety of assessment strategies, including performance and product-based assessments that are often more relevant in the technology-rich classroom."

- INTASC Principle 4 is reflected in the following performance indicator of Professional Skill 2: "The educator is skilled at identifying opportunities for improved student learning through technology and is capable of designing technology-rich learning activities that support the curriculum."

- INTASC Principle 10 can be found in the performance indicator for Professional Skill 3: "The educator is able to use technology to communicate with students, parents, educators and the wider community more effectively."

On another level, technology competency links not only with the performance of teaching standards, but also with the assessment of these performances. Chapter 2 described how preservice teachers at Purdue University create electronic portfolios to demonstrate not only their proficiency with technology, but also the level of compliance with the teaching standards. Indiana State University uses **electronic discussion groups** to triangulate evidence of preservice teachers' dispositions (an element of the INTASC Principles) toward teaching and students.

Developmental Stages and the Framework

We have called the top level of the framework Developmental Stages (see Figure 4.6). These developmental stages represent two different elements in the framework. First, the Professional Skills for the Digital Age Classroom are founded on "stages of instructional evolution," which were identified in the research done with the Apple Classrooms of Tomorrow (ACOT). The ACOT research identified five stages that teachers go through as they grow in comfort and ability with technology (Sandholz, Ringstaff, & Dwyer, 1997). The Milken Exchange on Education Technology elected to apply three of these stages to the Professional Skills for a Digital Age Classroom:

- *Stage 1: Entry.* At this stage, educators, students and the community are aware of the possibilities that technology holds for improving learning—but learning, teaching and the system remain relatively unchanged. Educators at this level lack access to technology and the requisite skills to implement and sustain significant changes in practice.

- *Stage 2: Adaptation.* Technology is thoroughly integrated into the classroom in support of existing practice. Educators at this stage have developed skills related to the use of technology, but have primarily applied these skills to automate, accelerate and enhance the teaching and learning strategies already in place.

- *Stage 3: Transformation.* At this stage, technology is a catalyst for significant changes in learning practice. Students and teachers adopt new roles and relationships. New learning opportunities are possible through the creative application of technology to the entire school community. (Milken Exchange, 1999, p. 11)

Each of the general performance indicators for the technology standards has a different description depending on the stage in the continuum. As an example, the stages of the Curriculum indicator for the Curriculum, Learning and Assessment Standard are described as follows:

- *Stage 1: Entry.* The educator is aware of the value of technology in the instructional program, but tends to use technology as a reward or as an end in itself. Educational software, when used, is often used out of context. The educator occasionally uses software and online services that are topically related to the curriculum being addressed, but little in-depth attention is paid to specific educational objectives of the software or the impact of its use. This software may be used in a lab rather than in the classroom under the direction of a "computer educator" or aide.

- *Stage 2: Adaptation.* The educator regularly applies technology that supports the existing curriculum standards. These applications typically reflect presentations of content or student activities that are similar to those found in the classroom prior to the introduction of technology.

- *Stage 3: Transformation.* The educator has become skilled at involving students in developing technology-enriched learning activities that are authentic, multidisciplinary and directly related to district, state and national academic standards. Strategies are aligned with standards both for efficiency of instruction and maximum student engagement.

The Resources section of this book contains information on accessing the full Milken Exchange document.

The second way that the developmental stages apply to the framework is through the stages of a teacher education program. Just as both NETS documents demonstrate that technology integration varies across developmental stages of K–12 and teacher preparation, we also believe that technology integration in a teacher education program can and should change across the developmental stages. Although no two teacher education programs are alike, we broke the category of teacher education into three major developmental components, regardless of the type of program (four-year, five-year, graduate, and so on):

Stage 1 (Entry): Courses and experiences might include general and university studies, speech communications, introduction to sociology or psychology, English composition, English literature, basic math, introductory physical science, introduction to child development, educational foundations, educational multiculturalism, education and special needs, classroom field observations.

Stage 2 (Adaptation): Courses and experiences might include advanced general studies, advanced sociology or psychology, specialized child development, content methods, teaching methodology, advanced content-area courses, history or philosophy of education, micro-teaching in the field, family and community or service learning.

Stage 3 (Transformation): Courses and experiences might include internship or student teaching and a capstone course.

Stages are an important element to consider in the design of a full, integrated technology approach. The ACOT research found that practicing teachers move through a series of stages in their use of technology. It is reasonable to assume that teacher education students will also need to work through similar stages. A SCDE that integrates technology to develop future teachers who can competently use technology in their classrooms should guide the teacher education students through the developmental stages. Much as the teacher education program is a process to guide preservice teachers through the development of being a good teacher, those same stages (presented here in three stages) will serve technology integration and development.

As the characters in the opening scenario said, and as we discussed in Chapter 2, the teacher education program encompasses more than the courses offered by the SCDE. Courses offered in the arts and sciences and other university divisions are all part of the program that a teacher education student must complete for a teaching degree or licensure and are part of the stages of a teacher education program. Therefore, to integrate technology throughout the teacher education program, the SCDE must work with the entire university.

Putting All the Pieces Together

When we put all of these elements together, as shown in Figure 4.6, we have combined instructional technologies with the main elements of the teacher education program. The elements of the framework are also adaptable to the specific standards of a SCDE. How the framework helps to guide the process of full technology integration is that each piece builds on the other. When teaching standards are considered in isolation, it is only by accident that technology skills will be melded into courses developmentally, or even at all. Chapter 9 discusses planning strategies; the framework presented in this chapter, or a similar one that considers all of these elements, should be a part of the planning process.

INTEGRATED
■ ■■ ■ TECHNOLOGY ACTIVITIES ■ ■ ■■ ■

The framework serves as a tool to demonstrate how elements of the teacher education program can be brought together to develop a cohesive, technology integration process. However, without specific examples, it may be difficult to conceptualize the framework and the interlinking of the elements. This section provides a number of activities that can be incorporated into the teacher education program and are then mapped to all of the elements of the framework.

Activities for Stage 1 of the Teacher Education Program (Entry)

During the first stage of the teacher education program, preservice teachers need to become familiar with the various technologies that are available and how to use them. Faculty and the courses should model the effective uses of instructional technologies while building student skills so they are ready to use technology to create knowledge products when they enter the second stage of the teacher education program. Although the following activities are presented as Stage 1 technology activities, they can continue throughout the program. These activities form a base to the model, with other technology skills built on this base. Table 4.2 maps the sample activities to the Milken Professional Skills for the Digital Age Classroom and the INTASC Standards.

Electronic Discussion Group for Each Teacher Education Cohort. If the SCDE uses cohorts in the teacher education program, an electronic discussion group can be effectively used to build a sense of community among the preservice teachers. Electronic discussion groups can also be used for individual classes. However, having the same electronic discussion that grows and evolves over the entire span of a preservice teacher's program encourages more community building and camaraderie.

When the cohort is formed, the electronic discussion group can also be formed and then facilitated or moderated by a SCDE faculty member. It is important for the faculty member to assume the role of facilitator for the discussion rather than direct the entire discussion. The purpose is to provide students an electronic forum in which they can share information about the program, provide peer assistance, share classroom strategies, and so forth. The conversation that takes place in the electronic forum will change depending on the developmental stage of the student. At the entry stage, conversation is likely to be based on reporting what students are experiencing. As they mature, students begin to discuss such issues as strategies employed in the field and classroom management and reflect on their own

	Milken Professional Skills	INTASC Principles
Table 4.2 Entry Stage Learning Activities		
1. Electronic discussion group for each teacher education cohort	1.2, 1.5, 2.4, 3.1, 3.2	5, 6, 9, 10
2. Peer teaching and coaching for computer skills	1.1, 1.2, 1.3, 3.1, 3.2	3, 4, 10
3. Virtual field trip to a variety of classrooms (e.g., developmental level, subject area, types of schools)	1.4, 1.5, 2.1, 2.3, 3.2, 3.3, 3.4, 3.5	1, 2, 3
4. Beginning of an electronic portfolio	1.1, 1.3, 1.6, 2.3, 2.5, 4.2, 4.3	1, 9
5. Digital recording of field observations	1.1, 1.3, 1.6, 2.3, 2.4, 2.5, 3.1, 3.2, 3.3, 3.4, 4.3	1, 2, 3, 4, 5, 6, 8, 9
6. Observation of technology-rich classrooms	2.1, 2.3, 2.4, 3.1, 3.5, 4.2	1, 2, 4, 6, 8
7. Electronic journaling	1.5, 3.1, 3.4	9
8. Web scavenger hunts for educational resources	1.2, 1.4, 3.4, 3.5, 4.1, 4.2	1, 2, 3, 10
9. Electronic sources for course assignments	1.1, 1.3, 1.4, 1.5, 3.1, 3.4, 4.2	1, 6, 10
10. Course web sites for grades, communication, announcements, and course materials	1.1, 1.3, 1.4, 1.5, 3.1, 3.4, 4.2	1, 6, 8, 10

teaching. As a facilitator, the faculty member's role is to make sure that conversations do not degenerate into petty concerns and to steer the conversation to relevant issues or make connections to relevant standards. Faculty throughout a teacher education program can suggest topics for on-line discussion. For example, a sociology professor could suggest that her teacher education students continue a discussion about school violence in the electronic discussion group, or the instructor for multicultural education could request that students gather examples of different cultural approaches to discipline through the discussion group.

Peer Teaching and Coaching for Computer Skills. When preservice teachers graduate, they will be expected to help their students learn about and use technology. An effective way to prepare teacher education students for that role, and also to ensure that all preservice teachers have the minimum level of technology skills, is to have students provide training for each other on a variety of computer skills and applications. Peer teaching also requires that teacher education students find effective ways to ensure that their classmates understand the technology. Particularly for students who struggle to understand instructional technologies, the peer teacher will need to find the right strategies and techniques.

Peer technology coaching can take place within small groups of five or six. The coaching and teaching provide the teacher education students with valuable experience with teaching about technology, and they give the faculty member some flexibility. For example, a life sciences instructor might want students to complete a computer simulation on frog dissection. Teacher education students who are comfortable with this or similar software can work with groups of students who have not previously used simulations. The instructor does not need to spend class time teaching how to use the software; the peer coaches can do the instruction outside class time. The instructor can instead use the class time to apply the knowledge obtained from the simulation. Also, combining several examples together, students can use the electronic discussion group to request peer coaching when needed.

Virtual Field Trip to a Variety of Classrooms. There are a myriad of classroom types that teacher education students will never experience. Perhaps a SCDE is located in a homogeneous community, thereby limiting the economically or culturally diverse classroom settings that the preservice teachers can experience. Furthermore, teacher education students who have already identified the grade level or subject area in which they plan to teach may never experience other types of classroom; they may never experience a grade or subject that is in fact a better personal fit.

The virtual field trip can be **synchronous** or **asynchronous**. The field trip can be conducted with video over the Internet (which can easily be done in the regular classrooms at both sites) or with one-way or two-way interactive video (which usually needs to be done in specialized classrooms with the necessary equipment). The asynchronous field trip can be conducted through videotape, through the Internet with digitally recorded video, or through computer-assisted instruction with digitally recorded video. Which option is selected depends on the instructional goals of the teacher education instructor and the tools available at the SCDE and in the field classroom.

If the goal is merely observation and reflection on what has been viewed in the classroom, the asynchronous virtual field trip will probably meet most needs. The asynchronous field trip also allows students to view the visited classroom multiple times if necessary. A recorded classroom visit allows the instructor to use the field trip several times within the same semester and over many semesters. A recorded field trip also ensures that the teacher education students are viewing classroom activities that achieve the desired outcomes. However, if the goal of the teacher education instructor is to have preservice teachers interact with the K–12 students in the field, synchronous is obviously the preferred method. At this early stage of the teacher education program, it is probably better if preservice teachers engage primarily in observation as they work to develop their technology skills and comfort, as well as their ability to work with students in the field.

Beginning of an Electronic Portfolio. Chapter 2 discussed the work at Purdue University to incorporate electronic portfolios into the teacher education program. As performance assessment increasingly becomes a central feature of teacher education programs, SCDEs turn to the use of portfolios to document preservice teacher performance. However, sheets of paper do not always provide an accurate reflection of teaching performance. Teacher education students find they must also include videotapes, photographs, printouts of computer presentations and worksheets, and even computer disks. It takes a tremendous amount of effort to tie all these elements together in a clear and understandable manner.

Electronic portfolios tackle two formidable tasks at the same time. First, they function as a paper portfolio and provide documentation of performance. Second, they provide substantial evidence of the teacher education student's proficiency with technology. Whether the electronic portfolio is in the form of an extensive web site, interactive multimedia, or an electronic portfolio software package (such as Scholastic's Electronic Portfolio), the ability to create an electronic portfolio is itself an artifact of the portfolio.

The formation of an electronic portfolio should begin in the entry stage of the teacher education program. Students may have only limited performance evidence to include at this point in the teacher education program. However, because they are in the process of developing the multimedia technology skills needed to create an electronic portfolio, the emphasis can be on the development of the portfolio framework. All faculty members throughout the teacher education program can suggest pieces to be added to the portfolio and can work with students to develop their skills. For the electronic portfolio to be effective, every faculty member of the teacher education program must participate in the development. Furthermore, there must also be a plan as to what parts of the portfolio are developed in specific classes.

SCDEs and faculty can model the use of electronic portfolios. Faculty must create documentation of their performance for the purposes of promotion, tenure, annual reviews, and performance pay. A SCDE that truly values technology and integrates technology into all aspects of the program should also promote the use of electronic portfolios by faculty.

Digital Recording of Field Observations. Field observations can be an effective way for teacher education students to understand how teachers function in a K–12 classroom. These observations can be used early in the teacher education program and can often help students decide if the teaching profession is the right choice for them. Unless the SCDE is using virtual field trips for classroom observations, it is unlikely that all students are observing the same class at the same time. When preservice teachers return to the college classroom, discussion and sharing of their observations is much richer if everyone else in the class could see some of those same observations. Video recording these observations allows for future sharing of these experiences.

The activity, however, specifies digital video recording. The difference is in some ways very minute; in other ways, the difference is significant for an integrated technology approach. Either way, the classroom observation has been recorded and can be used again. The digital recording has the advantage that it can be incorporated easily into the electronic portfolio. The recording can also be altered. One problem with recording of any type in the K–12 classroom is the privacy of children. Children's identities can be masked in a digital recording (e.g., by blurring their faces) while the elements of the teaching are still maintained.

Teacher education faculty can also model the use of digital video recording. Faculty who are in the process of creating an electronic portfolio can include digital examples of classroom practices, and digital recordings can be used for peer review and then incorporated into the portfolio.

Observation of Technology-Rich Classrooms. Teachers teach as they themselves have been taught and what they have experienced. At some point, it is important to break the cycle in order to change the teaching habits of teacher education students. One way for SCDEs to accomplish this task is by integrating technology into the teacher education program. The technology-rich classroom that teacher education students observe can actually be their own classroom. Full technology integration will have faculty modeling the use of technology. Another important element for technology integration, and to help preservice teachers understand how to employ technology effectively, is to expose them to technology-rich K–12 classrooms.

Teacher education students can observe technology-rich classrooms in several ways. One way is to place students in classrooms where teachers are using technology for teaching and learning. If it is difficult to find a sufficient number of K–12 classrooms and teachers where technology is central to the learning process, preservice teachers can virtually visit technology-rich classrooms synchronously or asynchronously. In fact, if the K–12 class is truly using technology in innovative ways, it will be natural for the students and teacher in the field to communicate with the teacher education students virtually.

Electronic Journaling. Journaling can be an effective way for teacher education students to capture their thoughts and reflect on their experiences as they grow as educators. Many SCDE faculty members require preservice teachers to keep a journal, and instructors may periodically collect these notebooks, read the entries, and provide feedback. This process, however, can be somewhat intrusive to the journaling process. While the faculty member has the journals, the students are unable to record new thoughts with the perspective of reading the old thoughts. There is also the drawback as to the length of time it might take to receive the feedback from the faculty member.

Electronic journaling can provide the same benefits of journaling and add some additional benefits. Through either an **intranet** or the Internet, a secure site can be established to which the faculty member and teacher education student have a password. Then at any time preservice teachers can post their reflections, and at any time the faculty member can log on and provide feedback and check the progress of students. This ability to log on at any point also prevents students from completing their reflections all at the same time and through hindsight. The electronic journal can also easily become a part of the electronic portfolio to highlight the teacher education student's ability to reflect.

Teacher education students may perceive some drawbacks to electronic journaling because they must be at a computer to capture their thoughts. The benefit of quicker feedback may not be sufficient to overcome these feelings. However, for technology integration to be successful, technology must be central to the course and the entire teacher education program. One option is to require computers, and perhaps laptops, for all teacher education students. Students can then take the laptop into the field with them to record their observations and reflections. The requirement of a laptop may still be too onerous for some SCDEs. There are less expensive alternatives that can still provide students with technology in the field for journaling and other uses. The SCDE can maintain an equipment pool from which teacher education students can check out laptops for field use. **Electronic keyboards,** which look like small, lightweight laptops but without a display (such as the AlphaSmart), can also be an inexpensive tool to be included in an equipment pool or required for teacher education students. This type of equipment is no more expensive than the average cost of textbooks for a typical course. To make technology integration successful, the technology must be in the hands of the teacher education students.

Web Scavenger Hunts for Educational Resources. At the entry stage of the teacher education program, preservice teachers are also at the entry stage for technology utilization. Technology activities need to help students grow in their comfort and confidence with the available information technology and resources. A simple way to accomplish increased familiarity with information technologies is to engage preservice teachers in web-based scavenger hunts. Teacher education faculty can construct web scavenger hunts in a number of ways:

- If the goal is to have teacher education students become more familiar with a course web site, instructors can embed clues and a prize into the site. As students work their way through the web site, moving from one clue to the next, they become more familiar with the features of the course web site. The last clue can direct them to some information that they forward via e-mail to the instructor to earn them extra credit points.

- To help students develop familiarity with an information technology resource that they will be expected to use many times throughout their teacher education career, such as the library, an instructor can develop a scavenger hunt that compels a student to use the database.

- The number of teacher resources available on the Internet is overwhelming. Teacher education students need to be familiar with these resources. When they begin lesson planning activities in the adaptation stage (Stage 2), these web sites will provide them with a wealth of information. Faculty can direct students to web sites that have teacher resources, educational **portals** and web sites that are specific to a course topic or content area.

- Teacher education students can also be asked to create their own scavenger hunt. In order to develop an original scavenger hunt, students will need to be very familiar with the web sites that are included. Depending on the teacher education course, the scavenger hunts can be created for other teacher education students or for students in the field.

Examples of scavenger hunts are available on the web site for this book.

Electronic Sources for Course Assignments. A wealth of electronic information is available to educators. Many journals are now available on the web. University libraries subscribe to a number of databases that provide full text articles. Many university libraries have a process established for the creation of electronic reserve materials whereby reserve readings are scanned and made available to registered students over the web. Instructors can include these information resources as part of required course readings.

Students can also be expected to use these electronic information sources as they prepare other course assignments. Teacher education students who are using information technology effectively should include these sources as they complete research papers and other assignments. In both instances, for student readings and assignments, electronic sources should not necessarily comprise the entire core of information sources used. Electronic information sources such as web sites can often be easier to access than traditional library sources—but ease of access does not necessarily translate into a better source of information, and instructors need to be clear on their expectations.

Course Web Sites for Grades, Communication, Announcements, and Course Materials. The copying budget of a SCDE can be substantial. The collection of syllabi, handouts, observation sheets, grading rubrics, worksheets, and other materials can create an overwhelming amount of paper. As students lose papers or documents are modified, multiple copies must often be made. Course communication materials are a prime example of how technology can be made a central component of a course.

All of these materials can be placed on a course web site for students to access at any time. The course web site can also allow teacher education students to access their course grade (password protected), an electronic discussion group, their electronic journal, electronic course materials, and links to related information. The site can include lecture notes to help guide students through face-to-face course time. To avoid the problem of students' printing out lecture notes and then skipping the class session, the lecture notes can appear on the web only partially completed. Students will then need to attend class in order to fill in key elements of the lecture notes. An effective course web site that demonstrates technology integration needs to be more than just a compilation of handouts. It needs to exemplify the power of the technology as a communication tool. One example of a comprehensive course web site is available on our book's web site.

Activities for Stage 2 of the Teacher Education Program (Adaptation)

In this second stage of the teacher education program, preservice teachers have completed most of their general studies and other introductory courses and are moving into advanced courses in their content area—courses that focus on teaching methodology and micro-teaching opportunities in the field. Technologies inside and outside the SCDE classroom need to support students as they learn about and practice lesson planning, assessment, instructional strategies, and classroom management and move along to the adaptation stage. Table 4.3 maps the sample activities to the Milken Professional Skills for the Digital Classroom and the INTASC Standards.

Collaborative Learning with Computer-Assisted Instruction. It can be useful for students to work with computer-assisted instruction (CAI) software tools so they become familiar with the software and work out strategies for using the technology. Teacher education students, working in collaborative teams, can cooperatively explore the software and develop curricular plans.

Table 4.3   Adaptation Stage Learning Activities

	Milken Professional Skills	INTASC Principles
1. Collaborative learning with computer-assisted instruction	1.1, 1.6, 2.1, 2.2, 3.5, 4.1, 4.2	1, 4, 6
2. Participating in and creating webquests	1.2, 1.3, 1.4, 1.5, 1.6, 2.1, 2.2, 2.3, 2.4, 2.5, 3.5, 4.1	1, 2, 3, 4, 5, 6, 7, 8, 10
3. Co-teaching in technology-rich classrooms	1.6, 2.1, 2.2, 2.3, 2.4, 2.5, 4.1, 4.2, 4.3	1, 2, 3, 4, 5, 6, 8
4. Continued development of the electronic portfolio	1.1, 1.3, 1.6, 2.3, 2.5, 4.2, 4.3	1, 9
5. Micro-teaching in the distance environment	1.5, 2.1, 2.2, 3.5, 4.1	1, 2, 3, 4, 5, 6
6. Field use of educational software	1.2, 2.1, 2.2, 2.3, 2.4, 4.1, 4.2	1, 2, 3, 4, 5, 6, 7

A commercial product is not always the best CAI to accomplish the instructional goals of a SCDE. Chapters 2 and 3 described some CAI tools developed at the Peabody School of Education at Vanderbilt University. Faculty can create their own CAI that meets specific programmatic goals. Teacher education students then work through the CAI classroom scenarios, for example, in collaborative teams. Students who have stronger technology skills can serve as peer coaches to students with more limited skills. As students learn from the CAI and the collaborative work teams, they also learn how to use CAI to facilitate learning goals. Furthermore, they develop a better understanding that they too can create CAI for their future students; if their instructor can create original CAI, so can they.

Participating In and Creating Webquests. Webquests, which emerged as a project out of San Diego State University (see **http://edweb.sdsu.edu/webquest/overview.htm**) in 1995, are inquiry-oriented projects designed for the K–12 classroom environment, where learners interact with information and resources from the web (Dodge, 1995). One such sample webquest that has been created for teacher education students has the instructor place students in four different small groups. Each group reviews a different type of Intenet activity that can be used in K–12 schools (such as scavenger hunts, webquests, collaborative projects, and quests). Each group becomes an "expert" on their assigned type of activity and shares this information at the end of the webquest with everyone else in the class through a presentation (see **http://train.rps205.com/tift2/index.html**).

There are two types of webquests: short term, which focus on knowledge integration and acquisition and are designed to be completed in one to three class periods, and long term, which have the goal of extending and refining knowledge and may take between one week and a month to complete. A learner analyzes a body of knowledge, transforms that knowledge, and demonstrates understanding by creating something to which others can respond. Webquests are typically group activities that emphasize collaborative work. Students are often asked to assume a role in a scenario in order to complete the task.

Although webquests are created for the K–12 environment, teacher education students can learn a great deal about the process by participating with peers in a webquest. By completing a webquest, they will better understand the process and how it can be used in a classroom. Some of the webquests that are available on-line are of sufficient complexity as to be suitable for college-level content methods course or general studies course. But the power of the webquest as an integrated technology tool for teacher education is not simply in the process of completion but also in the creation.

The creation of webquests can fulfill a number of technology and teaching standards, as Table 4.3 shows. At the very least, teacher education students demonstrate their ability to conduct a web search, create interactive multimedia through web site development, and demonstrate their understanding of how the technology tools link to the curriculum. The creation of a webquest is essentially the development of a curriculum unit (for a long-term quest) or at least a substantial lesson plan (for a short-term quest). A teacher education student who creates a comprehensive webquest will have considered learner differences, child development, assessment, and other factors. A

SCDE that seeks performance examples from its students will find that an activity like a webquest covers a variety of teaching and technology skills. In addition, because a webquest can cover any field or topic, it is adaptable to virtually any course in the teacher education program.

Co-Teaching in Technology-Rich Classrooms. One purpose of field observation, micro-teaching in the field, and student teaching is to have teacher education students work with master teachers: in-service teachers who exemplify their profession. A master teacher who also manages a technology-rich classroom can serve as a substantial role model for preservice teachers. If the SCDE has access to K–12 teachers who use technology to transform the teaching and learning process, all effort should be made to place field experience in these classrooms—not only for the purposes of classroom observation but also for teaching with the mentorship of the master teacher.

Classroom observations show teacher education students what can be done with technology in the classroom. The observation can help move the preservice teacher from the entry stage to the adaptation stage. However, in order to move from a level of adaptation to transformation, the teacher education student must experience what it means to plan instruction in the technology-rich classroom. Working side by side with a master teacher who uses technology can provide a working model for the preservice teacher, even if it occurs only during a brief field experience. The preservice teacher must experience firsthand how technology factors into planning, assessment, teaching, and communication.

Continued Development of the Electronic Portfolio. The electronic portfolio has its beginnings in the entry stage. Once teacher education students develop into the adaptation stage, they are prepared to move beyond the already developed framework. They will continue to call on their technology skills and will continue to hone those competencies as they add information regarding their ability to plan instruction, create assessment, and address learner differences.

During the adaptation stage of technology and the teacher education program, teacher education students are gathering information and resources specific to their teaching field and putting these materials to use. Therefore, they now manipulate the electronic portfolio to meet the specific needs of the early childhood major, the middle school science major, or perhaps the secondary choral major. Preservice teachers are participating in classes that guide them through the lesson planning process and have them experiment with different assessment techniques. This work may then be tested out in the field and then placed in the electronic portfolio.

Micro-Teaching in the Distance-Education Environment. Distance learning in the K–12 environment is part of a technology-rich classroom. Schools that take advantage of various distance technologies (interactive TV, Internet, satellite, audio) are using technology to bring students the best possible learning. Teacher education students may someday broadcast an advanced language class to multiple rural school sites or may facilitate a lesson that downlinks to a teacher in Antarctica, and so they need to experience the distance-learning environment.

Ideally, preservice teachers should have the opportunity to micro-teach in the field using the distance-learning technologies that are in the schools. However, because a field site may not have this equipment or a school is reluctant to allow micro-teaching on expensive distance-education equipment, a SCDE needs to find an in-house method to allow teacher education students to practice. One way is if the SCDE has distance-learning technologies similar to those in the schools. If that option is not available, distance-learning technologies can be simulated. For example, to simulate teaching in a one-way video, two-way audio environment, the teacher education student can be placed in one room in front of a video camera. The micro-teaching lesson is then projected into another room, and audio is run to and from each room. A great deal of cable is required, but the experience is similar to what might be experienced in the field.

Field Use of Educational Software. A previous learning activity had teacher education students working together cooperatively on commercially produced or instructor-produced software. The next step is for students to plan the use of educational software in the field. Unfortunately, educational software is often used in K–12 classrooms as a tool to keep students busy or as a reward. Under the guidance of university supervision and the master teacher, teacher education students need to practice incorporating educational software that addresses learner differences, makes learning meaningful, and supports critical thinking.

If a SCDE is working with technology-rich field placements, the computers and the software may already be in place in the schools, ready for use by the teacher education student. If that is not the case, the SCDE needs to supply the materials necessary for preservice teachers. The SCDE might find that making laptops available for student checkout is necessary. If the computing equipment is unavailable in the K–12 schools, it is likely that the software too is unavailable. Therefore, the SCDE will probably need to have a pool of software available for teacher education students to borrow and use temporarily in the field.

Activities for Stage 3 of the Teacher Education Program (Transformation)

In the final stage of the teacher education program, preservice teachers have moved out into the field for student teaching or an internship experience. Although they may have a remaining capstone course, the emphasis is on their putting into practice everything they have learned. Therefore, if technology has been a factor in all parts of the first two stages of the teacher education program, the preservice teachers will be prepared to apply those technology skills. Ideally the SCDE will place every student teacher in a technology-rich field placement; however, preservice teachers who have achieved the transformation stage and comfort level with technology can make effective use of whatever technology is available. Table 4.4 maps the sample activities to the Milken Professional Skills for the Digital Age Classroom and the INTASC Standards.

Distance Observation of Student Teaching. Distance technologies play an important role for the integration of technology during the transformation stage. One major factor of faculty and student interaction during the third stage of the teacher education program is student teaching contact and observation.

Table 4.4 Transformation Stage Learning Activities

	Milken Professional Skills	INTASC Principles
1. Distance observation of student teaching	2.5, 3.1, 3.2, 3.3, 4.3	9
2. Electronic links to other student teachers	1.4, 1.5, 3.1, 3.2, 3.3	9
3. Instructional strategies that encourage K–12 student development of knowledge products with technology	1.6, 2.1, 2.2, 2.4, 2.5	1, 2, 3, 4, 5, 6, 7, 8
4. Electronic communication with parents and community members	1.4, 1.5, 2.1, 2.2, 3.3	10
5. Virtual mentor	1.4, 1.5, 2.1, 2.2, 3.3	9, 10
6. Continued development of the electronic portfolio	1.1, 1.3, 1.6, 2.3, 2.5, 4.2, 4.3	1, 9

When student teaching assignments are at a considerable distance from the SCDE, faculty supervisors either spend a significant amount of time on the road or observe the student teachers only sporadically. With simple distance-learning technologies such as web-based **videoconferencing**, SCDE supervisors have the opportunity to meet synchronously with the student teacher, supervising teacher, and principal on a more frequent basis. Observation of classroom teaching is also possible in a similar fashion, although it may not be as effective. We are not advocating that all student teaching supervision take place at a distance, because that does not serve the student well. However, it can work to demonstrate the transformative nature of technology on the supervision process and provide much-needed contact between student teacher and SCDE supervisor.

Electronic Links to Other Student Teachers. A student teacher may be the only student teacher at his placement, and after years of constant contact with peers at the SCDE, she may suddenly feel adrift. An activity suggested at the entry stage was to develop an electronic discussion group with a teacher education cohort. Those discussions can continue into the student teaching period or the transformation stage.

At this stage, teacher education students are ready to extend their professional contacts, which they can do through nationwide electronic discussion groups for student teachers, such as the Teacher Training Listserv (**http://www.zusas.uni-halle.de/ resources/teacher_training_listserv.htm**) and NewTeacher. com (**http://www.geocities.com/Athens/Delphi/7862/**). Such groups are often open only to student teachers, with no faculty allowed to participate. The forums provide a venue for student teachers to make contacts and find support among peers all over the country. Teacher education students who have participated on an electronic discussion group throughout their teacher education program will be skilled at making the best use of more extensive discussions with peers.

Instructional Strategies That Encourage K–12 Student Development of Knowledge Products with Technology. The transformation stage means that "technology is a catalyst for significant changes in learning practice. Students and teachers adopt new roles and relationships. New learning opportunities are possible through the creative application of technology to the entire school community" (Milken, 1999, p. 11). If all the technology integration pieces have been in place throughout the teacher education program, then students entering the student teaching phase (the transformation stage) will be ready to use technology to create new learning opportunities. They need to be encouraged, by both the university supervisor and the cooperating teacher, to develop strategies that incorporate instructional technologies and to practice classroom management that encourages K–12 students to use technology to advance their knowledge and to create new knowledge. This work can then be documented in the electronic portfolio.

A teacher education program that uses an integrated technology approach has prepared the preservice teacher well to create these strategies. The student has experienced electronic communications, virtual field trips, CAI, collaborative learning with technology, knowledge generation through webquests, digital technology tools, and other activities. The student teaching period allows teacher education students to take the skills they have gathered and adapted to their needs, and then use those skills to transform their own teaching and the learning of their students.

Electronic Communication with Parents and Community Members. Student teachers need to practice effective communication with the parents of their students and the community in which they teach. In cooperation with the university supervisor and cooperating teacher, teacher education students can use the power of information technology to transform the classroom learning environment. Through the establishment of electronic contacts (with web sites, e-mail, and videoconferencing), student teachers can make parents active participants in their child's education. Community and business leaders can be invited into the class electronically to help make school-to-work connections for students, and other educators can make interdisciplinary connections to course work.

Virtual Mentor. There are times when a student teacher may need to seek advice. Peers may not have the necessary experience to provide insight. Other educators with whom the student teacher has contact, such as the university supervisor, principal, and cooperating teacher, are in a position to evaluate the preservice teacher. This supervisory role may prevent the student teacher from fully confiding any fears or concerns. What the preservice teacher needs is a "trusted friend."

Much as an electronic discussion group can be used to bring student teachers together with peers, an electronic discussion group can be developed to bring teacher education students together with experienced in-service teachers who have no connection to the evaluation of the student. The teachers who participate in electronic discussion groups such as this find the experience to be rewarding and energizing, as they reflect on their own teaching experiences and provide advice to future teachers. In turn, teacher education students feel free to ask a full range of questions without fear of reprisal.

Continued Development of the Electronic Portfolio. Teacher education students began to develop an electronic portfolio during the entry stage and then modified and adapted it during the second stage, adaptation. Here, in the transformation stage, the electronic portfolio is modified to provide evidence of how the preservice teacher uses technology and other teaching resources and transforms them to meet the individual teaching needs of students. The electronic portfolio at this stage also contains evidence of how the teacher education student has encouraged his own students to generate new knowledge products with the use of technology.

The electronic portfolio allows for easier capture of this type of evidence than the traditional notebook does. For example, if the student teacher in a secondary biology class uses an on-line frog dissection with his students and then has students create multimedia reports comparing frog anatomy to a variety of other animal anatomies, those projects can be captured and placed within the electronic portfolio. Using digital technologies (pictures, video, audio), capturing electronic discussions with peers, parents, and other teachers, and interactively linking evidence to other related evidence, the teacher education student can provide rich evidence of her ability to create meaningful learning experiences.

CONCLUSION

The learning activities presented in this chapter are by no means finite. The permutations these activities can take, as well as the added richness new technological innovations bring, provide an infinite number of possibilities. These activities serve as a starting point for SCDEs and can initiate discussion among all faculty in the teacher education program.

Although the learning activities are the easiest part of this chapter to put into action in the SCDE, it is not the important part of the process. It is far more critical for a SCDE to plan learning activities in courses that support teaching and technology standards adopted by the teacher education program and use a developmental approach to technology transformation. Ideas for activities are easy to find in journals such as *Technology and Teacher Education,* conferences like those sponsored by the Society for Technology in Teacher Education (SITE), and other resources recommended in the back of this book (see Resources) and on the book's web site.

The ideas presented here are not enough to create a successful technology integration program. The remaining chapters in this book, and in particular Chapter 9, add elements that are essential to a fully integrated technology approach.

■■■ REFERENCES ■ ■■

Dodge, B. (1995). Some thoughts about webquests. Available at: **http://edweb.sdsu.edu/courses/edtec596/about_webquests.html.**

International Society for Technology in Education Accreditation Committee. (1998). *Curriculum guidelines for accreditation of educational computing and technology programs.* Eugene, OR: International Society for Technology in Education. Available at: **http://www.iste.org/Standards/NCATE/intro.html.**

International Society for Technology in Education. (2000a). *National educational technology standards for teachers.* Eugene, OR: International Society for Technology in Education.

International Society for Technology in Education. (2000b). *National educational technology standards for students: Connecting curriculum and technology.* Eugene, OR: International Society for Technology in Education.

Milken Exchange on Education Technology. (1999). *Professional competency continuum: Professional skills for the digital age classroom.* Santa Monica, CA: Milken Exchange on Education Technology.

Quality Counts 2000: Who should teach? (2000). *Education Week 19*(18).

Sandholtz, J., Ringstaff, C., & Dwyer, D. (1997). *Teaching with technology: Creating student-centered classrooms.* New York: Teachers College Press.

5

Technology for Special Education Teachers

DIALOGUES WITHIN THE ACADEMY
What About Special Education?

Yunsun, one of the eight people introduced in Chapter 1, is the technology coordinator for a midsized school of education. She is responsible for purchasing and maintaining technology in the school, providing technical support, and offering professional development on technology to faculty and staff. Recently Joan, the chair of the Department of Special Education, the academic unit that provides courses and programs for both undergraduate and graduate students who wish to become special educators, arranged a meeting with Yunsun. Let's tune in to their recent conversation.

Joan: Thanks for finding time to talk to me. I am really frustrated by our efforts to make our undergraduate majors aware of the technology that can be used in special education. It's great that they are learning about general instructional technology applications, but they also need to learn how to use technology to support students with special needs.

Yunsun: I'm glad that you have brought this need to my attention. However, I should warn you that I know very little about assistive technology. We have provided some equipment on a case-by-case basis for a few of our preservice teachers to help them with their work, but I have not thought about this from the view of the special education professional. What can I do to help?

Joan: I am not sure what we will need later, but I do know where to begin. First of all, we need an instructional laboratory that contains the kind of assistive technology that special educators in K–12 schools are using now. When we have such a facility, our special education faculty can take students to the lab and demonstrate the use of some of the equipment, or they can assign students to become familiar with specific hardware or software and demonstrate its use to their peers.

Yunsun: I don't know where we will find the space to set up a special lab, but I will talk to the dean about the space issue.

Joan: If we can't support development of a completely new lab, we could start by adapting some of the existing computers in the educational technology lab with various devices that K–12 students with disabilities might use. Most assistive technology devices allow the computers to be used normally when the device is not in use.

Yunsun: That's an interesting idea. If you can provide me with a list of the equipment that you will need, I'd be happy to order it for you. If we can't purchase all that you need this year, we will complete the list in another year or two. That would give you an opportunity to update the list as new devices come on the market. Do you think that some of this equipment might also be useful to some of our undergraduates with special needs?

Joan: Of course, and they ought to have access to these devices throughout their teacher education program. Right now, we have students with visual impairments and physical disabilities enrolled in our program who have to do all of their computer work at home on their own adapted computers. Like classrooms and buildings, we should make our computer labs accessible to all students, including those with disabilities. Acquiring some of this equipment will help us to meet their computing needs, and it will support the training needs of our special education program. I'll have a list of the equipment we need in your hands by the end of the week. Thanks so much for your help!

SPECIAL EDUCATION
SERVICE DELIVERY

Peek into a typical K–12 classroom today, and you will undoubtedly see a richly diverse group of students embodying a broad range of cultural backgrounds, familial situations, academic strengths, and needs. Contributing to this diversity are students with disabilities who have been excluded traditionally from general education classes and curricula and instead received special education services in **pull-out programs**:

- **Resource rooms**
- **Self-contained special education classrooms**
- **Special schools**
- **Residential facilities**

Recent philosophical changes in the field of special education, coupled with legislative changes reflected in the 1997 amendments to the federal special education law (Individuals with Disabilities Education Act [IDEA] Amendments of 1997, P.L. 105-17), have led to widespread implementation of a more inclusive service delivery model, referred to as **inclusive education** or inclusion.

In inclusive education programs, students with disabilities remain in their neighborhood schools with their age-appropriate peers in general education classrooms. They participate as much as possible in the general education curriculum and receive their special education services right in the general education classroom. Instead of pulling students with disabilities out of the classroom for specialized services, inclusive education brings services in. General education teachers who serve one or more students with disabilities in their classrooms may be assisted by special educators who provide periodic consultation or come into the classroom and co-teach with them. In other cases, **paraeducators**, working under the direction of a special educator, may be assigned to provide additional support to individual students in inclusive general education classrooms.

The recent movement away from segregated services toward more inclusive educational programs for students with disabilities has required a concomitant change in the role and function of special education teachers. In the past, special educators worked essentially behind closed doors, maintaining sole responsibility for developing appropriate curricula, designing instructional programs, and delivering special education services to the students on their caseloads. With the shift toward inclusive service delivery models, many special education teachers now spend a large portion, if not all, of their time collaborating with general educators who serve students with special needs in inclusive classrooms. Increasingly special educators may not maintain their own classrooms, but may assist general educators to adapt and modify instruction to meet the needs of students with disabilities who are participating in the general education curriculum in inclusive settings. More than ever before, special educators are called on to consult about a wide range of disabilities and appropriate instructional modifications for individual students.

The Role of Technology in Special Education

Considerable research has shown that technology, including specialized hardware and software, can support students with physical, sensory, cognitive, or emotional disabilities (Flippo, Inge, & Barcus, 1995; Higgins & Boone, 1997; Hutinger, Johanson, & Stoneburner, 1996; Kinsley & Langone, 1995; Male, 1997; Okolo, Bahr, & Rieth, 1993; Ray & Warden, 1995). These technologies, referred to as **assistive technology**, not only support students in pull-out programs, but enable students in inclusive education programs to participate actively in the general education curriculum and achieve academic success.

Assistive technologies include both devices and services. As first defined in the Technology-Related Assistance for Individuals with Disabilities Act of 1988 (P.L. 100-407) and later adopted in the IDEA, an **assistive technology device** is "any item, piece of equipment, or product system, whether acquired commercially off the shelf, modified, or customized, that is used to increase, maintain, or improve functional capabilities of a child with a disability." **Assistive technology service** is defined as any service that directly assists a child with a disability in the selection, acquisition, or use of an assistive technology device. This term includes:

(A)   the evaluation of the needs of such child, including a functional evaluation of the child in the child's customary environment;

(B)   purchasing, leasing, or otherwise providing for the acquisition of assistive technology devices by such child;

(C)   selecting, designing, fitting, customizing, adapting, applying, maintaining, repairing, or replacing of assistive technology devices;

(D)   coordinating and using other therapies, interventions, or services with assistive technology devices, such as those associated with existing education and rehabilitation plans and programs;

(E)   training or technical assistance for such child, or where appropriate, the family of such child; and

(F)   training or technical assistance for professionals (including individuals providing education and rehabilitation services), employers, or other individuals who provide services to, employ, or are otherwise substantially involved in the major life functions of such child. (IDEA, P.L. 105-17, Section 602, Definitions)

Because the definition of *assistive technology* is broad, almost any type of technology device or service that is used to support the education of students with disabilities can be included. Assistive technology devices and services can be applied to a wide range of areas—for example:

- Positioning and mobility
- **Augmentative and alternative communication**
- **Assistive listening devices**
- Visual aids
- Computer access
- **Environmental control**
- Self-care
- Physical education
- Recreation, leisure, and play

The application of assistive technology can facilitate learning, independence, inclusion, productivity, and overall quality of life for individuals with disabilities. For school-age students, assistive technology can mark the difference between successful and unsuccessful inclusive education experiences and transition from school to adulthood. The following two cases illustrate the impact of assistive technology on special education service delivery, depending on the degree to which technology is integrated.

Case 1: A Typical Service Delivery Model. Ben is a sixth-grade student with a **learning disability** in the area of written language. Although he has normal intelligence and does not appear outwardly to have a disability, Ben has severe difficulty with reading and writing tasks. Even with text written at the second- or third-grade level, Ben reads very slowly and requires intensive assistance from his special education teacher to decode words. Because his decoding skills are so poor, Ben remembers very little of what he reads. He also has difficulty comprehending sixth-grade-level text read aloud to him. Ben can print the letters of the alphabet but has never mastered cursive writing. His spelling is extremely poor and his handwriting almost unreadable. Because Ben's disability is primarily in the area of language arts, he cannot read sixth-grade level math, social studies, and science texts, and thus his achievement in these subjects is also well below grade level.

Ben has been placed in a self-contained classroom for middle school students with mild disabilities. In his class are sixth-, seventh-, and eighth-grade students with a variety of disabilities: learning disabilities, mild **mental retardation**, **emotional or behavioral disorders**, **attention deficit/hyperactivity disorder**, and **low vision**.

Ben stays in the classroom with his special education teacher all day, except for a few hours per week when he is mainstreamed into general education art, music, and physical education classes. In those classes, Ben follows along passively and takes any assigned reading or writing tasks back to his special education class for completion.

In the special education class, Ben's teacher and a paraeducator provide instruction in basic academic subjects, along with daily living skills and social skills. They use third-grade textbooks and read most text aloud to Ben and his fellow students. Usually they allow students to dictate answers that they cannot write or simply have them circle or mark answers rather than write full sentences or paragraphs. The staff routinely simplifies concepts and learning activities so that all students can be successful in the classroom.

Ben does well in this setting and enjoys school, but his achievement scores in most subjects are on a third-grade level at best. There is little hope that Ben will pass the state's high school graduation qualifying exam in a few years. Because of his severe reading and writing problems, Ben's teacher does not think that he will ever be "terminated" from the special education program. Instead, she predicts that he will receive similar pull-out services in high school and continue to be labeled as a special education student. There is a slight chance that Ben will be placed in a diploma-track curriculum in high school. However, it is more likely that he will continue to participate in a special education curriculum and receive a certificate of completion rather than a high school diploma when he "ages out" of the special education program at age twenty-one, provided that he does not drop out before then.

Case 2: Technology-Supported Inclusive Education. In another middle school in the same town is Jacob. Like Ben, Jacob is a sixth grader with language-related learning disabilities. However, Jacob is participating in an inclusive education program supported by assistive technology. Jacob is assigned to a regular sixth-grade homeroom and attends classes with his general education peers. His special education teacher of record is part of the sixth-grade team and participates in all curricular and instructional planning with the other sixth-grade teachers. Jacob and several other students with mild disabilities take classes together with their general education peers and follow a similar daily schedule. Jacob's special education teacher co-teaches with his general education English, science, and social studies teachers on a regular basis. She also provides regular consultation to the math, art, music, and physical education teachers.

In the classroom, Jacob uses an array of technologies to assist him with language arts tasks. When assigned reading tasks, Jacob uses the classroom computer equipped with a scanner and headphones. His special education teacher has taught him how to scan text from his books and launch an electronic reading program called Kurzweil 3000 (Lernout and Hauspie). Jacob can see the text on the monitor and listen through the headphones as it is read aloud to him. As words are read, they are also highlighted on the monitor. Jacob follows along and can control the reading speed or direct the program to reread any portion that he did not hear or understand. He can also direct the program to start or stop reading at any point on the page. As the program reads to him, Jacob highlights sections of text in different colors, takes notes, and extracts the notes to produce a study outline. When finished taking notes, Jacob spell-checks his work and then prints it. Later, he uses the notes to participate in class discussions about the reading material.

When required to read short sentences or items on worksheets, Jacob often uses a portable, infrared reading pen called a Quicktionary ReadingPen (Seiko Instruments USA). He drags the pen over words that he does not know, and the device reads the words aloud.

For writing tasks, Jacob uses several computer programs to assist him with the process. To support brainstorming, he frequently launches a program called *Inspiration* (Inspiration) that allows him to create a concept map of his ideas. Jacob has used the software many times and is familiar with its capabilities to produce diagrams, maps, and figures with ease. This visual representation of his ideas helps Jacob to organize his thoughts before he begins writing. When he is ready to draft text, Jacob launches *DragonDictate* (Lernout and Hauspie), a **discrete speech recognition program**, and *Write:Outloud* (Don Johnston), a talking word processor. Using *DragonDictate*, Jacob speaks into a microphone attached to the computer. He is careful to speak the words clearly one at a time. When the program occasionally prints the wrong word on the screen, Jacob finds the correct word on a pop-up list and chooses the word he wants by number. Using *DragonDictate*, Jacob does not have to worry about how to spell what he wants to say. He simply talks, and the software types his words on the screen. Periodically Jacob rereads what he has written by selecting a button on the *Write:Outloud* menu telling the software to read a line or paragraph of text aloud.

As he travels from class to class, Jacob takes with him a small, portable keyboard called an AlphaSmart (Intelligent Peripheral Devices). Using this keyboard, Jacob copies notes from the board and enters his homework assignments. Because the keyboard stores eight files, Jacob has set up one for each of his classes. At the end of the day, he points the AlphaSmart to an infrared sensor on one of the classroom printers to print out his homework assignments and brief notes he has entered throughout the day.

Jacob's special education and general education teachers work together to design learning activities, instruct small groups within the classroom, provide individual assistance, and grade assignments. They routinely group students with and without disabilities together; some students do not even know which teacher is the special educator. Both teachers help the students with disabilities use the technology tools available in the classroom and ensure that they participate fully in all instructional activities.

Although the special education teacher originally recommended the assistive technology hardware and software that Jacob uses and initially trained him in its use, most of the general education teachers have assumed considerable responsibility for helping Jacob and others when they have problems or questions about the technology. The teachers recognize that the assistive technology supports have enabled Jacob to be successful in general education classes. At this point, they cannot imagine his being pulled out of general education classes to receive special education services in a segregated setting. The teachers provide Jacob with ample access to the assistive technologies that he needs and hold him to the same high standards that they have set for all of their students. His teachers expect Jacob to continue to use assistive technologies in high school as he pursues the general education curriculum and earns a high school diploma with his peers.

Reflection on the Cases. These two cases highlight the important role that assistive technology plays in the delivery of special education services. In Case 1, Ben's reading and writing difficulties led to his placement in a segregated special education classroom for the majority of the school day, a model that typifies special education service delivery of the past. In contrast, Case 2 showed how the use of assistive technologies can support students with disabilities in the general education curriculum. Like other teachers in leading schools today, Jacob's teachers prescribed assistive technologies that enabled him to read and write just like his peers. With appropriate assistive technologies, Jacob did not have to be segregated; he could participate in inclusive education, be held accountable to the same high standards as his peers, and look forward to the same opportunities for adult life.

The success of inclusive education for students with disabilities depends on many factors: administrative support, collaboration among general and special education teachers, well-prepared and supportive peers, a wide array of instructional modifications, and, as these cases illustrate, appropriate use of assistive technologies (Friend & Cook, 1993). In the absence of any one of these factors, inclusive education efforts may be doomed to fail. Now, more than ever before, special educators must know about and be able to use assistive technologies to help all students learn in a wide variety of classroom settings and across all subject areas.

Assistive Technology Competencies

Since the passage of the original federal special education law in 1975 (The Education for All Handicapped Children Act, P.L. 94-142; later renamed the IDEA), all students with disabilities are entitled to a "free, appropriate, public education," commonly referred to as FAPE. For the first ten to fifteen years after this landmark legislation was enacted, most special education teachers taught students without employing any type of technology. With very small caseloads in self-contained classrooms, teachers could modify and adapt instruction and accommodate students' individual needs through one-on-one assistance without relying on technology to provide instructional support. Ben's teachers, for example, accommodated his needs by reducing his workload, simplifying tasks, and reading and writing for him. In the special education class, those instructional strategies enabled him to experience success. However, Ben relied so much on his teachers that he was not able to perform at a level commensurate with other students his age, nor was he able to complete reading and writing tasks independently. Furthermore, there was a pervasive assumption that Ben would never progress very far in the general education curriculum and that he would not even earn a high school diploma after reaching twenty-one years of age.

Jacob, on the other hand, relied on technology to support him in the general education curriculum. His teachers spent less time modifying and adapting lessons for him and more time and effort developing and training him to use technology-based supports that could enable him to participate independently. In the long run, with continued assistive technology support, Jacob should be able to progress with his peers in the general education curriculum and may even pursue higher education.

With recent efforts to include students as fully as possible in the general education curriculum, as required by federal and state special education laws, special educators now must be knowledgeable about a wide array of assistive technologies available to support students with various disabilities. Recognizing the critical role that assistive technology plays, the IDEA Amendments of 1997 added a requirement for every Individualized Education Program (IEP) team to consider the assistive technology needs of students with disabilities when developing educational goals and instructional objectives. The IEP team must determine if assistive technology is needed for a student to receive a free and appropriate public education (IDEA Amendments of 1997, Section 614(d)(3)(B), Consideration of Special Factors). This new requirement marks a significant shift in how educators view assistive technology, which previously had been viewed almost exclusively within a rehabilitative context. Now technology is being considered as a viable tool for expanding access to the general education curriculum for all students with disabilities.

Of the IEP team members, it is most often the special educator who is called on to provide information about assistive technology and make recommendations about the provision of such devices and services. Special education teachers, who serve increasingly as consultants and co-teachers with general educators, must be prepared to evaluate students' individual strengths and needs, recommend and select appropriate technologies from among a vast array of tools, and train students with disabilities and the professionals and families who work with them to use these new technologies efficiently and effectively. They must have sufficient knowledge about instructional and assistive technologies, as well as skills in evaluating technology needs, installing and customizing hardware and software, providing training and technical assistance, and troubleshooting problems that may occur.

The Council for Exceptional Children (CEC), the foremost professional organization for special educators, specifies entry-level competencies for all beginning special education teachers in a document entitled *What Every Special Educator Must Know: The International Standards for the Preparation and Licensure of Special Educators* (Council for Exceptional Children, 2000). These competencies, presented as Knowledge and Skill Standards, are organized in eight categories:

1. Philosophical, historical, and legal foundations of special education
2. Characteristics of learners
3. Assessment, diagnosis, and evaluation
4. Instructional content and practice
5. Planning and managing the teaching and learning environment
6. Managing student behavior and social interaction skills
7. Communication and collaborative partnerships
8. Professionalism and ethical practices

The document includes a Common Core, specifying competencies for all beginning special education teachers, as well as Areas of Specialization competencies for teachers seeking licensure in specific disability areas. Several technology-related competencies are integrated in the Common Core, and others are sprinkled throughout the various Areas of Specialization. For example, one of the knowledge statements in the Common Core asserts that beginning teachers should know "ways to use technology in planning and managing the teaching and learning environment," and a skill for all beginning special education teachers is the ability to "choose and use technologies in the instructional process" (Council for Exceptional Children, 2000).

Under one of the Areas of Specialization, teachers of students with physical and health disabilities must know about "sources of specialized materials, equipment, and assistive technology," as well as "appropriate use of assistive devices to meet the needs of individuals with physical and health impairments." Furthermore, they must be able to "use appropriate adaptations and assistive technology such as switches, adapted keyboards, and alternative positioning to allow students with physical and health disabilities full participation and access to the core curriculum." They must "participate in the selection and implementation of augmentative or alternative communication devices and systems, including sign language, electronic devices, picture and symbol systems, and language boards, for use with students with physical and health disabilities." In another area, teachers of students with mental retardation or developmental disabilities must know about "assistive devices for individuals with special needs." In addition, they must demonstrate skills to "assist students in the use of alternative and augmentative communication systems" and "use and maintain **orthotic**, **prosthetic**, and **adaptive equipment** effectively." Teachers of students with visual impairments must know about "a variety of input and output enhancements to computer technology that address the specific access needs of students with visual impairments in a variety of environments." They must be able to "choose and use appropriate technologies to accomplish instructional objectives for students with visual impairments, and integrate the technologies appropriately into the instructional process." They must also be able to "use **Braillewriter**, **slate and stylus**, and computer technology to produce Braille materials." Other specialization areas contain similar technology-related knowledge and skill statements.

Because the knowledge base for special educators changes rapidly, CEC updates the profession's Knowledge and Skill Standards regularly. The CEC Knowledge and Skills Subcommittee has validated, and the Professional Standards and Practice Standing Committee has approved, several additional technology-related competencies to be included in the Common Core. They have also developed a new set of competencies for Special Education Technology Specialists that will be included in the next edition (Lahm, 2000). These new competencies describe advanced knowledge and skills for educators who seek to develop specific expertise in this area and to serve as technology specialists for students with disabilities in their school systems. Typically, training for Special Education Technology Specialists is offered at the graduate level.

To fulfill their new roles adequately, special educators must be familiar with the general education curriculum and meet the educational technology standards required of all teachers, as prescribed by such entities as the International Society for Technology in Education (ISTE), the National Council on Accreditation of Teacher Education (NCATE), the Interstate New Teacher Assessment and Support Consortium (INTASC), and individual state teacher licensing agencies. In addition, special educators must acquire assistive technology knowledge and skills, as identified by CEC, to address the needs of students with disabilities. These assistive technology competencies must build on educational technology competencies rather than supplant them.

PREPARING TEACHERS TO USE TECHNOLOGY IN SPECIAL EDUCATION

Recent reports indicate that few teachers use technology in a substantial way in their classrooms (National Center for Education Statistics, 1999b; U.S. Congress, Office of Technology Assessment, 1995), and only one in five report feeling well prepared to integrate technology into teaching (National Center for Education Statistics, 1999a). Special education teachers, who must be knowledgeable about and proficient users of assistive technologies, in addition to mainstream educational technologies, also have significant unmet training needs (Cramer, 1992; Edyburn & Gardner, 1999; Hutinger et al., 1996; Lesar, 1998; McGregor & Pachuski, 1996).

What can be done to turn this situation around? How can SCDEs adequately prepare teachers to incorporate assistive technologies into their programs for students with disabilities? What is the knowledge base that should be covered? How can SCDEs incorporate this knowledge base into preservice special education programs? What is the role of graduate assistive technology education? Is it necessary? How can it best be delivered? These are important questions that must be addressed thoroughly if we expect students with disabilities to achieve high levels of academic success and, more importantly, become fully participating members of society with control over their own lives.

The remainder of this chapter provides recommendations for the design and implementation of special education technology education for preservice and graduate-level teachers.

Special Education Technology Curricula

CEC's technology competencies, integrated throughout the Knowledge and Skill Standards for Beginning Special Educators (Council for Exceptional Children, 2000), lay a strong foundation for building special education technology curricula. According to CEC, beginning-level teachers should know about the ways that technology can be used to plan and manage the teaching-learning environment for students with special needs. They must also demonstrate skills in selecting and using appropriate assistive technologies to accomplish instructional objectives and to help students with disabilities participate in the general education curriculum. Most important, they must engage in ongoing professional development to stay abreast of changes in the field of assistive technology.

Preservice special education technology programs must build curricula that enable students to learn about a wide range of assistive technologies. All special education teachers should be familiar with an array of technology devices that are available to assist students in various domains. Because the field of assistive technology is still in what could be considered a dinosaur age, and commercially marketed assistive technology products change daily, it is difficult to prescribe precisely which devices students should learn to use. What is available today will certainly not be used tomorrow. Conversely, devices that have not yet been dreamed of will one day enable individuals with disabilities to engage in activities previously deemed impossible. Recognizing that assistive technology is in a state of constant change, technology education programs should focus more on the types of devices that are available and less on the specific products.

Table 5.1 offers a framework that SCDEs can use to guide the development of assistive technology course work for preservice special education teachers. The first three columns define the types of disabilities, tasks, and major categories of devices that should be included in an assistive technology education program. The last column provides examples of specific products that are currently available. The entries in this column will depend on the availability of products that the particular school owns or can borrow from agencies or K–12 schools in its local community. As new products are acquired, the specific examples to which students are exposed will certainly change.

Use of this framework as a guide for building course work will ensure that preservice special educators learn about an array of assistive technology solutions to address a wide range of student needs. Teachers who have a solid awareness of the types of devices that are available and the tasks for which they can be used will have a schema for assimilating new products into their understanding. With thousands of devices on the market at any given time, it is less important for new teachers to be familiar with specific products than it is for them to understand the range of devices that are available, the tasks for which they can be used, and resources for further information.

In addition, special educators must be able to integrate instructional and assistive technologies into the context of a student's IEP. They must have experience in assessing students'

(Text continues on page 172.)

Table 5.1 Framework for Assistive Technology Devices

Type of Disability	Task	Assistive Technology Device Category	Examples of Specific Products
Cognitive/Learning	Reading	Electronic reading machines	*WYNN* (Arkenstone) *L&H Kurzweil 3000* (Lernout & Hauspie)
	Reading	Portable reading pens	*Quicktionary ReadingPen* (Seiko Instruments USA) *Scan-a-Word* (BrightEye Technology)
	Reading	Portable hand-held dictionaries	*Speaking Language Master* (Franklin Electronic Publishers) *The American Heritage Dictionary with Organizer, Alarm, and Spell Checker* (Seiko Instruments USA)
	Reading	Instructional software	*My Reading Coach* (MindPlay) *Reading Who? Reading You! Something Phonics, Something New* (Sunburst Communications)
	Language arts	Instructional software	*Simon Sounds It Out* (Don Johnston) *The Sentence Master* (Laureate)

(continued)

Table 5.1 Framework for Assistive Technology Devices *(cont.)*

Type of Disability	Task	Assistive Technology Device Category	Examples of Specific Products
	Writing	Word cueing and prediction programs	*Co:Writer* (Don Johnston) *textHELP! Read & Write* (textHELP Systems Ltd.)
	Writing	Speech synthesis software	*Write:Outloud* (Don Johnston) *Intellitalk II* (Intellitools)
	Writing	Speech recognition software	*DragonDictate* (Dragon Systems) *ViaVoice* (IBM)
	Writing	Spelling, grammar, and style checkers	*Write This Way* (Hartley)
	Notetaking	Portable keyboards	*AlphaSmart 3000* (Intelligent Peripheral Devices) *DreamWriter* (New Technologies for Schools)
	Mathematics	Instructional software	*Math for Everyday Living* (Educational Activities) *Math Sequences* (Milliken Publishing Company)
	Mathematics	Talking calculators	*Radio Shack Talking Calculator* (Radio Shack)
	Auditory memory	Portable prompting devices	*Mobile Digital Recorder* (Voicelt) *StepPAD* (Attainment Company)

Table 5.1 Framework for Assistive Technology Devices *(cont.)*

Type of Disability	Task	Assistive Technology Device Category	Examples of Specific Products
Visual	Reading	Video magnifiers (CCTV)	*Aladdin Pro+* (Telesensory) *Magni-Cam* (Innoventions)
	Reading	Scanner/OCR systems (reading machines)	*L&H Kurzweil 3000* (Lernout and Hauspie) *Reading Edge* (Telesensory)
	Reading	Braille translation software	*Duxbury Braille Translator* (Duxbury Systems) *MegaDots* (Duxbury Systems)
	Reading	Speech output hardware and software	*Braille 'n Speak 2000* (Blazie Engineering) *Jaws for Windows* (Henter-Joyce) *OutSPOKEN Solo 3.0* (Alva Access Group)
	Computer access	Screen magnification software	*Vista PC1* (Telesensory) *ZoomText Xtra* (Al Squared) *MAGic* (Henter-Joyce)
	Mobility	Low-tech aids	Long cane
	Mobility	Electronic aids	*Mowat Sensor* (Pulse Data International Ltd.)

(continued)

Table 5.1 Framework for Assistive Technology Devices *(cont.)*

Type of Disability	Task	Assistive Technology Device Category	Examples of Specific Products
			Sonic Pathfinder (Perceptual Alternatives)
Hearing	Listening	Assistive listening devices	Hearing aids (various manufacturers)
			Personal FM Educational System (Auditech)
			Easy Listener (Phonic Ear)
Communication	Augmentative communication	Dedicated AAC (augmentative and alternative communication) devices	*DynaVox 3100* (DynaVox Systems)
			Liberator II (Prentke Romich)
			Lighthawk (ADAMLAB)
Hearing/ communication	Speech	Speech training software	*Speech Viewer III* (IBM)
Physical	Seating and positioning	Forms and cushions	*Tumble Forms* (Sammons Preston)
			PinDot Comfort-Mate Cushion (Invacare)
	Mobility	Powered wheelchairs	*Action Storm Series Power Chairs* (Invacare)
			Bruno Power Chair (Bruno Independent Living Aids)
	Environmental control	Environmental control units	*PowerLink 3 Control Unit* (AbleNet)

Table 5.1 Framework for Assistive Technology Devices *(cont.)*

Type of Disability	Task	Assistive Technology Device Category	Examples of Specific Products
			Relax II (TASH International)
	Activities of daily living	Low-tech devices	Various reachers and grippers
	Computer access	Keyboard modifications	*Accessibility Options* (built into Windows operating system; Microsoft) *Easy Access* (Apple Computer Corporation)
	Computer access	Alternative pointing devices	*Headmaster 2000* (Prentke Romich) *NoHands Mouse* (Hunter Digital, Ltd.) *CrossScanner* (RJ Cooper and Associates)
	Computer access	Alternative keyboards	*Intellikeys* (Intellitools) *BAT Personal Keyboard* (Infogrip)
	Computer access	Alternative input method —switch with scanning	*WinScan 2.0* (Academic Software) *WiVik2 with Scanning* (Prentke Romich) *Switch Clicker Plus* (Don Johnston)
	Computer access	Alternative input method —speech recognition	*Dragon NaturallySpeaking* (Dragon Systems) ViaVoice (IBM)

strengths and needs and determining potential technology solutions to address those needs. They must also be able to design instructional programs that incorporate instructional and assistive technologies in the teaching-learning process. In short, it is not sufficient for preservice teachers to learn about an array of devices. They must also learn how to apply those devices to the learning needs of real students. Thus, technology education programs for special educators must incorporate knowledge about a wide range of assistive technology devices, as well as skill in applying assistive technology services. Such skills can be developed only through field experiences, practica, or student teaching components.

Packaging Assistive Technology Content

Whenever new teacher competencies are adopted, one of the most difficult tasks that faculties of education face is determining how to integrate the new knowledge and skills into the teacher preparation program. One of two approaches can be taken: (1) create a stand-alone course to address the new competencies, or (2) infuse the new competencies into a broad range of new or existing courses in the program—referred to, respectively, as the concentration versus infusion approaches. Of course, there are benefits and liabilities to either approach.

Lawrence Tomei (1999), special assistant to the dean for teaching and technology at Duquesne University in Pittsburgh, summarizes some of the arguments in this age-old concentration versus infusion debate. The concentration approach provides learners with a complete bag of tools that they can use throughout their program. Providing such a course early in the program can level the playing field for students by equipping everyone with the same skills at the same time. The concentration approach also recognizes that the topic of study—in this case, assistive technology—is a legitimate discipline in itself. It can also facilitate group work and peer tutoring. In addition to Tomei's arguments, concentrating assistive technology competencies into a stand-alone course requires one faculty member rather than many to stay abreast of changes in the field. It is also easier to monitor and evaluate the extent to which the competencies are addressed when they are packaged together in a concentrated course.

Arguments in support of the infusion approach suggest that it is easier to offer a broad range of alternative delivery methods when the content is chunked into smaller modules. When competencies are infused into other courses, students master the competencies in context, when they need them, and they are able to use those new skills immediately. Using an infusion approach, assistive technology competencies could be addressed in other courses when they are relevant. For example, **word prediction software** could be introduced when students learn about writing tools in a language arts methods course; augmentative communication devices could be addressed when students learn about various communication modes in a communication disorders class.

Certainly it is more efficient to deliver a concentrated, stand-alone assistive technology course to preservice teachers than to infuse the competencies across an entire program. With a stand-alone course, one instructor can be responsible for developing the syllabus, coordinating lab resources and equipment, and delivering instruction. A stand-alone course devoted to assistive technology can elevate the status of the subject matter and allow students to focus attention on it. Because most SCDEs offer at least one educational technology course for teachers, a stand-alone assistive technology course could follow, ensuring that students first have an understanding of the use of mainstream technologies on which to build their assistive technology knowledge and skills. It is difficult to argue that a stand-alone course would not be more efficient from both faculty and student perspectives.

Although a stand-alone course is efficient and relatively easy to manage administratively, there are strong pedagogical reasons to infuse assistive technology competencies across many courses and field experiences. Because learning is a process of making connections, the infusion model has clear benefits over the concentration approach. If preservice teachers are to make connections between teaching and learning, as effective teachers must do, then we must stop packaging content in narrowly defined courses. Instead, we must allow preservice teachers numerous opportunities to work with real students—to design and implement instructional activities with them, evaluate performance, and model exemplary teachers. We must help them to make connections between what they know and what they do in the classroom, between what they teach and what their students learn. Infusing assistive technology competencies across a variety of courses and field experiences will ensure that preservice teachers make these connections as they learn.

Both the concentration and infusion approaches are being used to address assistive technology competencies in special education preservice programs today. For example, the University of South Carolina, which trains special educators at the graduate level only, requires all students seeking special education licensure to take a course entitled "Technology for Special Populations." This three-credit-hour course introduces preservice teachers to a variety of technology applications for students with disabilities, including assistive technologies, and to an array of personal productivity tools for special educators. Students develop skills in basic computer and software operations, use of productivity tools, telecommunications, multimedia, and assistive devices. Throughout the course, they learn how technology can be used to support the learning needs of students with various types of disabilities. Typical course requirements include weekly journal entries, participation in e-mail and web-based discussion forums, weekly skill assignments to demonstrate competence in the use of various hardware and software applications, a curriculum integration project requiring students to create a thematic unit with a series of lesson plans integrating technology for students with disabilities, a technology presentation, and a culminating technology performance competency-based assessment. Cheryl Wissick, the course instructor, requires students to write their own rubrics for the competency-based assessment (personal communication, April 21, 2000), thus demonstrating their breadth and depth of understanding about technologies that can be used to support students with disabilities.

This special education technology course is taught in the Educational Technology Center (ETC) in the College of Education at the University of South Carolina. The ETC houses a classroom, allowing faculty to model teaching with technology in a traditional classroom setting. It contains training labs where students gain hands-on experience with educational technology, and it serves as a software preview center for the local education community, housing a large collection of software for pre-K through adult education. In addition, the Center for Excellence in Special Education Technology (CFE/SET) is housed within the ETC. Modeling an inclusive environment, the CFE/SET provides several computer stations equipped with assistive technology hardware and software. Integrated throughout the ETC, these stations provide examples of assistive technologies for students with disabilities: speech recognition, **switch control**, **head-controlled mouse**, **touchscreen**, **Braille translation**, **alternative keyboards**, word prediction software, and talking word processors.

In contrast to the stand-alone course model, the Department of Special Education in the College of New Jersey's School of Education has adopted an infusion model for technology training in its special education program. Each course in the special education curriculum includes one or more modules that address technology-related knowledge or skills. Instead of one faculty member's teaching all of the special education technology content, many instructors share responsibility for infusing selected competencies into their courses. For example, in a course on moderate and severe disabilities, students complete a module entitled "Using Simple Technology to Increase Independence and Participation." They rotate among eight to ten stations, each equipped with some kind of device (e.g., battery-operated toys, cassette player, hair dryer) and switch set-up (pneumatic switch, button switch, air cushion switch). As they explore the equipment at each station, they answer questions on a "Switch Review Form"—for example: "What is the purpose of this set-up?" "What motor skills are required to use this set-up?" "Who might benefit from this set-up?" This activity relates directly to the course content, addressing instruction on **functional skills**, **partial participation**, and adaptations for students with physical impairments.

In another course on multiple disabilities, students complete a module entitled "Access to Computers." They view two short videotapes about adaptive computing hardware and software, then explore a variety of alternative input devices, such as an Intellikeys keyboard (Intellitools) with ABC overlay, an Intellikeys keyboard (Intellitools) with Math Pad (Intellitools), an **on-screen keyboard** with an adapted track ball, a **headpointer**, a

WinMini (TASH), a **Touch Window** (Touch Window), and a **Discover:Switch** (Don Johnston) with scanning. Students work in pairs to determine the cognitive and motor demands of each input device, as well as the benefits and limitations.

Some of the other modules infused into the special education curriculum include such titles as "Awareness and Benefits of Assistive Technology for Students with Disabilities," "Making Computers Accessible," and "Facilitating Writing with Computers." As courses develop and the technology changes, the Plan for Infusion is continually updated and revised. Nevertheless, each module in the plan adheres to a standard format:

1. Introduction to the module
2. Evaluation of the module
3. Training activities
4. Required reading for students
5. Out-of-class assignments
6. Resources for trainers

To support its technology training efforts, the College of New Jersey publishes a newsletter about assistive technology: *TECH-NJ, Technology, Educators, and Children with Disabilities—New Jersey.* The articles in the newsletter are written and edited by undergraduate and graduate students enrolled in the special education program. The newsletter is distributed free of charge to anyone who is interested in receiving it. Not only is *TECH-NJ* an excellent source of information about technology applications in special education, but it also provides an authentic learning experience for students enrolled in the College of New Jersey special education program and serves as a model for other institutions.

According to Amy Dell, a faculty member who serves as editor-in-chief of the newsletter and coordinates the department's extensive software collection, the infusion model works especially well for developing basic knowledge and broad awareness among students about the uses of technology in special education. Because preservice teachers are exposed to technology applications in a variety of courses, they understand how technology, particularly assistive technology, can be used to support students across the curriculum.

Levels of Training for Assistive Technology

Another question that faculty of education encounter when developing technology training is how much depth and breadth the program should address. What should general education preservice teachers learn about assistive technology? What must special education preservice teachers know and be able to do? What content areas can be reserved for graduate education or for students wishing to become Special Education Technology Specialists?

Although general education preservice teachers should be prepared to address the learning needs of all students, few teacher preparation programs include more than a course or two in special education for their preservice general education teacher candidates. Typically general education preservice teachers may take an introductory course providing an overview of disabilities or the field of special education. Some SCDEs offer course work that prepares general education candidates to include students with disabilities in the general education classroom. The ISTE National Educational Technology Standards for Teachers (2000) suggest that prior to the culminating student teaching or internship experience, prospective teachers should "identify and use assistive technologies to meet the special physical needs of students." Upon completion of the teacher education program, such candidates should be able to "design and facilitate learning experiences that use assistive technologies to meet the special physical needs of students." Clearly SCDEs must ensure that some instruction in assistive technologies, specifically as it relates to physical disabilities, is included in courses or field experiences that are offered to general education teacher candidates.

Preservice special education teachers must develop additional knowledge and skills related to the use of assistive technologies. CEC's *Essential Knowledge and Skills for Beginning Teachers* (2000) integrates technology-related knowledge and skills across the knowledge base for all beginning-level special education teachers. According to CEC, all special education teachers should have basic knowledge and skills in integrating instructional and assistive technologies into the educational programs of students with disabilities. In practice, many special education K–12 school systems are developing assistive technology teams to assist general and special educators to assess students and to select and use appropriate assistive technologies. These teams may consist of a special education or **assistive technology specialist**, an occupational therapist, a physical therapist, an administrator, a computer specialist, a rehabilitation engineer, or other professionals with special interest and expertise in assistive technology. Most beginning teachers probably will not serve on these district-wide assistive technology teams early in their careers. Rather, they will work collaboratively with assistive technology team members to find solutions for their students. As classroom teachers, they may also find themselves the recipients of training from the team and be expected to use specific assistive technologies with their students.

In small school districts, however, or in systems that have not yet developed district-wide assistive technology teams, special educators, whether neophyte or experienced, will be called on to provide information to the IEP team about assistive technologies. Because assistive technology consideration is now a required part of the IEP process, it cannot be overlooked or skipped because the school system does not have assistive technology experts on staff. The IEP team must consider assistive technologies and more frequently than not will turn to special educators for advice. Thus, it is crucial that all special educators have more than a passing familiarity with assistive technology devices and services. Although we cannot expect beginning teachers to be assistive technology specialists, they must have sufficient knowledge and skills to fulfill their role on an IEP team. In addition, they often will be responsible for training students to use their technologies and providing assistance to general education teachers who work with students with special needs.

Jacob's special education teacher, for example, recommended his assistive technologies and trained him and his general education teacher to use them. General educators must have some awareness of the benefits of assistive technologies, be willing to learn about the assistive technologies that their students with disabilities use, and be able to provide students with disabilities ongoing support to use their tools.

For teachers or **related services** personnel who wish to develop focused expertise in the area of assistive technology, several colleges, universities, and organizations offer graduate education in this area. The University of Kentucky, for example, offers STATE-KY (Specialist Training in Assistive Technology for Educators in Kentucky), a distance-education program in central and eastern Kentucky. The program prepares graduates to deliver assistive technology services in rural Kentucky. Leading to an educational specialist (Ed.S.) degree, the program is offered to individuals who hold a master's degree in special education or a related field (e.g., administration, physical therapy, occupational therapy, speech-language pathology, or regular education). It is designed for persons already employed and offers distance-education experiences in the evenings and summers so that educators can receive advanced training without leaving their jobs.

The University of Kentucky also offers assistive technology degree programs at the master's, educational specialist, and doctoral levels. Most noteworthy is a postdoctoral fellowship program for special education leadership personnel who are interested in developing skills in the application of technology in special education. The fellowship program is a full-time, individually planned program of studies that blends didactic instruction, observation and field experiences, independent study, consultation, and research related to the use of technology.

Another institution that has responded to the need for advanced training in the area of assistive technology is the Center on Disabilities at California State University–Northridge (CSUN). In conjunction with the university's College of Extended Learning, the Center on Disabilities developed a 100-hour course, Assistive Technology Applications Certificate Program (ATACP), in early 1997, which allows students to obtain a certificate in assistive technology applications from CSUN in just one week. The training experience, offered in various locations throughout the United States and the rest of the world, consists of 40 hours of live instruction over five days, 52 hours of on-line instruction, and 8 hours credit toward a required written project to be completed within 90 days of completion of the program. American Speech-Language-Hearing Association (ASHA) and university continuing education units (CEUs) are also available.

Another program that offers advanced training in assistive technology is RIATT@NASDSE. In 1997, the Research Institute for Assistive and Training Technologies at the University of New Mexico merged with the National Association of State Directors of Special Education to form RIATT@NASDSE, a professional development program that delivers assistive technology training via distance education to school administrators, teachers, therapists, and psychologists. Students can earn NASDSE Competency Certificates, American Speech-Language-Hearing Association (ASHA) CEUs, National Association of School Psychologists (NASP) continuing professional development credits (CPD credits), and graduate and undergraduate credit and degrees from several university programs. The program offers nine different assistive technology certificates that focus on specific areas of study including: Basic, Severe/Profound, Preschool/Early Childhood, Educators, Occupational/Rehabilitation, Communication, School Psychology, Administrator, and Paraprofessional. The Basic Competency Certificate covers those competencies that have been recommended by the National Association of State Directors of Special Education to each State Department of Education as the minimal competencies required by those providing assistive technology services. This certificate can be obtained by completing 11.4 CEUs or 114 contact hours of study.

Each course in the RIATT@NASDSE program is offered in a four-week format. Course work is completed through Accessible Learning Kits (ALKs) that include a combination of consumable materials (e.g., course information booklet, video guide, worksheet packet, and a competency check) and nonconsumables (e.g., reading materials, video and audio tapes, CD-ROMs, **hyperstacks**, portfolio assignments, and hands-on equipment or materials). RIATT@NASDSE also sells the ALKs to a variety of agencies, including universities that offer courses for graduate or undergraduate credit, state departments of education that offer professional training, and school districts that train paraprofessionals.

Similar on-line assistive technology training is offered by Equal Access to Software and Information (EASI), an organization of the Teaching, Learning, and Technology Group, which itself is an affiliate of the American Association for Higher Education. EASI serves as a resource to the education community by providing information and guidance about adaptive computer technology to colleges, universities, K–12 schools, libraries, and workplaces. In conjunction with the Rochester Institute of Technology in Rochester, New York, EASI delivers on-line workshops on a variety of topics that focus on adaptive computing technology, creating accessible web pages, learning disabilities, and access to the disciplines of science, engineering, and math. Courses are four weeks long and are provided over the Internet via e-mail. CEUs can be obtained through the Rochester Institute of Technology.

Assistive Technology Practitioner Credential

Only a handful of universities offer degree programs in assistive technology, and states do not yet offer licensing in this area. Some professionals who want to serve as assistive technology specialists complete a degree or certificate program, but most develop the requisite knowledge and skills by participating in professional development workshops and on-the-job training. One organization that is working diligently to professionalize the role of assistive technology specialist is the Rehabilitation Engineering and Assistive Technology Society of North America (RESNA). RESNA is a not-for-profit professional organization comprising an interdisciplinary association of people with a common interest in technology and disability.

In 1995, RESNA developed a voluntary credentialing program for assistive technology service providers that promotes an entry level of expertise in the field of assistive technology. Its purposes are to ensure consumer safeguards and increase consumer satisfaction. Initial certification is valid for five years. If a certified Assistive Technology Practitioner (ATP) desires to renew his or her certification, documentation regarding relevant work experience and ongoing professional development must be submitted. Although the ATP credential is not a license, it indicates that the professional has passed a rigorous competency test in assistive technology service delivery.

Resources and Equipment

Developing a special education technology training program, even a single course, is an expensive venture. To ensure that students are provided hands-on experience with a variety of assistive technology devices, SCDEs must either purchase equipment or make arrangements to borrow devices from agencies and P–12 schools in the community. Many states, with funding from the Technology-Related Assistance to Individuals with Disabilities Act of 1998 (P.L. 105-394), as amended and administered by the National Institute on Disability and Rehabilitation Research (NIDRR), have developed statewide systems to provide assistive technology devices and services to individuals with disabilities. SCDEs may be able to develop partnerships with these state projects to help them locate equipment, place students in field sites, or find instructors and guest speakers. In addition, many states house one or more Alliance for Technology Access (ATA) sites. The ATA is a network of community-based assistive technology resource centers dedicated to providing information and support services to children and adults with disabilities, and increasing their use of standard, assistive, and information technologies. Centers are located across the country and may be a resource to SCDEs for information, loan equipment, or instructors.

Depending on the size of the school and the range of degree programs offered, some SCDEs may choose to consolidate resources across several programs and create a technology center that serves students in several different majors. For example, Western Michigan University created a separate computing facility, the Multipurpose Enabling Technology Lab. Rather than supporting individual, departmentally based labs, the university pooled computing resources for several departments (special education, blind rehabilitation, occupational therapy, and speech-language pathology) and created a facility that could serve students enrolled in several majors. The lab provides adaptive computing devices for PC and Macintosh computers, such as screen reader software, Braille translation software, scanners, **Braille embossers**, switches, scanning programs, speech recognition software, and alternative keyboards. In addition to serving as an instructional facility, the lab is used for adaptive computing by students, faculty, and staff who have disabilities themselves, such as low vision, blindness, and physical disabilities.

An assistive technology adaptive computing facility can provide students with valuable hands-on experience with computer access devices. However, students also need to have access to augmentative communication devices, which may be housed in a speech pathology unit; assistive listening devices, which may be housed in an audiology unit; **low-tech assistive devices,** for activities of daily living (ADLs), which could be housed in an occupational therapy unit; and devices for low vision and blindness, which may be housed in a blind rehabilitation unit. Even engineering programs can be a source of assistive technology resources. Engineering students, who are often required to develop projects to address real-life engineering problems, could partner with special education students to identify assistive technology needs and design new devices to address those needs. In short, to serve the assistive technology training needs of their students adequately, SCDEs must develop partnerships with other academic units that can assist them in finding appropriate devices and sharing expertise.

An alternative to providing students with hands-on experience on campus is to arrange for them to visit sites in the community where assistive technology devices are being used by individuals with disabilities. Although this option ensures that students see authentic use of devices, it can be difficult to coordinate, especially for a large number of students, since few sites have a sufficiently large range of device types in one place. SCDEs can also collaborate with local sales representatives for assistive technology device manufacturers to arrange for product demonstrations on campus. Sales representatives may visit classes, lend equipment, or participate in technology fairs and expositions on campus. For many educational institutions, a combination of approaches—access to on-site equipment, visits to off-site centers, borrowing from agencies and schools, and linking with local sales representatives—will best meet their instructional needs.

■■■ CONCLUSION ■■■

Like all teachers, special educators must be adequately prepared to integrate technology into their instructional programs. In addition, they must understand and be able to use a wide array of assistive devices to support the physical, sensory, cognitive, and emotional needs of students with disabilities. Increasingly, special educators are called on to consult with general educators and families about appropriate assistive technology hardware and software for students with special needs, many of whom are participating in inclusive general education classes.

SCDEs that prepare special educators must ensure that their graduates have developed knowledge and skills in assistive technology assessment, selection, use, and evaluation. To support this training, SCDEs must acquire faculty who have expertise in assistive technology applications, allocate sufficient laboratory resources including a wide array of assistive technology devices, develop strategies for including assistive technology course work and field experiences in the special education curriculum, and create tools to assess students' knowledge and skills. Numerous resources and training models are available to guide the development of these critical competencies in special education teacher preparation programs. With appropriate training in instructional and assistive technologies, special educators will be able to support the diverse needs of all students with disabilities and enable them to participate as fully as possible in the mainstream.

■■■ REFERENCES ■■■

Council for Exceptional Children. (2000). *What every special educator must know: The international standards for the preparation and licensure of special educators* (4th ed.). Reston, VA: Author.

Cramer, S. F. (1992). Assistive technology training for special educators. *Technology and Disability, 1,* 1–5.

Edyburn, D. L., & Gardner, J. E. (1999). Integrating technology into special education teacher preparation programs: Creating shared visions. *Journal of Special Education Technology, 14*(2), 3–20.

Flippo, K. F., Inge, K. J., & Barcus, J. M. (1995). *Assistive technology: A resource for school, work, and community.* Baltimore: Paul H. Brookes.

Friend, M., & Cook, L. (1993, November–December). Inclusion: What it takes to make it work, why it sometimes fails, and how teachers really feel about it. *Instructor,* pp. 52–56.

Higgins, K., & Boone, R. (Eds.). (1997). *Technology for students with learning disabilities: Educational applications.* Austin, TX: PRO-ED.

Hutinger, P., Johanson, J., & Stoneburner, R. (1996). Assistive technology applications in educational programs of children with multiple disabilities: A case study report on the state of the practice. *Journal of Special Education Technology, 13*(1), 16–35.

International Society for Technology in Education. (2000). *National Educational Technology Standards for Teachers* (3rd ed.). Eugene, OR: Author.

Kinsley, T. C., & Langone, J. (1995). Applications of technology for infants, toddlers, and preschoolers with disabilities. *Journal of Special Education Technology, 12*(4), 312–324.

Lahm, E. A. (2000). Special education technology: Defining the specialist. *Special Education Technology Practice, 2*(3), 22–27.

Lesar, S. (1998). Use of assistive technology with young children with disabilities: Current status and training needs. *Journal of Early Intervention, 21*(2), 46–59.

Male, M. (1997). *Technology for inclusion* (3rd ed.). Boston: Allyn & Bacon.

McGregor, G., & Pachuski, P. (1996). Assistive technology in schools: Are teachers ready, able, and supported? *Journal of Special Education Technology, 13*(1), 4–15.

National Center for Education Statistics. (1999a). *Teacher quality: A report on the preparation and qualifications of public school teachers.* Washington, DC: Author, U.S. Department of Education.

National Center for Education Statistics. (1999b). *Status of education reform in public elementary and secondary schools: Teachers' perspectives.* Washington, DC: Author.

Okolo, C. M., Bahr, C. M., & Rieth, H. J. (1993). A retrospective view of computer-based instruction. *Journal of Special Education Technology, 12*(1), 1–27.

Ray, J., & Warden, M. K. (1995). *Technology, computers, and the special needs learner.* Albany, NY: Delmar Publishers.

Tomei, L. A. (1999). Concentration and infusion: Two approaches for teaching technology for lifelong learners. *THE Journal, 26*(9), 72–76.

U.S. Congress, Office of Technology Assessment. (1995). *Teachers and technology: Making the connection.* Washington, DC: U.S. Government Printing Office.

6

Preparation of Technology Specialists

■■ ■ **DIALOGUES WITHIN THE ACADEMY** ■ ■
Trying to Do It All

Cathy, a professor of instructional technology, is working with Jerry, a faculty member in elementary education, to help compose their institution's thoughts on the governor's request. Cathy was one of the few committee members who thought there were some positive aspects to the proposed legislation, and she felt a responsibility to put some of her views down on paper. To ensure that her thoughts were representative of the faculty she works with and not just reflective of her own desire to integrate technology, she invites a faculty member who is not a frequent user of technology to work with her. While clarifying their thoughts and what technology in teacher education should look like, Jerry also finds the opportunity to learn more about Cathy's field.

Jerry: Doesn't your department already do all of the technology preparation for teacher education? The technology course all of our students take comes from your department. What preparation do we need beyond that? Also, I thought that the instructional technology department trained graduate students for K–12 schools.

Cathy: In reality, to prepare teachers to use instructional technologies effectively, we need to have more than just one course on technology. And those are some of the options that we are discussing, both on this committee and in my professional organizations. Second, our instructional technology majors go out into the marketplace in a variety of capacities. We prepare them for corporate training, software development firms, and organizational consulting. But we do have a number of students each year who are interested in the K–12 arena. Some of our doctoral students are studying instructional technology in order to work as faculty in teacher education programs. We also have master's students who want to be leaders for technology in school systems. Most of these students already have teaching certificates, so they can easily move into the schools.

Jerry: If we have people like that already in the schools, why do teachers need to have the additional training with technology? Programs like yours seem to be providing the necessary individuals to bring technology into the schools.

Cathy: The specialists we train are rarely found in the classroom in direct contact with students. Our teacher education students need to know about technology integration so they can use it effectively when they teach. They need to know how to use it for learning, assessment, and personal productivity.

Jerry: I remember when I was on a curriculum committee and we talked about a library media program—or something like that. Don't you do that too?

Cathy: There used to be a library media program in the library sciences college, but that program was eliminated a couple of years ago. The program originally helped students achieve certification to be a school librarian. But libraries in schools have now become less a traditional library and more a media center. Library media specialists help teachers and students to work with a variety of media tools to access information.

Jerry: It seems that there are a whole lot of people in the school system who are already specialists in technology. We can prepare the teachers to be specialists too, but it starts to seem like technology overkill to me.

PREPARING THE
■ ■ ■ TECHNOLOGY SPECIALIST ■ ■ ■ ■

Does Jerry have a point? If there are a number of professionals in the schools who are specifically trained to be experts with technology and applications for technology in the schools, why do classroom teachers also need to be experts? The reason is precisely because of the title: classroom teachers. The technology specialists are in the schools to assist teachers and students with technology and to add their own specialized skills and talents to the mix. However, the teachers are in the classroom with students on a daily basis, and it is their knowledge and experience with technology that will have an impact on student learning. Conversely, the technology specialists throughout the school organization are there to work with and support the teachers to make sure that technology is used effectively and efficiently.

Although different states use different titles for technology specialists, the majority of the personnel fall within the broad titles of teachers with computer endorsements, technology coordinators, and library media specialists. In this chapter, we discuss the important roles that various technology specialists play in the schools. In addition, we examine how a teacher education program that elects to prepare technology specialists might structure its program. You will find Table 6.1 a useful reference tool. It compares the technology roles of three types of technology specialists and the differences among preparation programs. The table and the discussion in this chapter focus on what the roles *should* be for the various technology specialists if technology is effectively integrated and a priority.

The Classroom Teacher and Computer Endorsements

The majority of this book is about how to prepare teacher education students to use technology to enhance their teaching and therefore the learning of their students. In many ways, teachers must be de facto technology experts within their own classrooms. They need to be able to weave technology seamlessly in and out of the many activities that take place during the school year. Technology specialists are in the school to work with other

Table 6.1   Comparison of the Preparation and Roles of Technology Specialists

	Computer Literacy Endorsement	Technology Coordinator	School Library Media Specialist
Preparation			
Degree program	Generally not	SCDE advanced degree	SCDE or school of library and information science—generally an advanced degree
Computer literacy	Yes	Yes	Yes
Media literacy	Yes	Yes	Yes
Technology integration	Yes	Yes	Yes
Technology leadership	No	Yes	Yes
Media center management	No	No	Yes
Networking	No	Yes	No
Teaching certification	Yes	Recommended	Yes
Additional preparation	No	School and technology law	Library focus
Role in schools and school districts			
Technology mentor	Yes	Yes	Yes
Technology leader	Yes	Yes	Yes
Technology trainer	Yes	Yes	Yes
Change agent	No	Yes	Yes
Budget/finance and purchasing	No	Yes	No
Training for students	Yes	No	Yes

(continued)

Table 6.1 Comparison of the Preparation and Roles of Technology Specialists *(cont.)*			
	Computer Literacy Endorsement	Technology Coordinator	School Library Media Specialist
Information management	No	No	Yes
Strategic planning for technology	No	Yes	No
Focus in classroom	Yes	No	Somewhat
Focus in school	No	Yes	Yes
Focus in district	No	Yes	No
Technology infrastructure management	No	Yes	No
Web presence	Class	District	School

teachers to help facilitate the integration of technology. A classroom teacher may be the person who fills this role. These teachers have added an extra endorsement to their license, often called a *computer literacy endorsement.* In many states, the computer endorsement allows teachers to teach computer courses.

The way that many SCDEs approach the preparation for a computer literacy endorsement is reflected in the title of the endorsement. The traditional approach was an emphasis on computer literacy. A decade or so ago, when the use of educational technology was in its first generation, the focus on computer literacy was appropriate. SCDEs needed to prepare preservice and in-service teachers alike to use basic computer applications and educational software. However, as we have seen in this book so far, technology in the schools is more than just knowing how to use a variety of software applications. In this second generation of technology use, the emphasis is more on using technology to transform the teaching-learning process. We want teachers who hold a computer literacy endorsement to do more than be able to create web pages or use grading software. We want them to use the web in engaging ways in their curriculum (perhaps students post reports to the web for peer review), with the technology enhancing the assessment and feedback loop (perhaps an **electronic grade book** is placed on the web, where a password allows parents and students to access grades and class averages). Therefore, why do many SCDEs continue to provide teachers with a special endorsement in computer literacy with a focus on the use of **application software** instead of the use of technology to transform teaching and learning?

The endorsement needs to evolve along with the technology. Literacy is still an important piece of this endorsement. However, instead of computer literacy—how to use a computer—the issue is more one of **media literacy** (Rafferty, 1999). With the vast amount of information technology available, teachers who have a computer literacy endorsement must be educators who have the skills to help students, teachers, and all other constituents of the school system understand, manage, and interpret the variety of information that technology bombards them with every day. Not only must the media-literate person determine how to use advanced technologies, but must also apply the "When?" "Why?" "Where?" and "For what purpose?" questions. Media-literate teachers are able to do more than just teach computer applications courses; they can provide technology guidance and leadership to teachers and students throughout the school.

We have already introduced the foundational technology standards developed by the International Society for Technology in Education (ISTE) for teachers. ISTE has also created a set of standards for the *Basic Endorsement in Educational Computing and Technology Literacy* (1998). Although ISTE uses the terms *computing and technology literacy,* a careful reading of the standards shows that they encompass concepts embedded in media literacy. Teachers seeking the endorsement in computing and technology literacy must first meet foundational standards (as described in Chapter 4) and then fulfill additional performance standards. An abbreviated version of these standards are presented in Figure 6.1.

Figure 6.1   Basic Endorsement in Educational
Computing and Technology Literacy

- **Specialty Content Preparation in Educational Computing and Technology Literacy**. Professional studies in educational computing and technology provide concepts and skills that prepare teachers to teach computer/technology applications and use technology to support other content areas.
  - *Social, Ethical and Human Issues*. Candidates will apply concepts and skills in making decisions concerning social, ethical, and human issues related to computing and technology.
  - *Productivity Tools*. Candidates integrate advanced features of technology-based productivity tools to support instruction.
  - *Telecommunications and Information Access*. Candidates will use telecommunications and information access resources to support instruction.
  - *Research, Problem-Solving, and Product Development*. Candidates will use computers and other technologies in research, problem solving, and product development. Candidates use a variety of media, presentation, and authoring packages; plan and participate in team and collaborative projects that require critical analysis and evaluation; and present products developed.

- **Professional Preparation**. Professional preparation in educational computing and technology literacy prepares candidates to integrate teaching methodologies with knowledge about use of technology to support teaching and learning.
  - *Teaching Methodology*. Candidates will effectively plan, deliver, and assess concepts and skills relevant to educational computing and technology literacy across the curriculum.
  - *Hardware and Software Selection, Installation and Maintenance*. Candidates will demonstrate knowledge of selection, installation, management, and maintenance of the infrastructure in a classroom setting.

Source: ISTE, 1998.

To emphasize further the move to media literacy, some key features of these standards should be highlighted. Although there is still an emphasis on advanced knowledge of technology and software, the teacher is more than just an endorsed computer instructor; the teacher with this endorsement becomes part of the technology leadership of the school by advising on policies and procedures in the school. The SCDE that provides this endorsement must teach the principles of instructional design that can be applied to product development. There also needs to be a high degree of familiarity with K–12 student technology standards, as well as changes in trends in standards and technology.

Finally, it is important to note that only a small portion of these standards are devoted to the issue of maintenance. In fact, only the final performance indicator in the hardware and software section requires the teacher to be able to configure a computer system, and even then with only one or more software packages. All of the other performance standards under this section on maintenance require the technology-endorsed teacher to assume the important role of designing and recommending strategies.

What does the SCDE need to do to prepare preservice teachers (as well as in-service teachers) with a technology endorsement? First, the courses offered to fulfill the endorsement must be examined to determine if they meet the standards. These courses therefore need to do more than focus on software. Preservice teachers must be able to apply evaluation techniques, have strong communication and leadership skills, and understand a variety of teaching methodologies that use technologies. The SCDE that offers an endorsement must have a mechanism for updating the courses and the endorsement as necessary (because the course that successfully fulfills the endorsement needs in 2001, may be hopelessly outdated in 2004). Software, hardware, and other technologies evolve and change frequently. The SCDE must be able to update the courses in the endorsement, and even revise the endorsement if necessary, to respond quickly to changes in the field of educational technology. A teacher with a technology endorsement who is not prepared to assume that role will not be an effective leader.

The University of Sioux Falls in South Dakota prescribes a specific set of courses for the technology endorsement for its preservice teachers, with some minor variation depending on whether the teacher education student is majoring in elementary or secondary education. Preservice teachers completing the technology endorsement program are expected to:

1. Demonstrate knowledge of basic computer technologies and networking concepts, terminology, tools, and applications;

2. Study the design, operation, and maintenance of computer technologies and networking systems;

3. Develop skills with current productivity and multimedia tools for education;

4. Demonstrate competency with integrating educational technology to support teaching and learning; and

5. Study equity and ethics associated with the use of educational technology in schools. (http://www.thecoo.edu/~apeter/endorsement_program.htm)

The program balances technical knowledge, computer applications, and the integration of technology and provides the background necessary for endorsed teachers to play a leadership role for change in schools.

Otterbein College in Westerville, Ohio, has a program for a computer technology literacy endorsement designed specifically for practicing teachers, not preservice. The program is comprehensive, with six required courses, a practicum, and two or three elective courses. The courses cover the important content areas: "Multimedia Applications for Teaching and Learning," "Telecommunications for the Classroom," "Hardware/Software Management and Maintenance," "Instructional Design for Technology Training," and "Effective Models for Software Applications." Elective courses cover specific computer applications and can be selected to fit a teacher's specific classroom needs. The purpose of the practicum is to require the teacher to apply the technology knowledge and practice in the classroom. Although the number of credits for the endorsement is extensive, teachers can apply this course work toward a master's degree at Otterbein (program information available at: **http://www.otterbein.edu/dept/educ/tech.htm**).

Technology Coordinator

Technology coordinators and library media specialists fulfill unique and important roles in the school setting that require differing modes of preparation. Both positions are similar in that they form the core of technology leadership in the schools. With their specialized knowledge and experience, in conjunction with classroom teaching experience, technology coordinators and library media specialists are change agents for instructional technology. In this section, we examine the preparation of technology coordinators, and in the next we look specifically at library media specialists.

To understand better how a SCDE should prepare teachers for the role of technology coordinator, we refer to a familiar set of performance standards. ISTE has also developed a set of standards for the technology coordinator. Specifically, the standards are for Educational Computing and Technology Leaders. An abbreviated version of the standards is presented in Figure 6.2.

These standards emphasize that the knowledge and abilities of the technology coordinator (or similar position) go further than those of teachers who hold the computer endorsement. Teachers who earn an advanced degree in educational computing and leadership must meet not only the technology standards that all preservice teachers must fulfill and the standards completed by teachers with computer endorsements, but must also fulfill performance standards that demonstrate a greater depth of knowledge of, experience with, and application of educational technology. These graduates are being prepared to be the technology leaders and change agents in the schools.

A teacher who assumes the role of technology coordinator must be cognizant of the research and theories surrounding the use and application of educational technology in the schools. The role of technology leader requires the teacher to be able to apply the research and theory to the effective design of technology-based products. A technology coordinator must also be able to use research and theory to provide effective staff development on educational technology. These roles are enormous and are what make the technology coordinator a change agent in the

Figure 6.2   Advanced Programs in Educational
Computing and Technology Leadership

- **Specialty Content Preparation for Educational Computing and Technology Leadership.** Professional studies in educational computing and technology leadership prepare candidates to exhibit leadership in the identification, selection, installation, maintenance, and management of computing hardware and software and the uses of computers and related technologies throughout the curriculum.
  - *Research and Theories.* Candidates will identify and apply educational technology-related research, the psychology of learning, and instructional design principles in guiding use of computers and technology in education.
  - *Instructional Design and Product Development.* Candidates will evaluate authoring and programming environments for use in the classroom. They will apply instructional design principles to develop, implement, and test interactive multimedia instructional products using authoring environments.
  - *Information Access and Delivery.* Candidates will implement information access and delivery resources in K–12 schools to support the curriculum.
  - *Operating Systems.* Candidates will install, customize, and configure the operating systems of computers and computer networks in school settings.
  - *Software and Hardware Selection, Installation, and Maintenance.* Candidates will identify and implement software in both classroom and administrative environments. They will investigate issues related to school and site planning, purchasing, and technology integration.
- **Professional Preparation in Educational Computing and Technology Leadership.** Professional studies in educational computing and technology combine leadership skills and concepts with knowledge about use of computers and related technologies in schools. Advanced programs preparing educators for a specialty in educational computing and technology require studies of and experiences with leadership, staff development, and supervisory concepts and skills as they relate to use of technology-based systems in K–12 education.

(continued)

- *Instructional Program Development.* Candidates will develop curricular plans based on local, state, and national standards for the use of computers and other associated technologies.
- *Teaching Methodology.* Candidates will apply effective methods and strategies for teaching the use of technology tools.
- *Staff Development.* Candidates will demonstrate knowledge of issues and models related to leadership in staff development. Candidates will plan and design staff development activities for educational settings.
- *Facilities and Resource Management.* Candidates will demon-strate knowledge of issues related to facilities and resource management.
- *Managing the Change Process.* Candidates will demonstrate knowledge of strategies for and issues related to managing the change process in schools.
- *Field Experiences.* Candidates will participate in field experiences that allow them to (1) observe the use of technology to support instruction, the management of technology resources in educational settings, and the evaluation of effectiveness of technology resources for teaching and learning; and (2) apply technology resources to support instruction in classroom settings.

Source: ISTE, 1998.

schools. SCDEs must ensure that their programs are creating leaders who are able to work within, and possibly outside, the system to improve student learning.

Network and technical skills are also an important component of the preparation of the technology coordinator or educational computing leader. Smaller school systems use the technology coordinator as both a "techie" to maintain and fix computer systems and an instructional technology consultant for teachers and administrators. Larger school systems should be able to hire technical staff to provide the day-to-day maintenance that is necessary to keep the technology functioning.

Although a technology coordinator might need to play the role of "techie" from time to time and will need the necessary technical expertise to make wise technology purchases, the instructional application of technology is an equally critical element. In its preparation program, the SCDE must not place an emphasis on the "techie" aspect of the position to the detriment of the research, theory, and instructional application of technology, or even vice versa. The power of teachers with these advanced degrees is in their ability to be technology leaders and change agents. Their ability to fix a network and maintain a system will not move systemic change forward if they are expected to perform this task all day, every day. Alternatively, the instructional technology specialist who does not understand the nuances and quirks of the systems being purchased can also hinder change and technology utilization. The trained teacher who possesses both knowledge sets will be in a better position to help revolutionize classroom learning, create instructional materials, and provide staff development to move K–12 technology integration forward.

David Moursund of ISTE (1992) provides an outline of the types of course work that should compose an advanced program in educational computing and leadership. In the case of a thirty-two-credit-hour graduate degree, approximately half of the course work is dedicated toward computer programming and networking, educational technology leadership, and current research and theory in the field. This sequencing allows teachers who are seeking the advanced degree to meld together programming, instructional uses of technology, and the administrative uses of technology. The remainder of the credit hours are used for general graduate education course work, practicum experiences, and graduate theses or projects. Such an advanced program provides a balance between the pedagogical components and the technical aspects of the degree.

You will note that we have used the word *teacher* multiple times in this discussion when referring to the technology coordinator role. This use is intentional; the technology coordinator is still a teacher, and preferably even a licensed teacher, with classroom experience. To be a change agent, the technology specialist must be able to communicate effectively with those who are involved in the change process. A licensed teacher will be able to identify and relate to other licensed teachers. There exists a shared understanding and camaraderie.

Valley City State University (VCSU) in North Dakota initiated a program specifically for technology coordinators that is fashioned following the ISTE guidelines. In 1993, it began to offer both a minor and a major in instructional technology for students who seek technology coordinator positions. This concentration can then be paired with the elementary education major or the secondary education program to prepare the technology coordinator appropriately. VCSU has placed an emphasis on preparing teachers first, who can then fulfill the position of technology coordinator. The content has an emphasis on programming and networking, in addition to educational theory and foundations.

California State University at Hayward has developed a master's degree program targeted to the development of technology coordinators. The degree is in educational technology leadership and is a collaborative effort of California State University at Hayward, the Alameda County Office of Education, and the Contra Consta County Office of Education. The university already has a graduate program in multimedia technology and design; in contrast, the educational technology leadership program specifically targets the integration of technology in education and combines the concepts of technology, human factors, and design and planning for technology to create effective educational technology leaders.

Approximately 90 percent of the program participants are licensed teachers, and at least 60 percent of the teachers are nominated to the program by the county offices. Program participants are required to have a working knowledge of technology prior to admittance. Graduate students who have the necessary technology skills take up to two courses during the summer prior to admittance that teach a variety of computer authoring languages. Six core courses form the nucleus of the program: "The Web as an Interactive Educational Tool," "Learning Theories and Multimedia Design," "Planning and Change," "Research in Technology," "Technology and Culture" (on the social aspects of technology), and "Educational Interface Design." Beyond these courses, students have four elective courses that they can choose from around the university and must complete a thesis or master's degree project.

Library Media Specialist

Many readers can probably conjure up memories of school libraries: shelves upon shelves of books, rows of card catalogues, and nary a computer or any other advanced technology. We might recall the librarian reading to a group of students or helping students sort through the many encyclopedias and almanacs to find reference materials for a research paper.

School libraries today present a sharp contrast to this image. First, the school library is now often called the *media center.* Although there are still rows and rows of shelved books, the card catalogues have been replaced with multiple computer stations with **multimedia computers**. Students now search electronically for school resources, as well as the library resources available throughout the entire school system, throughout the state, possibly in area colleges and universities, and even at national libraries such as the Library of Congress. The reference materials that students use (encyclopedias, dictionaries, and so forth) are now accessed through CDs (such as Microsoft *Encarta*). Using Internet connections, students can search throughout the world to find information to enhance their learning. You may still see the librarian reading to groups of young students or working with older students to help them search for information, but the library media specialist is using computer technologies to facilitate those information searches. The specialist is also working with students and teachers to develop instructional units and projects that use a variety of media technologies. Because the media center is also the repository for specialized instructional technologies, such as digital cameras, computer projectors, video cameras, and AlphaSmarts (electronic keyboard), the library media specialist not only maintains this inventory of special equipment, but trains others in the building to use it as well and to find ways to use it to enhance the curriculum.

Library media specialists might be called the technology anchors of the school. They are intimately involved with technology throughout the school day and may be the most experienced educators in the school with the use of technology as an information tool who are also working directly with students. Therefore, SCDEs are preparing more than librarians; they are creating teacher-librarians who are important members of the school technology leadership team.

The American Library Association has developed a set of standards that have been adopted by NCATE. The portion of the standards that are directly relevant to technology are presented in Figure 6.3 (the full standards can be found at **http://www.ncate.org/standard/programstds.htm**).

A look at these standards probably leaves the reader saying, "I didn't see that much related to technology mentioned." To a degree, that is correct. There is little explicit mention of technology. However, embedded in the performance standards presented in Figure 6.3 is the implicit fact that the school library media specialist must be a technology specialist in addition to a librarian. In order to perform these many tasks successfully, a teacher-librarian must fully use all the technologies available.

School libraries today rely on technology to deliver current resources. Books are still important, but newspaper and periodical subscriptions are more cost-effective and timely when accessed through information technologies such as CDs or through the Internet. The same is true for reference materials. Few school libraries maintain shelves of encyclopedias anymore, opting instead for digital versions that are updated yearly. The curriculum resources that a librarian must be familiar with, purchase, and catalogue refer also to educational software. The school library media specialist must be able to evaluate, choose, train, and provide instructional application assistance on these many software titles. A library media specialist who is truly a technology leader would not allow *SIMCITY* (a simulation software program that allows users to create all aspects of a city while dealing with crises that befall it), for example, to be used only for students who finish their work early. Instead, the technology change agent would point out the benefits of this program for problem solving and work on group dynamics. Then she would work with the teacher to find the appropriate ties to the curriculum or suggest another technology tool that might be even more effective at achieving instructional goals.

Figure 6.3   Abbreviated School Library
Media Program Standards

1. Professional studies in teacher education provide an understanding of the principles and methods of teaching and learning and candidates meet appropriate state licensure requirements for teaching.

2. **Professionalism**: The ability to demonstrate a commitment to personal professional growth. . . .

3. **Communications and Group Dynamics:** The ability to communicate effectively with students, faculty, staff, administrators, parents, other colleagues and the general public. . . .

4. **Collection Management:** The ability to apply basic principles of evaluating and selecting resources and equipment to build and maintain a resource collection that includes both internal holdings and external information access points to support the educational goals of the school is shown by candidates who can:
   - Develop, implement, monitor, and revise selection policies and procedures at the district level and collection development policies that reflect the school's philosophy, goals and objectives.
   - Identify and apply criteria appropriate for evaluating resources and accompanying equipment in all formats and at all grade levels.
   - Use appropriate collection management principles and procedures for need analysis, evaluating, selecting, and discarding resources (e.g., collection mapping, teacher interviews, on-site preview, use of reviews, and bibliographic tools) in collaboration with classroom teachers.
   - Evaluate both internal holdings and external information access points, and the needs of the students and faculty to coordinate the selection of appropriate resources to meet the educational goals and objectives of the school.

5. **Collection Utilization:** The ability to use resources to support the personal, developmental and curricular needs of students, and the instructional development needs of faculty is shown by candidates who can:

(continued)

- Develop a partnership with faculty to ensure that the evaluation and selection process provides curriculum-related resources appropriate to learner characteristics such as abilities, interests, needs, and learning styles.
- Ensure that the evaluation and selection process provides curriculum-related resources that reflect instructional strategies, learning styles, and teaching styles.
- Recognize the characteristics unique to each information format and select items according to their specific contribution to learning objectives or personal, developmental needs.

6. **Production Management:** The ability to assist faculty and students to design and produce resources is shown by candidates who can:
   - Apply criteria to determine the appropriateness of producing local resources as opposed to selecting commercially produced resources.
   - Apply basic principles of instructional design in producing resources for specified learning objectives.
   - Apply evaluative criteria for locally produced media for inclusion in the internal holdings.

7. **Organization:** The ability to implement policies and procedures for effective and efficient acquisition, cataloging, processing, circulating, and maintaining equipment and resources to ensure access is shown by candidates who can:
   - Select appropriate systems for circulation and access including automated systems
   - Implement procedures for ongoing inventory and maintenance of resources and equipment.

8. **Administration:** The ability to develop, implement, and evaluate school library media programs to meet educational goals, including the management of personnel, resources, and facilities is shown by candidates who can:
   - Participate in planning, arranging, and using school library media facilities to support the instructional program.
   - Advocate, initiate, and implement formal and informal agreements providing for increased availability and accessibility of information through resource sharing.

(continued)

- Evaluate in collaboration with faculty, administrators, and other library media professionals the instructional effects of the school library media program.
- Apply appropriate research findings to improve teaching and learning throughout the school and specifically within the school library media program.
- Conduct action research to assist in the development and implementation of an exemplary school library media program.
- Monitor, assess, and employ existing and emerging technologies for management applications.
- Participate in school-wide instructional leadership efforts.

9. **Instructional Leadership:** The ability to serve as a learning facilitator within schools and as a leader of faculty, administration, and students in the development of effective strategies for teaching and learning is shown by candidates who can:
   - Participate, as an educational leader, an equal partner, and a change agent in the curriculum development process at both the building and district levels.
   - Work with other faculty to identify appropriate instructional strategies and creative uses of resources.
   - Collaboratively plan with other faculty to provide activities and opportunities for elementary and secondary students to assume responsibilities for planning, undertaking, and assuming independent learning.
   - Anticipate the need for specific information and resources in response to information needs identified in the curriculum development process.
   - Share with other faculty the role of motivator, coach, and guide for elementary and secondary students in the development of reading, listening, and viewing competencies, including critical thinking skills, for lifelong learning.
   - Participate as an equal partner with faculty in designing, evaluating, and modifying teaching and learning activities, and in evaluating student mastery of these activities.
   - Assist elementary and secondary students and faculty in developing independence in retrieving, analyzing, interpreting, organizing, evaluating, synthesizing, and communicating information and ideas.

(continued)

- Promote the design of production activities, including adapting resources for new purposes, to assist in the development of skills for analyzing, evaluating, synthesizing, and communicating information.
- Monitor, assess, and employ existing and emerging technologies for possible applications to the instructional program.
- Plan and implement staff development activities to increase competence in locating, using, and producing resources for teaching and professional growth.
- Cooperatively plan with other faculty to ensure that information skills are taught and practiced as curriculum integrated learning experiences.

10. **Access:** The ability to develop a school library media program dedicated to providing access to information and ideas is shown by candidates who can:
   - Develop and monitor selection policies and review procedures that ensure unrestricted access to information and ideas needed in a globally concerned, diverse and multicultural democratic society.
   - Provide for a reevaluation process for addressing expressed concerns about school library media resources.
   - Enhance accessibility to all types of resources and equipment by identifying, evaluating, establishing, and using delivery systems to retrieve information in all formats and for all ability levels.
   - Comply with the copyright law and program standards, advocate compliance, and share interpretations with the school's publics.
   - Communicate concepts presented in basic access documents.
   - Identify, select, and use appropriate external information access points.
   - Protect confidentiality and ensure information security as well as the rights of users.
   - Provide for equity of access to information and ideas.

Source: Adapted from http://www.ncate.org/standard/programstds.htm.

Media literacy on the whole is a critical issue for school library media specialists. Helping teachers and students to understand and evaluate the breadth of information they have access to is a key element of the position. When students are able to gather information from a seemingly infinite number of sources, both good and bad, the library media specialist assumes the role of helping a student, and perhaps his teacher, to pick the information that is being accessed and teaching how to decide which information to use and which to discard. Beyond these many important functions, there is still the large, demanding task of managing the media center itself, as well as being a central resource center for the school and community.

The preparation required for the library media specialist who can do all of this is daunting. Many library media programs have been eliminated from SCDEs and schools of library and information science, due either to a lack of enrollment or the daunting and expensive task of preparation. In addition to all the specialist training, the library media teacher is still in fact a teacher and must be also appropriately prepared. The American Association of School Librarians has set out the following position statement regarding the preparation of school library media specialists:

> School library media specialists have a broad undergraduate education with a liberal arts background and hold a master's degree or equivalent from a program that combines academic and professional preparation in library and information science, education, management, media, communications theory, and technology. The academic program of study includes some directed field experience in a library media program, coordinated by a faculty member in cooperation with an experienced library media specialist. Library media specialists meet state certification requirements for both the library media specialist and professional educator classifications. While there may be many practicing library media specialists who have only an undergraduate degree and whose job performance is outstanding, the master's degree is considered the entry-level degree for the profession. (http://www.ala.org/aasl/positions/ps_prepschool.html)

The issue of prior teaching experience is not a new one for this field (Haycock, 1995). Teachers tend to respond and work better with a media specialist who has had classroom experience. The media specialist is in fact the information educator of the future (Pappas & Tepe, 1995). The library media specialist as an information manager must assume four distinct and overlapping roles: curriculum consultant, teacher, manager of an information center, and a leader for staff development. These roles are synchronous with the standards provided by the American Library Association. Furthermore, a consultant's classroom experience can be a critical element in teacher acceptance of the consultant's advice and assistance on the use of technology to enhance teaching and learning.

The SCDE that undertakes the preparation of the library media specialist must understand what that preparation entails. First, it is preparing a teacher who must understand pedagogy, educational foundations, child development, and other traditional foundations of teacher education. Next, it is simultaneously preparing a technology specialist who must be aware of research and theories surrounding technology integration, instructional design issues, software evaluation, multimedia computer applications, media literacy, information technology access, computer ethics and responsibilities, and hardware and software maintenance. Third, it is preparing a librarian who must understand the cornerstones of that field and issues behind resource management and cataloguing. Finally, and just as important, the SCDE is preparing a leader who will assume an important role in school reform issues. None of these preparation roles is more or less important than another. To do them all equally well is a daunting task for a SCDE or school of library information science.

Western Maryland College's graduate School Library Media Program integrates technology and emphasizes the importance of technology to its students (**http://www.fac.wmdc.edu/ HTMLpages/Graduate/graduate/drafts/gp-lib.htm**). Western Maryland expects that educational references required of applicants for admission will speak not only to a student's ability to perform at the graduate level, ability to teach, and ability to organize but also to that student's ability to use technology. The program makes it clear that library media specialists need to have an excellent command with technology, not only for their own use but also to work with others:

Your ability to teach is critical to your success as a school librarian. You teach every child in a school building. This means you must be able to teach children of all ages and abilities. Also, you will be responsible for instructing teachers on technology and ways to incorporate it into the curriculum. If you do not have teaching experience, please consider teaching before continuing graduate studies in this field, or at least substitute in classrooms, or secure a position as a school library assistant. (http://www.fac.wmdc. edu/ HTMLpages/Graduate/graduate/drafts/gp-lib.htm)

Technology is used in all courses in the program, and a number of core courses, including "Multimedia Presentation and Design" and "Telecommunications and the Internet," provide students the skills they will find necessary to use and teach about technology. In addition, the courses on media selection focus not only on appropriate choices of books and magazines for children but also computer media. Finally, the comprehensive examinations for the degree revisit and reemphasize technology by expecting students to refer to the skills and knowledge they have acquired regarding technology use in schools and library media centers and to support instruction.

At Rutgers University in New Brunswick, New Jersey, school library media specialists are educated in the Department of Library and Information Science at the School of Communication, Information and Library Studies. The department prepares professionals for leadership in a world of digitized information. The master of library service (M.L.S.) program, where school media services is one specialization, requires basic technological competency for matriculation. Students build expertise through integrated technological use throughout their program of study. Because of the emphasis on technology, they need to be proficient with electronic communication, word processing, and **user interfaces** in order to be successful in the program.

CONCLUSION

Different states have different licensure requirements for teachers seeking computer endorsements or for individuals who want to work as library media specialists or technology coordinators. The SCDE must understand its state's expectations for these professionals and create a program that strives to educate the best technology specialists possible for K–12 settings. In order for these educational professionals to serve as catalysts for change and reform in the schools, they must be more than just adequately prepared.

Readers of this chapter might have felt that they know of numerous excellent graduate programs in instructional technology. There are many outstanding programs that prepare students at the graduate level in instructional technology. In fact, both of us are proud of our relationships with many of these exceptional programs. However, it is the focus of the advanced programs specifically for K–12 technology leadership that is the topic of this chapter. For example, we discussed the preparation of library media specialists as change agents, not just library information science majors who may work in a variety of library settings. We discussed the preparation of technology coordinators who will serve as technology leaders for their school system, not the preparation of an instructional technology student who may go into corporate training or e-commerce or the educational setting.

Instead, the point of this chapter is to highlight the preparation needs of technology specialists who will serve K–12 schools. These needs extend beyond the advanced degree itself or extra computing courses. Course work and degrees in educational technology are a high demand area for SCDEs, and the offering of courses or a program can be particularly appealing if increased student numbers are a concern. However, if SCDEs are truly concerned about the application and integration of technology in K–12 schools and have a concerted interest in playing a role in encouraging and leading systemic reforms with educational technology, then SCDEs must pay particular attention to the preparation of teachers who will be the leaders of change.

REFERENCES

Haycock, K. (1995). Research imperatives for information professionals: Developing foundations for effectiveness. In B. J. Morris (Ed.), *School library media annual* (Vol. 13). Englewood, CO: Libraries Unlimited.

International Society for Technology in Education Accreditation Committee. (1998). *Curriculum guidelines for accreditation of educational computing and technology programs.* Eugene, OR: International Society for Technology in Education. Available at **http://www.iste.org/Standards/NCATE/intro.html.**

Moursand, D. (1992). *The technology coordinator.* Eugene, OR: International Society for Technology in Education.

Pappas, M. L., & Tepe, A. E. (1995). Preparing the information educator for the future. In B. J. Morris (Ed.), *School library media annual* (Vol. 13). Englewood, CO: Libraries Unlimited.

Rafferty, C. D. (1999). Reconceptualizing literacy for learning in the information age. *Educational Leadership, 57*(2), 22–25.

7

Technology for School Administrators and Counselors

■■ ■ DIALOGUES WITHIN THE ACADEMY ■ ■
Administrators and Counselors Next

Following is a brief conversation that took place among colleagues within one SCDE about two weeks following the meeting with the governor and commissioner of education described in Chapter 1. The participants are Bill, who attended the meeting at the capital and is a professor of educational foundations; Carolyn, who chairs the Department of Counseling and Educational Psychology; and George, who heads the graduate program in school administration. Following is a portion of their conversation.

Carolyn: Bill, I have heard nothing about your recent meeting with the governor and the commissioner of education. How did it go?

Bill: It was awful, and I'm still angry! The purpose of the meeting was to warn us of pending legislation. If it's passed, it will require every new teacher to show competence in the use of technology. Those who fail to demonstrate competence will be denied a teacher license and the opportunity to teach in any public school in this state. Current teachers will have three years in which to become technologically competent; those who don't will lose their license and their job.

Carolyn: Wow! I don't blame you for being angry. Could this really happen?

Bill: Wait, there's more. The law will also demand that every professor who teaches courses that are taken by preservice teachers will be required to show competence in the use of technology. A professor shown to be lacking technology skills will no longer be allowed to instruct teacher education students.

George: It is hard to imagine that such a bill could win support in the legislature. I am certainly glad that it won't apply to school administrators.

Bill: The governor seems pretty confident that he has the votes. Moreover, he thinks that the school boards association and the various administrator organizations will support the legislation.

Carolyn: What about school counselors? They are neither classroom teachers nor school administrators.

Bill: I don't know about the status of counselors in the proposed bill. But I know this: The governor is serious about increasing the role of technology in schools. Administrators and counselors may not be included in the current bill, but I bet that they will appear in the next round of legislation.

WHY SHOULD WE BE CONCERNED ABOUT THE TECHNOLOGY COMPETENCE OF SCHOOL ADMINISTRATORS AND COUNSELORS?

Although this book is about the role of technology in preservice teacher education, teachers are not alone in schools. Their work is led by administrators and supported by school counselors. One reason that reform advocates stress the role of technology in schools is they want to change the way schools do their business, that is, to modernize schools. Because the main business of schools is to teach and to help students learn, the initial focus nationally has been on the classroom use of technology. But schools constitute a system of interrelated parts. It is inconceivable that one part of a school system would become modern and technologically advanced while the remaining parts stay as they have been in the past.

Moreover, building principals, curriculum directors, and superintendents—to name only three of the most prominent school administrators—are expected to provide leadership for others. Clearly it is not reasonable to imagine that teachers, the "followers," are going to get very far ahead of the "leaders," their administrators. Of course, one is more likely to find technology used in administrative offices than in classrooms. The first place that technology was employed in school systems was on the management side of schooling: keeping financial, personnel, and student records. Secretarial staff to administrators have often had computers before teachers did. Thus, the use of technology for the management side of schooling is well accepted and advanced. This does not mean that school administrators as a group are leaders in the classroom application of technology or even in the use of technology for their own work. The advantage that administrators have is that they can employ people who are skilled in the use of computers and data processing, can set up the systems that manage financial, personnel, and student records, and can keep them in operation. A superintendent or building principal can remain a technology novice so long as there are skilled people available to maintain the systems.

School counselors are in the business of assigning students to courses, advising students on their academic and career plans, and helping to solve personal and social problems. Counseling is highly personal work, not the kind of activity that anyone can easily turn over to a machine. Nevertheless, counselors cannot truly meet their obligations to students without taking advantage of the many resources available to them through technology. Computer-based assessments, national databases relating to career choices, and electronic information concerning college strengths and admission requirements are but three resources available to counselors that touch their daily activities.

We agree with Bill's statement in the preceding scenario. It is inconceivable that efforts to strengthen the role of technology in schools will be limited to creating technology competence among teachers. Thus, although this book focuses primarily on what SCDEs are doing to provide sound instruction about technology for preservice teachers, no SCDE can afford to ignore the preservice training it is providing to school administrators and counselors. Furthermore, if many SCDEs have been slow to provide appropriate training for K–12 teachers, they have been even slower to alter training programs for administrators and counselors. Preservice technology training for administrators and counselors lags behind technology training for teachers.

For purposes of this chapter, we are treating all school administrators as being essentially the same. We are quite aware that there are substantial differences in the role and responsibilities of an elementary school principal, for example, and the superintendent of a district with two dozen schools and twelve thousand students. We also know that the business manager, the director of food services, and the director of transportation are also administrators, but the administrators we shall focus on here are those who provide schoolwide (principals) or districtwide (superintendents) leadership. Their roles are significant because they can have a huge influence on whether and how technology is employed in their school or school district. Collectively, their role is also substantially different from that of a classroom teacher. Furthermore, whether their training is at the master's, specialist, or doctoral level, their graduate training is substantially different from the training teachers receive and leads to different licensure.

THE IMPACT OF TECHNOLOGY ON THE ROLE OF SCHOOL ADMINISTRATORS

One way to gain a picture of what administrators must be able to do with technology to meet their responsibilities is to follow a hypothetical school superintendent through a typical working day. Dr. John Williams is the superintendent of a medium-sized district with both elementary and secondary schools. He has been in the position for five years and is known as a technology advocate.

A Day with Dr. John Williams

8:00 A.M. Dr. Williams arrives at work. After greeting his secretary and pouring a cup of coffee, he moves into his office and begins at once to read his e-mail, responding to those messages that require a quick response. Here are a few of the two dozen or so messages awaiting him:

- A message from a school board member congratulating him on his interview that appeared in the local newspaper.

- A message from the director of transportation that one of the school buses had broken down that morning but because all of the buses are connected by radio and are equipped with geopositioning map software, it was possible to reroute two buses swiftly. No student arrived late to class.

- A message from the director of building services reporting an attempted break-in at one of the middle schools during the night. The electronic security system worked: police were notified promptly, and the potential intruder was frightened away before gaining entry.

- A note from the director of special education notifying him that Channel 8 would include a two-minute news item at 6:00 P.M. on the impact of recently purchased assistive technology on the education of several physically disabled children in the district. She wanted him to watch the broadcast because the technology featured included some tools he had recommended for purchase.

- A report from the director of libraries and media services. Williams had asked her recently to inform him about the use of the Internet by students.

8:30 A.M. Conference call with building principals. Williams has a scheduled conference call with building principals one day each week. The agenda is open, and the meeting ordinarily runs less than a half-hour. Each person participates from his or her own building and is not required to travel to another location.

9:00 A.M. Meeting with Don Jenkins, associate superintendent for business. Jenkins, who has responsibility for all bids and contracts, wants to discuss a bid he is preparing that will integrate all communication services—voice, data, and video—and assign the task to a single vendor. Thus far, the school system has used separate vendors for each service. Consolidation and integration should lead to better service and cost less.

10:00 A.M. Williams has set aside an hour and a half to catch up on office work. He dictates replies to some letters, signs documents, and works on the "Superintendent's Opinion" column for the next newsletter for parents. Williams sends his own notes by e-mail, but he relies on his secretary to word-process letters for him; it saves him time, and the letters appear to be more professionally done when his secretary produces them. The newsletter, sent to all parents in printed form, is published in his office. The school system maintains a web site and posts items there, but nearly a third of the parents do not have access to the Internet.

Noon Williams attends a Rotary Club meeting, where he is the invited speaker. In his talk about his vision for the district, he uses his computer to provide PowerPoint slides. A high school intern had produced the final product to make it a better show. Williams uses a computer whenever possible in public presentations.

1:30 P.M. Williams conducts a two-way video teleconference with four other superintendents who constitute a committee of their state professional association. The state provides the technology infrastructure to support video teleconferencing; the superintendents employ it to conduct business whenever possible because it saves travel time and money.

3:00 P.M. Williams meets with Jane Thompson, director of personnel, who is in charge of district-wide recruitment and employment of teachers and administrators. They discuss his belief that all prospective teachers and administrators should be expected to demonstrate their technology competence before being considered for employment by the district.

3:30 P.M. Williams attends a meeting of the Professional Development Committee. He is not a member of the committee and rarely attends its meetings. However, on this day the committee is considering some new approaches to professional development—approaches that seem suited to assisting teachers gain confidence in and competence with technology than some of the more traditional approaches they have used in the past. Williams believes the school system must do more to assist teachers in their use of technology and therefore decided to attend the meeting to promote his ideas.

7:00 P.M. Meeting of the board of education. Williams is presenting the final draft of the technology plan that faculty and staff have been working on for nearly a year. Each board member is equipped with a laptop computer, and the plan has been loaded onto each computer. An executive version has been printed and distributed in advance. The electronic version contains many data tables and graphs; it also contains scenarios of the future, subject to several variables. Williams uses a PowerPoint presentation to show the board how greater investments in professional development, technical support, and other facets will lead to the desired result: better use of technology for teaching and learning.

11:00 P.M. Williams drives home at the end of another long but productive day.

What can we conclude about the influence a school administrator can have on the use of technology within a school system? First, the administrator can model the use of technology. In our scenario, Williams depended on technology for communication with his staff and others; whenever possible, he also used technology when making presentations. Second, an administrator can make certain that appropriate systems are in place to make the school system operate efficiently. In the scenario, there were systems to manage transportation and security, as well as records of various kinds. Third, an administrator can make certain that others in the system understand the importance of using technology well. Williams met with the district business manager to plan the integration of voice, data, and video communication; he asked the director of libraries to give him a report on student Internet use; and he spoke to the personnel director about the importance of employing only teachers and administrators who were competent in technology. Fourth, a school administrator provides leadership for establishing a vision for technology use and creating a technology plan that makes it possible for the vision to become a reality. In the scenario, Williams is presenting a technology plan that is the product of months of work by faculty and staff. And, finally, an administrator can provide some direction for professional development to ensure that all faculty and staff have appropriate command of technology befitting their responsibilities.

It is not necessary for a superintendent or a building principal to be a "techie." It is enough that administrators use technology in their own work, support the use of technology by others, promote its use, understand issues affecting technology use in schools (e.g., matters of copyright, censorship), articulate ways technology can be used effectively for instruction, explain to laypeople their vision for schools using technology effectively and lead others to achieve the vision, and be sufficiently aware of leading-edge technologies that they can make sensible choices among new opportunities for employing technology. Although these skills do not require that an administrator be expert in technology, it is no longer possible for administrators to be both naive about technology and be a good school leader.

THE ROLE OF TECHNOLOGY IN SCHOOL ADMINISTRATION GRADUATE PROGRAMS

Most school administrators are acquiring their knowledge of technology on the job and through various professional development programs available to them through vendors, professional associations, and colleges and universities. Few principals and superintendents had the opportunity to learn about technology when they were pursuing graduate studies. Even today, graduate programs in school administration vary greatly in the attention they give to providing administrators the knowledge and skills they require to serve as leaders of technology-rich schools or school districts.

Graduate school programs generally are doing a poor job in preparing school principals and superintendents to be technology leaders. It is possible to obtain a principal's license without knowing anything about technology. Very few programs that prepare school administrators require that the candidate take a course on technology or demonstrate any competence with technology. In the majority of cases, technology is treated only incidentally. For example, during a course on school law, the instructor may include cases that arise from an electronic school environment—cases dealing with **pirating** software, use of **filters** to screen out pornographic web sites, and inappropriate use of e-mail. Nevertheless, some professors are doing more than merely providing incidental reference to technology. They are redesigning their courses to employ technology and thus model its use; a few are designing their courses in such a way that the skills taught are immediately applicable to the administrator in the school. A few programs now require that all administrator candidates enroll in one or more courses on technology, and a few SCDEs are giving technology a high profile in their programs at both the master's and specialist level of training.

The examples of these efforts that follow are representative of some professors of school administration who have recognized the need and are responding to it.

Bruce D. Baker, Assistant Professor, Department of Teaching and Leadership, School of Education, University of Kansas. Bruce Baker, who teaches courses in school finance as well as other courses in school administration, believes that school administrators must learn to use technology because of the impact it will have on their work. Baker is also motivated to use technology in his graduate courses in school administration because of his prior experience as a middle school science teacher. He observed the interest his students had in technology and the effectiveness of his instruction when he organized it around problem-based learning. Thus, he has brought his interest in problem-based, collaborative learning to his work as an instructor of prospective school administrators. Technology is fundamental to Baker's course; he can teach the way he wants only through the use of technology. This requires also that he take seriously the requirement to pay close attention to what his students need to be able to do with technology to succeed in his courses.

For example, "School Resource Management" is a four-week, eight-session (six hours each) course in school-based financial management. The majority of class time, about four hours of each class session, is spent analyzing school-based budgets, deciding whether to lease or purchase, and finally, constructing a school-based budget. Typically, a class session concludes with PowerPoint presentations by student teams.

In another course, "School Finance: Policy and Practice," Baker has collaborated with Craig Richards, professor of education at Teachers College, Columbia University, in the development of teaching simulations both as custom applications in Microsoft Excel and more recently dynamic systems modeling software (ITHINK 5.0).

Baker and Richards have been at work since the mid-1990s developing what they describe as "flight simulators" for school finance. They use the software ITHINK in order to model a state-driven school finance system and enter many variables to affect the outcomes. From printed cases about school finance decisions, students are often unable to appreciate the many political and economic variables that affect the results. Therefore, Baker and Richards have created a simulation of school finance policymaking in New Jersey as that state struggles to achieve parity in per pupil spending. As the simulation proceeds, students are able to adjust policy levers—for example, by regulating the rate of spending growth by wealthy districts and changing the state's share of aid to poor districts. Following the simulation, their students prepare policy briefs on the strategies they attempted and the results of their efforts.

Baker also uses technology to communicate with students and distribute information about his courses. He provides web-based support for all of his courses, including the site for "School Finance: Policy and Practice," which also functions as the web site for the course that Richards teaches at Teachers College. His web-based course support is more extensive than the typical site. Students may download lecture outlines and many readings in advance of any class session. They are also able to download all of the simulations. Listservs are maintained for all courses to inform students of upcoming events. Baker provides students with timely one-to-one feedback on their work by using electronic communication and **file transfer**.

Baker's students, like those in school administration courses generally, vary widely in age, their personal comfort with technology, and their basic quantitative analysis skills. Baker begins "School Finance: Policy and Practice" with an open-ended problem and a web address where students can find the data they are to use. Then he assigns a short policy paper on the data, due by the next class session. The paper is not graded but is used as a preassessment. On the basis of the skill level that each student demonstrates by the preassessment, Baker makes suggestions for on-line reading that students can do to overcome deficiencies. In subsequent course assignments, he also provides tasks that call for differing levels of skills, so that quicker, more skilled students are not bored, while the less skilled can do tasks that are within reach for them. Baker believes that wherever possible, technology instruction should be individualized, and he practices that belief with his own graduate courses.

Everything Baker undertakes in his courses is designed to demonstrate to school administrators how technology can be employed effectively for instruction, thereby planting the seed for what can be done in their own schools by teachers and students who have access to technology and the skills and support to use it well. Baker is also showing administrators that modern businesses depend on the information that technology can provide. School administrators today are expected to have the capability of using every electronic management tool available to them.

All of Baker's courses make use of technology, but they vary somewhat in the technology skills required of the students and the ways technology is employed. Table 7.1 provides a list of his courses, an indication of whether the course is for master's or doctoral students, the role technology is employed, the software required, and the support provided on the web. These courses are among the most advanced in the use of technology for preparing school administrators and provide a glimpse at what future training programs for school administrators may become.

Table 7.1 Courses and the Role of Technology, University of Kansas

Course	Program	Role of Technology	Software*	Web-Based Support[†]
"Analysis of Administrative Problems"	Master's in Ed. Admin. (required for principal's certification)	Heavy emphasis on spreadsheet applications and dynamic systems models. Technology instruction provided within course. Baker and Richards book used. Concludes with practical exam/data-driven case analysis. Time in presence of computers: 50% or more.	MS Excel (H) ITHINK (M) MS PowerPoint (L)	All lecture notes (PPT and PDF) All data sets (XLS) Simulation models (ITM) Links to data sites Supplementary readings and support materials (PDF)
"School Resource Management"	Master's in Ed. Admin. (required for principal's certification)	Eight-session summer course in budget planning and development (each session is 6 hours). All problem-based learning, where the primary tool for financial analysis is MS Excel. Teams are given analyses to perform each	MS Excel (H) MS PowerPoint (M) MS Access (L)	All lecture notes (PPT and PDF) All data sets (XLS) Links to data sites Supplemental readings and support materials (PDF)

Course	Degree	Description	Software use†	Materials
		class period. Analyses done in Excel; findings presented in PowerPoint. Some direct instruction provided. Time in presence of computers: 50% or more.		
"School Finance Policy"	Ed.D. in Ed. Admin. (required for district certification)	Custom spreadsheet simulations and templates and dynamic systems models used for finance policy analysis. Data access from on-line sources and analysis in spreadsheets required for student projects (policy options briefs). Tech-savvy pretest given. Tech-IEP written and support materials provided via web. Time in presence of computers: 20–25% class time.	MS Excel (H) ITHINK (M) Web-based data (H) PowerPoint (L)	All lecture notes (PPT and PDF) All data sets (XLS) Simulation models (ITM) Links to data sites Supplemental readings and support materials (PDF) State-by-state guide to web-based data
"District Business Management"	Ed.D. in Ed. Admin. (required for district certification)	First half of course similar to "School Resource Management." Involves	MS Excel (H) ITHINK (M) Web-based data (H)	All lecture notes (PPT and PDF) All data sets (XLS)

(continued)

*Key to software use: (H) heavy, (M) moderate, (L) light.
†PPT: PowerPoint; XLS: Excel; ITM: ITHINK software.*

Table 7.1 Courses and the Role of Technology, University of Kansas (*cont.*)

Course	Program	Role of Technology	Software*	Web-Based Support[†]
		preparing a district budget (rather than school budget). Students access school-level demographic and other data on-line from KSDE (Kansas State Department of Education). Then using templates (or their own spreadsheets depending on IEP), prepare enrollment and revenue forecasts and construct, analyze, and present budgets. In second half of course, students have a two-session unit on technology planning.	PowerPoint (L)	Simulation models (ITM) Links to data sites Supplemental readings and support materials (PDF) Links to KS data sites.

*Key to software use: (H) heavy, (M) moderate, (L) light.
[†]PPT: PowerPoint; XLS: Excel; ITM: ITHINK software.

N. Kathleen O'Neill, Director, Leadership Preparation Initiative, Southern Regional Education Board. Kathleen O'Neill was formerly associate professor of education policy studies and director of instructional technology in the College of Education at Georgia State University (GSU) in Atlanta. Perhaps her dual appointment at GSU contributed to her sensitivity to the role of technology in schools and the importance of preparing school administrators who are confident in their own use of technology.

The effort at GSU to give more attention to technology in the school administration program was prompted by a 1996 Georgia study, *Two Miles Down a Ten Mile Road,* that provided a status report on the use of technology in Georgia schools. One of the obstacles the study identified was the absence of visionary technology leadership in the educational community. The report noted that where technology was used well in schools, a visionary leader was responsible. When it was used poorly, no such leaders could be found. Therefore, for Georgia to make the advances it wanted, greater attention had to be paid to the training and cultivation of visionary leaders who could lead their schools to use technology well.

GSU, a major site for preparing school administrators for the state's schools, decided that it would take the lead in attempting to overcome this deficiency (O'Neill, 1999). Its solution was to redesign the beginning leadership course, "Leadership in Education Organizations," required for students in school administration, to make it the vehicle for teaching the students about technology while introducing them to fundamentals of leadership. Dr. Carol McGrevin, a faculty member in educational leadership, agreed to work with O'Neill in designing the new course.

At first they focused on infusing technology into the existing leadership course. Students were required to use e-mail, word-process their work, employ presentation software, search the Internet, and demonstrate their competency in other areas. Students were also expected to describe what schools of the future might be and what demands these schools would place on school administrators. The main challenge the instructors faced was keeping the course focused on leadership and not transforming it into a course on technology.

Building on their initial success, the two instructors elected to extend their use of technology. In 1998, they decided to expand their use of on-line resources by using **WebCT** software. Their goal was to allow their students to experience an "anytime, anywhere" approach to instruction. This phrase is popular among distance learning proponents. It means *anytime* you wish to access the site and *anywhere* in the world in which you have an Internet connection.

Today students enrolled in the course are expected to obtain information from a variety of web sites, communicate with the instructor and other classmates by e-mail, and complete assignments electronically. The course, which has become a combination of face-to-face and on-line experiences, ensures that all candidates for school administrator positions take at least one course in which they must learn to use technology. The fact that the content of the course is school leadership is to reinforce the notion that schools require leaders who are comfortable with technology.

Terence R. Cannings, Associate Dean and Professor of Education, Graduate School of Education and Psychology, Pepperdine University. Pepperdine University began as a small, undergraduate, liberal arts college based in southern California. It was founded in 1937 by George Pepperdine, who wished to launch a coeducational college based on Christian values. In 1971, with the addition of professional schools, George Pepperdine College became Pepperdine University. Today it offers bachelor's, master's, and doctoral degrees. It enrolls more than eight thousand full-time and part-time students, of whom approximately three thousand are undergraduates, and it has a full-time faculty of more than three hundred. It is a Christian university with a special relationship to the Churches of Christ.

In addition to Seaver College, the undergraduate college, there are four professional schools: the George L. Graziadio School of Business and Management, the School of Law, the School of Public Policy, and the Graduate School of Education and Psychology (GSEP). GSEP offers both master's and doctoral degrees in education and in psychology. In education, at the master's degree level, GSEP offers a master of arts in educational technology, which is provided on-line; a master of science in administration, which also makes graduates eligible for the California Preliminary Administrative Services Credential; and a master of science in administration with a concentration in school business. At the doctoral level in education, GSEP offers four tracks: educational technology, organizational leadership, organization change, and educational leadership, administration, and policy. Those who are preparing to obtain their principal's license would ordinarily pursue the master of science in administration and Preliminary Administrative Services Credential. The typical terminal degree for school superintendents is the doctoral degree in educational leadership, administration, and policy.

Terence Cannings has been a technology leader at Pepperdine University since his appointment to the faculty in 1981 and has become a spokesperson on behalf of technology in education. He has published numerous articles on educational technology, spoken widely on the topic, and is in demand as a technology consultant. At Pepperdine, he has been one of those responsible for the establishment of the master of arts in educational technology degree and for the doctoral track in educational technology. Along with his colleagues, he has also been an important influence in ensuring that technology is represented in the other degree tracks as well.

The master of science in administration and Preliminary Administrative Services Credential is a cohort program that extends over eleven months. A cohort program is one that admits a group of students at one time and keeps the group together throughout their period of study in the program. This can be compared to admitting students as individuals and allowing them to pursue degrees at their own individual pace. Because the program serves students who have full-time jobs, classes meet mainly in the evenings and on weekends. All students have e-mail accounts and must be able to use computers when they enter the program. Each student must work on a project for his or another school as part of the academic work. Many choose to develop technology plans for their school or district. At the end of the program there is a required oral exam when each candidate is expected to employ one or more of the following: overhead transparencies developed with a presentation program like Persuasion or PowerPoint, a short video, slides, or a presentation developed on HyperStudio or HyperCard. Thus, each person seeking an administrator's license must demonstrate skill in using presentation technologies. All educational doctoral candidates, regardless of degree, are required to take "Communication and Information Technology." This course, taken during the first two trimesters of the program, stresses the development of computer skills and understanding Pepperdine's technology and software applications.

One of the remarkable aspects of the Pepperdine program is the degree to which educational technologists and school administration professors appear to collaborate. A second feature is the degree to which Pepperdine is experimenting with distributed learning and problem-centered learning as important features of their preparation programs for school administrators. Distributed learning is often used to stand for a type of distance learning; in this case students take a portion of their work in a distance learning mode and other parts on a face-to-face basis.

Ronald M. Stammen, Associate Professor of Educational Leadership, School of Education, College of Human Development and Education, North Dakota State University (NDSU); Director, NDSU Teaching Support Center; NDSU Coordinator, Tri-College University Educational Leadership Program. North Dakota has long recognized the value of technology for instruction and was among the first states to employ technology for purposes of distance learning. Stammen returned to North Dakota in 1990 with the responsibility for creating the statewide **Interactive Video Network (IVN)**, which uses two-way video and two-way audio to deliver courses leading to degrees and professional development courses to students scattered across the state. Since 1996, he has also been chair of SENDIT, a statewide, K–12 computer network funded by the state legislature. Stammen's responsibilities for statewide leadership in telecommunications and his role as associate professor of educational leadership have influenced his views regarding what school administrators need to know about technology.

NDSU is located in Fargo, the largest population center in North Dakota and just across the border from Moorhead, Minnesota. Fargo and Moorhead jointly provide a regional shopping, recreational, medical, and educational center.

Three decades ago, North Dakota State University, Concordia College, and Moorhead State University formed the Tri-College University (TCU), a consortium through which students share classes, facilities, events, and a coordinated bus service. Students can take courses on any of the three campuses while being registered at the home campus. All course fees are treated as in-state fees regardless of where the course is taken.

The graduate program in educational leadership is shared between Moorhead State University and NDSU faculties, with oversight by the TCU provost. The school administration program is provided by faculty of the two institutions who provide courses leading to a master's degree (intended especially for elementary and secondary school principals) and a specialist degree (intended primarily to prepare superintendents). TCU educational leadership faculty also jointly coordinate with the University of North Dakota to provide a planned sequence of IVN-based courses for graduate students located in the middle and western sections of North Dakota.

The master's and specialist programs are organized according to the Reasoned Action Leadership model of development, which holds that the primary function of schools is teaching and learning and the primary responsibility of school administrators is to support teaching and learning. Both the master's and specialist degree programs are competency based. The curriculum is structured according to six blocks of study: Block I, Personal and Professional Development; Block II, Instructional Leadership; Block III, Organizational Leadership; Block IV, Political and Community Leadership; Block V, Systems for Leadership and Instruction; and Block VI, Specialty Options. All students are expected to complete all of the courses in each of the first five blocks and complete six hours of their choosing from Block VI. The courses required for the master's degree are different from those of the specialist degree, but the courses in both degrees are organized according to the same six blocks.

NSDU's Instructional Technology Service provides training for students in Microsoft Office, web authoring software, **Blackboard's Course info**, and other applications upon request. Therefore, the TCU educational leadership program can move students into applied applications of these skill areas rather than teaching catch-up skills.

Students who are pursuing the master's degree are required to take "Technology and Information Systems" as part of Block V (Systems for Leadership and Instruction), and those pursuing the specialist degree must take "Computer Data Management and Decision-Making." Whatever degree they are pursuing, all candidates must take a required course in technology for administrators. Candidates taking both the master's and specialist degrees from TCU are required to take two courses on technology for administrators.

"Technology and Information Systems" was taught by Mark Schmidt, a lecturer in NCSU's College of Human Development and Education in spring 2000. Schmidt assigned course grades to students according to three performances. First, each student, participating as a member of a team, was to produce a technology plan for an actual school. The plan was expected to include an external scan to identify current possibilities and future needs regarding technology; an internal assessment covering the instructional needs of the student body; stated goals aimed at meeting the needs; a vision statement describing how technology will address the need; a design for the system needed to meet the goals and address the need; a description of the staff training required to implement the plan; a description of the equipment and software that will be purchased and installed and a timetable for implementation; and an evaluation design to measure the effectiveness of the plan. This task counted for one-third of the grade. Another third of the grade required that each student develop a scenario that describes how teachers can use various technologies (e.g., computers, laser disk players, CD-ROMs) for effective instruction. The scenario was intended to reveal the student's understanding of the kinds of equipment available and their appropriate application to learning. And the final third of the grade was determined by a portfolio prepared by each student that exhibited his or her ability to use publishing software to produce a final product. The portfolio had to show use of graphs, figures, and tables; spread-sheet; a map of a school district or bus route; a PowerPoint presentation; and other items. The aim of this course is to equip administrators with complex skills that they can use in their own school systems.

"Computer Data Management and Decision-Making" is required of all those who are seeking a specialist's degree. This course emphasizes computer applications that manage data, present information, organize instruction, and solve problems. In the past, the course has also given greater attention to communication networks than has "Technology and Information Systems." Each student is expected to devise an individual educational plan that is tailored to fit his or her own professional circumstances. One-third of a student's grade is based on creating a report that would be useful in the school district where the individual is employed—for example, an evaluation of a technology plan, a detailed school budget, a technology plan, or a demonstration of the ways to employ various microcomputer programs. The report must be presented in a way that demonstrates the student's command of technology.

Few other school administration programs have moved as aggressively as that offered by North Dakota State University and Moorhead State University to ensure that students are prepared to provide leadership with and through technology.

THE IMPACT OF TECHNOLOGY ON THE ROLE OF SCHOOL COUNSELORS

At first glance there seems to be something about the relationship between a school counselor and a student client that makes technology appear alien. The link between a student seeking guidance and an adult counselor providing advice is very personal, very human, and very nonmechanical. It is similar to the relationship between a physician and a patient, and this analogy may help illuminate the relationship of counseling to technology.

When we visit a doctor, we expect personal attention. We want the doctor to pay close attention to our aches and pains and prescribe a treatment that fits our situation. We want the doctor to treat us as a unique individual with a particular history and special needs and concerns—not unlike the expectations students might have for a counselor. Yet we would have little faith in a doctor who knows nothing about and cares little for modern medical technology. Our doctor must be able to monitor our temperature and blood pressure and listen to our heart and lungs. And doctors must know when more complex tests are necessary, sending us to specialists who can provide more complex examinations. However humane doctors may be, they are useless, perhaps even dangerous, if they do not employ advanced medical technology.

To see the technology that is available to school counselors and how they can use it, we will follow a hypothetical high school counselor through a typical working day. Her name is Carmella Lopez, and she is the head counselor in a senior high school of fifteen hundred students, serving grades 9 through 12.

A Day with Carmella Lopez

7:10 A.M. Ms. Lopez arrives at her office. Although classes do not begin until 8:00, she often has appointments at 7:30 so that parents and teachers can participate. By arriving early, she has the opportunity to open her voicemail and e-mail, responding to many of the messages before she begins to see people. She depends on e-mail. It is the principal form of communication among school staff. Students and parents also use it to communicate with her. Today her e-mail includes the following messages:

- A note from a former student who shares a humorous anecdote about something that happened to her recently. Relatively few graduates stay in touch, but some do. Messages from former students are especially welcome to Lopez.

- A note from a grateful mother thanking Lopez for her skill in handling a recent problem affecting her son.

- A message from Sam Kahler, the high school principal, asking her to take responsibility for assembling data on the school's recent National Merit Scholar Award winners. He wants to release the information to the newspapers by the end of the week.

- A request from a new teacher who is having problems with classroom control. The teacher wonders whether Lopez can give him some ideas for classroom management. She responds by directing him to a couple of web sites that provide the kind of help he is seeking.

After reading her e-mail, she brings up her calendar to see what appointments she has and what tasks lie ahead. For each student she will see today, she calls up the student record and prints it out so that it will be available at the time of each appointment. She realizes that this process is a waste of paper, but she finds it easier to counsel students if she is not looking constantly at the computer screen. All paper records are shredded at the end of the day.

7:30 A.M. Lopez has her first appointment, this one with a student who has been having serious academic problems in two of his classes. The student is accompanied by his parents, and all of his teachers are also present. Lopez has assembled the student's dossier; it includes grade reports, standardized test scores, records of attendance and discipline, and examples of his work. Using her computer, Lopez has produced graphs and charts that indicate his behavior and performance during his three years in the school.

8:00 A.M. Jim, another counselor, enters Lopez's office to tell her about new software he has recently found. The software contains a database of items that provide practice exercises for students preparing for college entrance exams. He proposes that the school purchase a site license for this software and load it onto computers in the Library/Media Center and the Career Center so that students can use it at their convenience. Lopez asks him to give her the details, and she will suggest to the principal that they purchase it.

After Jim leaves, Lopez brings up a counselor listserv that she consults regularly. The listserv alerts her to forthcoming professional meetings and provides information about new resources for counselors. She bookmarks the Web sites that she uses regularly—mainly sites that deal with career counseling and financial aid. Today she found a site that will provide her with information on renewing her counselor license.

8:30 A.M. Alex arrives. Alex is a senior, and Lopez conducted an interview with him earlier in the year. She and her colleagues interview each senior individually during the first month of the school year in order to make certain they are on course to graduate on time and have plans in place for the future—college, work, military service, or other options. Alex requires some extra attention. He has an interest in photography but is uncertain how to build a career in the field. Is a college education required? If so, what colleges are best for this purpose? What will it cost to get the education he needs? When Lopez met him a few weeks ago, she thought that maybe he was allowing his interest in his hobby limit his career choices and suggested that he take advantage of a software package to construct a personal interest inventory. The resulting profile could then be connected to occupational choices, career training options, and appropriate colleges or other institutions of higher education. Alex has arrived with computer printouts in hand and a keen desire to discuss what he has found.

9:00 A.M. Lopez meets with Sam Kahler, the principal. He asks her to give him a report that he can use for public presentations to indicate that the high school focus on student results is producing good outcomes. He wants to compare the current situation with results five and ten years previously. He asks her to assemble data on attendance, dropout rates, student mobility, standardized test scores, statewide graduation test scores, college attendance rates, and whatever else she has in her files that the public might find interesting and would build confidence in the school. Fortunately, all of these data are stored electronically, waiting to be assembled and displayed as needed.

10:30 A.M. Lopez returns to her office. In the few minutes before her next appointment, she responds to telephone calls and answers her e-mail. She has a policy of refusing calls while an interview is underway yet seeks to respond to calls as quickly as possible. Voicemail and e-mail enable her to practice this policy.

11:00 A.M. Lopez meets with a parent and her daughter. The girl is having considerable trouble with her schoolwork. In the past she had been a good student. Her recent problems in class have begun to affect her attitude toward her parents, school, and even her friends. Lopez suggests that the first step should be to look for a physical explanation for the problem and advises a checkup and tests on her eyesight, her hearing, and whatever else her physician may recommend. Once the results of these tests are available, Lopez suggests that they meet again.

Noon Lopez meets with a group of students over lunch in the cafeteria. This self-appointed group called SAVE (Students Against Violent Events) has been working hard to combat violence in the school. Lopez, their faculty adviser, offers a number of suggestions for web-based sources of information on conflict management.

1:15 P.M. Lopez meets with the school's student web master. The high school found a student who is skilled in web development. He relies on teachers and administrators for the web content and contacts key individuals once a week in order to update the various web pages. Lopez provides him with information about scholarships, career opportunities, and scheduled test dates that will be entered on the counselor web page.

1:30 P.M. Lopez conducts a very delicate session with Alice, a student who has questions about her sexuality. After twenty minutes, it becomes obvious that a face-to-face discussion is difficult for Alice, so Lopez suggests a piece of software that will enable Alice to ask her questions. Lopez has found that students often find it difficult even to frame the questions they want to ask about sexual matters without feeling embarrassed. Alice works alone on a computer in Lopez's office for about thirty minutes. When Alice leaves, she seems visibly relieved and tells Lopez that most of her questions have been answered.

3:15 P.M. Lopez attends a faculty meeting. She has been invited to make a PowerPoint presentation to the faculty on course-taking trends among students. She also uses the opportunity to report on two new support groups that students have organized: one on grief and the other for children of divorced parents.

4:00 P.M. Lopez returns to her office to enter notes into the records of all of the students she met that day. The information is stored electronically. She tries to enter her notes at the end of each school day or she falls very far behind.

4:30 P.M. Lopez logs onto a graduate course in counseling that she is taking from a state university. The course will help her in the renewal of her counseling license.

5:30 P.M. Lopez closes her office and leaves for home, carrying her laptop computer for work that evening. She is developing a PowerPoint presentation to be given to current juniors to help them understand what lies ahead for them in their senior year. She presents at all junior English classes in order to reach all of the junior students. The PowerPoint presentation is designed to be sufficiently interesting to hold their attention; it also enables her to be consistent across all of the presentations. Because she finds it difficult to set aside time during the school day to work on such matters, this becomes her "homework."

School counselors are responsible for three types of counseling activities: academic, personal and social, and career planning. The scenario shows Lopez's involvement in each of these arenas. We are also provided with evidence of ways she benefits from the use of technology. Counselors are relied on as sources of accurate information. Much of the information students and administrators need is predictable and can be packaged. For example, we should expect that the school's Career Center contains up-to-date software that permits students to analyze their strengths and weaknesses and links them to occupations consistent with their strengths and interests. The Career Center also has videotapes from various colleges and universities advertising their programs. Students can also check out videos that provide insights into careers and occupations.

Technology can help with resolving personal problems. Alice is experiencing physical and emotional changes in her life. She is reluctant to talk to her parents about her feelings and too shy to be frank with Lopez. Sometimes the impersonality of a computer-based program provides the anonymity that a student needs. Alice was able to ask the computer any question she wanted without feeling that someone was judging her.

It is also obvious from the scenario that Lopez uses technology for her own productivity. Many of the tasks she is asked to undertake would have been nearly impossible, given the demands on her time, if she lacked access to modern information technology.

How do school counselors acquire the knowledge and skills in the use of technology their jobs require? Becoming a fully certified school counselor requires completing a master's degree in an accredited counselor education program in a SCDE. School counselors are often classroom teachers before they become counselors. Therefore, they may have learned a portion of what they might know about technology while they were preparing to teach or even on the job. However, we should expect that good counselor education programs would ensure that their candidates have the knowledge and skill they will need to be successful as school counselors.

THE ROLE OF TECHNOLOGY IN COUNSELOR EDUCATION GRADUATE PROGRAMS

The Association for Counselor Education and Supervision (ACES) Technology Interest Network has developed, and the ACES Executive Council has approved, "Technical Competencies for Counselor Education Students: Recommended Guidelines for Program Development." According to the document:

> At the completion of a counselor education program, students should:
>
> 1. be able to use productivity software to develop web pages, group presentations, letters and reports;
> 2. be able to use such audiovisual equipment as video recorders, audio recorders, projection equipment, video conferencing equipment, and playback units;

3. be able to use computerized statistical packages;

4. be able to use computerized testing, diagnostic, and career decision-making programs with clients;

5. be able to use e-mail;

6. be able to help clients search for various types of counseling-related information via the Internet, including information about careers, employment opportunities, educational and training opportunities, financial assistance/scholarships, treatment procedures, and social and personal information;

7. be able to subscribe, participate in, and sign off counseling-related listservs;

8. be able to access and use counseling-related CD-ROM data bases;

9. be knowledgeable of the legal and ethical codes that relate to counseling services via the Internet;

10. be knowledgeable of the strengths and weaknesses of counseling services provided via the Internet;

11. be able to use the Internet for finding and using continuing education opportunities in counseling, and

12. be able to evaluate the quality of Internet information. (Bloom & Walz, 2000)

It is difficult to be certain as to what degree counseling education programs are meeting these requirements. Although the ACES competencies seem to be widely accepted by counseling programs, it is not clear that they are being implemented. Some studies raise serious doubts about the degree to which counselor education programs are attending to computer-related counseling skills (Lambert, 1988; Granello, 2000).

It is not that counselor education programs have ignored the value of technology. Indeed, audiotape recorders have long been used to record counseling sessions, and videotaping is employed in counselor education to debrief counseling students after clinical sessions.

Counseling education programs have also made limited use of simulations from time to time. Simulations are valued because they allow students to practice counseling techniques without placing clients at risk. Some early examples of simulating counseling processes were *Client I, The Great Therapist Program,* and *SuperShrink. Client I,* developed in 1975, sought to manipulate various emotional and demographic factors, allowing students to test various approaches to diagnosis. *The Great Therapist Program* gave students an opportunity to compare their approaches with leaders in the field. The program provided a statement from a hypothetical client; students could type in their responses to the statement, and the program would respond by providing feedback according to the congruence of the student's statement to those of one of the master therapists (Carl Rogers, Frederick Perls, Alan Goldstein, and Albert Ellis). *SuperShrink* simulated a counseling session in which the student was the counselor and the computer was the client. All of these programs made efforts at being truly interactive, but limitations imposed by the technology of the time placed constraints on their level of interactivity.

A more recent example, *Basic Counseling Responses: A Multimedia Learning System for the Helping Professional,* developed in 1991, has been favorably reviewed (Casey, 1999). It employs compressed video of seven client sessions representing a wide range of student populations. Fifteen basic counseling responses (e.g., opening or closing, giving feedback, clarifying) are developed along with three therapeutic intents (to acknowledge, explore, or challenge) and five focuses (client experience, client feeling, client thought, client behavior, and immediacy). Students select one of the sessions and view it completely. After viewing a session, a student can view it again, segment by segment. Following each segment, the student is asked to identify the type of response, the intent, and the focus of the interaction he observed. Students are given immediate feedback regarding the accuracy of their observations.

Although simulations such as these have proved valuable for training, it is not apparent how widely they are used. Cost factors and lack of faculty training appear to be constraints.

The Internet and desktop computing appear to be growing rapidly in importance in counselor education because they are relatively inexpensive and ubiquitous. The Internet is especially valuable because a major factor in counselor effectiveness is gaining access to good information. In the past, information for counselors came mainly from books and journals. Today counselors have access to such resources as **virtual libraries**, created by ERIC Counseling and Student Services (ERIC/CASS). Information in them is available electronically in full text and can be easily downloaded. Each "library" targets high-priority counseling topics that are updated every two to four weeks. Topics for virtual libraries include career development, student achievement, cultural diversity, conflict resolution, school violence, youth groups, and depression and suicide (Walz & Reedy, 2000).

Another indicator of the interest of the Internet among counselor educators is the appearance of a relatively new electronic journal, *Journal of Technology in Counseling*. The journal, which began publication in fall 1999 (Jencius & Baltimore, 2000), is sponsored by the Department of Counseling and Educational Leadership at Columbus State University and can be accessed at the university's web site **(http://jtc.colstate.edu/issues.htm).**

One of the leaders in the use of technology for counseling and education is Peggy Hines at Indiana State University.

Peggy Hines, Assistant Professor of Education and School Counselor Program Director, Department of Counseling, Indiana State University. Indiana State University is one of six universities in the United States to receive funds from the Dewitt Wallace-Reader's Digest Fund. Its project, Transforming School Counseling, is a joint effort by Indiana State University and the Vigo County School Corporation.

The master's degree for school counselors is a forty-eight-credit-hour program that requires two years to complete. The program admits a cohort of fifteen students each June and graduates the cohort two years later.

The program uses a combination of face-to-face and distance-learning technology. Each summer, the group spends six weeks on the Indiana State University (ISU) campus engaged in full-time study. During the academic year, the students return to campus one weekend each month (all day on Saturday and Sunday) for a total of five sessions each semester. When they are not in session during the academic year, they are engaged in individual assignments and group projects. They are expected to share their materials electronically and participate in chat rooms and listservs. Many of their assignments require researching web sites.

Each cohort draws students from throughout the state of Indiana, but the instructors divide each cohort into learning communities that have geographical propinquity, thereby facilitating communication among subgroups of the cohorts. The program also works with school systems to find internship placements for their students. Each student is assigned to a feeder system within the school system, that is, an elementary, a middle, and a secondary school. Thus, each counselor education student gains experience at each level of K–12 education while remaining within the same system.

Because the counselor education students must possess basic computing skills to participate in the program, Hines and her colleagues have established a set of computer competencies required for admission. Those who cannot demonstrate proficiency in each of these competencies are required to take a course that provides the basic competencies that school counselor education students need to survive in the program. The course can be taken for credit, but the credit does not apply toward the master's degree in school counseling. Following are the competencies expected of all students admitted to the program. Students lacking these skills are required to take the basic competencies course.

Word Processing/Desktop Publishing

1. Use word processing and desktop publishing to create printed documents.
2. Cut and paste information from an electronic source into a personal document complete with proper citation.
3. Upload and use computer-generated graphics and digital photos in various print and electronic presentations.
4. Scan document and import into word processing software.
5. Create mail merge documents.

Database and Spreadsheet

6. Use database management software to create original databases.

7. Use spreadsheet software to create spreadsheets, charts, tables and graphs.

Multimedia Presentation

8. Use presentation software (e.g., PowerPoint and Hyper-Studio) to create electronic slide shows and to generate overheads.

9. Import graphics, charts, and pictures into presentations.

10. Connect and operate technology needed for presentations.

Electronic/Internet Resources

11. Able to send and receive e-mail messages and attachments.

12. Able to subscribe and search electronic discussion lists.

13. Able to search the Internet, analyze, and filter electronic information in relation to the task, rejecting non-relevant information.

14. View, download, decompress, and open documents and programs from Internet sites.

15. Properly cite electronic sources of information.

16. Able to upload reports, presentations, etc. to the Internet.

17. Able to use electronic library search technology.

18. Able to join and participate in chat rooms.

Hines thinks of these competencies as minimum competencies; much more is expected as students proceed through the program. Each course contains assignments that require students to use technology. For example, each student is expected to conduct research on some topic within the school system where he or she is working. The research products are then presented to the school administration or the school board, or both. The presentation is usually a PowerPoint presentation that uses Excel or other software.

It is unlikely that technology will replace counselors, but it is not only likely, it is also necessary, that technology be employed to enhance the counselor's work. When giving advice to a student who is having trouble in school, a counselor needs as much information about the student as possible before prescribing a solution. These data may be taken from an anecdotal record of the student's history at school, previous course grades, scores on a variety of standardized tests, hearing and vision tests, and many other sources. A counselor needs a relational database that assembles such information in order to discern patterns.

When providing career advice, a counselor needs access to tests that may provide clues to a student's occupational interests and databases that provide information about occupational trends and the entry qualifications for various careers. When advising a student on college choices, counselors need to help students scan a wide range of educational institutions and their academic strengths, admission requirements, availability of scholarships, and tuition expenses. A counselor also needs to be able to advise students on ways to develop resumés for employment and college admission and to file applications electronically. Each of these tasks can be done better with the help of technology.

A counselor's job is not only to be friendly, patient, and wise, although these qualities are vital. A counselor must also have a firm grip on the tools that will provide the best information available to client students.

■■■ CONCLUSION ■■■

SCDEs are giving greater attention than before to the preparation of classroom teachers who can use technology effectively. This task is a big challenge and deserves the attention it is receiving. Nevertheless, SCDEs cannot overlook the preparation of school administrators and counselors with regard to technology. School systems that lack leaders who understand and use technology do not succeed in the classroom either. Technology is the catalyst that will lead to modern school practices. It is not enough for classroom teachers to use these tools; they must also become the everyday practice of counselors and school administrators as well.

■■ REFERENCES ■ ■

Bloom, J. W., & Walz, G. R. (Eds.), *Cybercounseling and cyberlearning: Strategies and resources for the millennium.* Alexandria, VA: American Counseling Association, and Greenboro, ND: CAPS.

Casey, J. A. (1999). Computer assisted simulation for counselor training of basic skills. *Journal of Technology in Counseling, 1*(1), 1–8.

Granello, P. (2000). Historical context: The relationship of computer technologies and counseling. In J. W. Bloom & G. R. Walz (Eds.), *Cybercounseling and cyberlearning: Strategies and resources for the millennium* (pp. 3–16). Alexandria, VA: American Counseling Association, and Greenboro, ND: CAPS.

Jencius, M., & Baltimore, M. (2000). Professional publication in cyberspace: Guidelines and resources for counselors entering a new paradigm. In J. W. Bloom & G. R. Walz (Eds.), *Cybercounseling and cyberlearning: Strategies and resources for the millennium* (pp. 185–199). Alexandria, VA: American Counseling Association and Greenboro, ND: CAPS.

Lambert, M. (1988). Computers in counselor education: Four years after a special issue. *Counselor Education and Supervision, 28,* 100–109.

O'Neill, N. K. (1999). Preparing technology-competent leadership. *Teaching in Educational Administration, 6*(2), 1–5.

Walz, G. R., & Reedy, L. S. (2000). The international career development library: The use of virtual libraries to promote counselor learning. In J. W. Bloom & G. R. Walz (Eds.), *Cybercounseling and cyberlearning: Strategies and resources for the millennium* (pp. 161–170). Alexandria, VA: American Counseling Association, and Greenboro, ND: CAPS.

8

Distance-Learning Technologies in Education Courses

DIALOGUES WITHIN THE ACADEMY
Out on the Road

Right before the meeting with the statewide conference on teacher education and the subsequent dinner meeting with his colleagues, Lee had agreed to help out the director of teacher education at his small, private college and supervise a student teacher, Terry. Lee, the provost at the college, had agreed in part at Terry's request because she is one of the President's Scholars, a small corps of academically elite students. Unfortunately, Terry was placed at a high school that was over sixty miles away from the college. Now, for the third time this semester, Lee had had to cancel appointments for the entire afternoon so he could meet with the supervising principal at the high school. At the end of the meeting, Lee felt it necessary to let the principal know that as the semester became busier, he might not be able to drive up for as many meetings with the student teacher, cooperating teacher, and principal. Let's join their conversation.

Lee: I really do apologize, but I think you understand my predicament. When I agreed to supervise Terry, I didn't know it was so far away, and my duties as provost will make it difficult for me to make time to come up here much more this semester. Terry, her cooperating teacher, and you deserve a field supervisor who can devote the necessary time. I enjoy seeing Terry in her history classes and would really like to keep doing the supervision, but I don't think it will be best for everyone.

Principal: I understand your predicament, but I think there are alternatives.

Lee: Oh. That's gracious of you to offer to come to campus for our meetings? I would still need to come up here to observe every once in a while, but not as often, and the student teacher could also come to campus for our meetings. Yes, that could work!

Principal: That was not quite what I had in mind. I was thinking more along the lines of using some of the technology that we all have in our schools to make this work. The principals in this school district regularly meet with the superintendent using a webcam and video-conferencing over the web. Our teachers have also held web conferences with other teachers in the state for professional de-velopment, and we have had guest speakers into our classes with this technology. Here let me show you. [The principal provides a quick demonstration: a conference between his desk and the secretary in the outer office.] You can get somewhat of an idea from this.

Lee: Well, it looks like an interesting idea, but even assuming we have this technology at our college, I can't imagine doing the classroom observation with it.

Principal: You're right; classroom observation would probably not be as effective with a tiny webcam. However, at our end, we can hook up a regular video camera to the computer and the Internet. You wouldn't want to do all your observation that way, but it is a good interim tool. Then you can use it to meet with Terry, Mr. Coleman, and myself when individual meetings are necessary. Terry is also do-ing some interesting applications with distance learning in her class. For example, there is no reason you can't observe the class sessions she has planned for an on-line conference with a Jeffersonian scholar from Monticello from your own computer. And I know that you do have it available at your college. We had a life sciences pro-fessor from your college do an in-service workshop for our science department over web conferencing just a few weeks ago.

Lee: Thanks for the idea. It looks as if you aren't going to let me off the hook that easily. I will contact our technology director when I get into the office tomorrow and start making arrangements. This really adds a new dimension to student teaching supervision, doesn't it?

DISTANCE LEARNING IN
HIGHER EDUCATION

How do **distance education** and **distance-learning** technologies affect higher education? Distance education on the whole is not a new phenomenon to education. Correspondence schools emerged as a valid teaching method in the late 1800s, and in 1883, the Chautauqua Institute was recognized by New York State as a source for degrees (Moore & Kearsley, 1996). In the 1950s and 1960s, distance education developed further through the use of radio and television. In 1978, the University of Phoenix was established as an accredited institution offering undergraduate and graduate degrees at a distance.

The U.S. Department of Education reports that 90 percent of higher education institutions with enrollments of more than ten thousand students and 85 percent of those institutions with student populations of three thousand to ten thousand offered distance-education courses in 1998. To extend this growth, Michael P. Lamber, executive director of the Distance Education and Training Council, predicted that by 2001, most college teachers would be involved in distance teaching and distance learning (Olsen, 1996). Much of this rapid growth can be attributed to advances in **distance-learning technologies**. Newer technologies that use **ATM**, the Internet, or video conferencing enable institutions to deliver and students to receive distance learning in many more easy and inexpensive ways.

All of this rapid growth and change are presented in terms of distance-education courses. It does not include the use of distance-learning technologies within courses delivered face-to-face. Teacher education itself is already engaged in some of these activities. For example, in an earlier chapter, we discussed technology applications like electronic discussion groups. These types of asynchronous communication tools are in effect distance-learning technologies. A facilitated discussion that takes place beyond the traditional classroom walls falls under the definition of distance education. If teacher education is already successfully using some distance-learning technologies, then why not embrace distance-learning and distance-learning technologies in the teacher education curriculum?

WHY DISTANCE EDUCATION?

We hope that by this point in the book, we have developed a strong argument for why technology should be integrated into teacher education programs. This chapter explains why distance education and distance-learning technologies can help SCDEs do their work and thereby integrate technology. We start this section with the question, "Why distance education?" because when distance education is considered in concert with teacher education, the question is bound to emerge. Most teacher education faculty understand why technology should be integrated, although they may not be sure how to accomplish that task. However, distance education is not as readily accepted in teacher education.

SCDEs should move to incorporate distance-learning technologies for three primary reasons. First, these technologies will enable them to reach new teacher education students and provide existing students with learning opportunities they were not able to have access to previously. Second, school corporations increasingly use distance-learning technologies to teach students in different ways and also to provide them with educational opportunities to which they may not previously have had access. Third, these technologies provide yet another tool and opportunity for SCDEs to integrate technology in the teacher education program and model effective uses of technology. To address why these are good reasons for integrating distance-learning technology, we look at how these are done.

Expanding the Reach of Teacher Education

A SCDE has a number of possible student constituencies. Those students eighteen to twenty-two years old whom you might see in your mind's eye when you imagine a college student are not necessarily the typical student anymore. In addition to these traditional students, we also see returning adult students, who may have job and family responsibilities; the greatest responsibility of these students may not be sitting in a classroom to have knowledge imparted to them. A SCDE that has a large contingent of nontraditional students may have a great deal of success, and generate a great deal of goodwill as well, using distance-learning technologies in conjunction with face-to-face instruction to meet the needs of these students. Lectures can be offered to students on videotape. Class discussion can take place through electronic communication. Faculty can hold office hours in web-based chat rooms. Class notes can be uploaded to the web. Then on-campus time can be reserved for more active learning opportunities and exercises.

There is also the possibility that a SCDE can use distance-learning technologies not to fill the needs of students but to fill a curricular hole. Few SCDEs have the unlimited resources necessary to offer a full range of learning experiences and information to their teacher education students. Generally they can take advantage of the resources at another institution to assist with the education of its students. CaseNET at the University of Virginia is one such example.

CaseNET is a set of courses developed at the University of Virginia and delivered using distance-learning technologies to other SCDEs, as well as in-service teachers and school administrators. The program uses the web, Internet videoconferencing, electronic discussion groups, and e-mail, as well as videotape and print materials, to deliver course content. The courses are not truly delivered at a distance because students meet at a site at a given time with an on-site instructor. The technologies are used to deliver cases that guide the learning in the course and provide real-life applications, and they are also used to bring together the students in the many sites around the country to expand everyone's learning.

K–12 School Use of Distance-Learning Technology

K–12 schools have been using a variety of distance-learning technologies in the classroom for well over a decade. K–12 students now turn to web-based classes to complete requirements for high school or to have a jump-start on college-level courses. In addition, innovative teachers have found that the classroom application of these tools may not use the label of distance-learning technology, but this is in fact what they are doing.

One project that is available to all teachers around the world is called *keypals*. Essentially an electronic form of the pen-pal concept, keypals matches classrooms of students in the United States with other classrooms around the world. Using e-mail and the facilitation of their teachers, students send messages back and forth to each other as they learn more about school, food, culture, and life in other countries and cultures. Teachers can locate keypals through an organization **(http://www. keypals.com)** or use contacts they already have, or the school might have a sister school in another country that might be willing to partner as a keypal.

The University of Virginia developed a distance-learning technology tool to enable elementary and middle school children to learn more about history during the time of Thomas Jefferson. Staff and faculty created and operated an e-mail address to which students could send e-mail questions directed to "Mr. Jefferson." The children learned a great deal about history and life during the time Jefferson was alive, and the staff and faculty who answered the questions also learned a great deal as they researched the students' questions.

There are numerous examples that use e-mail as a vehicle. The Great Canadian Trivia Contest has students across North America researching the answers to questions. Students and teachers may also use the Internet to collect data from different parts of the country about family, food, weather, and other topics. The data can then be used to teach authentic applications of graphing and statistics. For example, a middle school team may create an interdisciplinary curriculum unit about acid rain. Through Internet surveys, students collect rainfall amounts and acidity levels from other children around the country. For science, they learn about the effects of acid rain. For social studies, they study the geographic regions where they are collecting data and the historical developments that have brought about acid rain. For math, students graph the results of the survey and complete projections with spreadsheets. For language arts, students write the electronic communications, which are sent out across the country, and publish an electronic version of their findings.

Asynchronous distance technologies have a great deal of value in that the communication does not need to be tied to a specific time or place. However, synchronous technologies are also a factor in K–12 classrooms. Think of the video footage you might have seen of students sitting in an auditorium watching live video of the space shuttle astronauts on a space walk. That is a passive use of distance-learning technology. However, these same students can also have the opportunity to talk to the astronauts, send them questions, and perform simultaneous experiments with the astronauts while they are in space through a combination of synchronous and asynchronous distance technologies

Synchronous communication out into space is truly long-distance technology. Synchronous distance-learning technologies can be used more locally too. For example, there are regular opportunities for students to web-conference with researchers or teachers in residence at the Antarctic research base. Libraries set up videoconferences between authors and young readers. Authors such as Marc Brown (of the *Arthur* series) read their books to early readers and may sponsor on-line contests for young readers to decide storylines.

Teachers themselves can deliver the distance-learning technologies. There are now a number of virtual high schools around the country. These virtual schools are used by students who are home-schooled, but course work is often prepared and delivered by a licensed teacher. Smaller schools have found **two-way video and two-way audio** technologies to be a cost-effective way to expand their curriculum. A school may not have sufficient numbers of students for Advanced Placement (AP) or language courses. Using advanced television technologies, multiple schools can pool their resources together and offer an AP Biology course, for example, and pull students into the course from four area high schools.

A SCDE must determine if it is preparing future teachers who can perform these same functions and encourage these same types of learning experiences. The preservice teachers being prepared in SCDEs must be able to do at the very least these same types of applications. Ideally, teacher education students will also be prepared to find additional applications of distance-learning technologies that they can integrate into their curriculum in order to advance student learning.

Distance-Learning Technologies as a Model for Technology Integration

Take a moment to glance back over what you just read in the previous two sections, and then we will consider this third reason that distance-learning technology should be integrated. If a SCDE were to try to reach out to nontraditional students or extend the existing curriculum by sharing resources with another SCDE, could this be done without distance-learning technologies? Or if a school wanted to collect data on acid rain from around the country and then report results back to participants, could it be done without distance-learning technology? Of course, it could! Could it be done as expeditiously and effectively? The answer is an emphatic "no" to the first part of the question and a "most likely not" to the second part.

We are not technocrats who are advocating that technology should be used in all instances, no matter what. However, if technology can enable teaching and learning to occur that is more realistic (case-based instruction, analysis of real data, access to learning otherwise unavailable), then a SCDE that did not use technology, and in the case of these examples, distance-learning technologies, would be remiss. When a faculty member expands the boundaries of her classroom and uses distance-learning technologies to access more resources and make learning more authentic, then not only has the teaching and learning changed in that teacher education program, but the faculty member has also modeled the power of technology (and distance-learning technology in particular) to change the learning environment. Those learning experiences will therefore change not only what the teacher education student learned, but also how he learned it and how he might envision teaching in the future.

A MODEL FOR MERGING DISTANCE-LEARNING TECHNOLOGY AND TEACHER EDUCATION

Can distance-learning technology and teacher education be merged together? After what you have already read, we hope the answer is a resounding yes! The previous examples of what has been done in K–12 education should be more than enough to provide that answer. We could now suggest that you go forth and do good work, and some in teacher education are so excited by the possibilities of distance-learning technologies that it will happen. Perhaps some are motivated by the challenge of designing and delivering instruction for a new form of delivery, or the desire to reach new students, or the appeal in not being face-to-face with students. Whatever the motive or interest, the numbers presented at the beginning of the chapter demonstrate that there are many interested in distance-learning technology, and web-based instruction in particular. Others in teacher education may have no negative feelings toward distance learning, but feel strongly that it is not an appropriate method for teacher education where preservice teachers need to experience excellent face-to-face instruction and that direct observation of the teacher education student is necessary, thereby making distance learning impossible. And a handful of teacher educators believe that distance education is not appropriate at all in the academy. Regardless of where any teacher education faculty may fall within these groups, the SCDE still needs to make it work at its institution.

We need a framework of how distance learning and teacher education work together, some examples of how it is being done, and additional ideas for using distance-learning technologies. Figure 8.1 offers an example of how distance learning, teacher education, and technology work together.

The diagram shows how the three components function independently, as well as with each other. There is a point where distance learning has nothing to do with teacher education and technology. For example, traditional correspondence courses do not use computer technology. Technology can exist outside teacher education and distance learning. Engineering programs make high use of technology and are traditionally not part of the teacher education program. And teacher education can also exist without the influence of distance learning or technology (it is

Figure 8.1   The Distance-Learning, Teacher Education, and Technology Environment

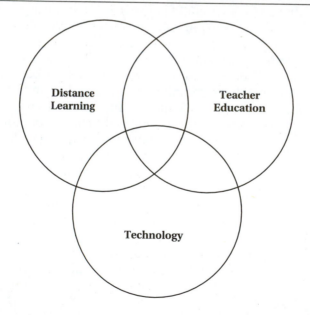

important to note that it *can* exist without technology; however, we hope that by now readers agree with us that it *should not* exist without technology).

Figure 8.1 also shows that two of the areas can intersect without involving the third. Therefore, technology and teacher education can (and should) have a union, and so can technology and distance learning. This intersection is seen in the distance-learning tools themselves, such as one-way and two-way video, web-based videoconferencing, and web-based instruction. Currently most distance learning is delivered through technology. And there is also an intersection between distance learning and teacher education. There are teacher education programs that are using traditional distance-learning techniques to enhance their programs, as we will see in an example in this chapter.

Finally, the three elements also work together. Technology and distance learning can be tools to enhance the preparation of teacher education students. Not only can it happen, but also in a world where there are virtual high schools, teachers who teach to home-bound students, and teachers who need to engage in professional development consistently to stay current, it *should* happen.

What should be noted in particular about Figure 8.1 is that this framework does not prescribe an all-or-nothing approach. For example, nowhere does the diagram say that all courses throughout a teacher education program should be web based. The move to a program offered fully through distance-learning technologies needs to be deliberate and carried out with a great deal of care and instructional design expertise. However, if carefully implemented, a teacher education program can effectively use distance-learning technologies for part, or even all, of its program. When courses are carefully designed and implemented, student learning is not hindered in distance-learning environments; in fact, there is evidence that learning may be enhanced (Mory, Gambill, & Browning, 1998; Business Wire, 1999). A highly interactive, well-designed web-based course also has the added advantage of developing self-directed learning skills and practice at technology utilization (Romiszowski, 1997).

A discussion of how to design effective, interactive distance-learning courses is beyond the scope of this book. There are numerous resources available to provide that information. What we will do here is provide a variety of examples of distance-learning programs that represent different parts of Figure 8.1, as well as a number of ideas of distance-learning strategies that can be employed in teacher education programs.

What Is Available for Preservice Teachers at a Distance?

A simple web search reveals numerous teacher education and general education courses taught at a distance, primarily through web-based instruction. The vast majority of these are offered at the graduate level and available to teachers who already are licensed and are seeking professional development course work. This phenomenon is due in large part to the any-time, anywhere learning needs of graduate students who may also work full time. The following examples represent different segments of the model in Figure 8.1.

Intersection of Distance Learning and Teacher Education. Figure 8.2 shows the point where distance learning and teacher education can work together without the benefit of advanced technologies. Saint Mary-of-the-Woods College (SMWC) in Indiana has been using a distance-learning program for more than twenty-five years. Over nine hundred students are enrolled in the Women's External Degree Program (WED). The women range in age from twenty to over sixty-five; the majority are married, employed full time, and have children under the age of eighteen; approximately 20 percent are single mothers. These women thus represent a population that is traditionally unable to consider a college degree; a distance-learning program is often their only option for higher education. The WED program, which is accredited by the North Central Association of Colleges and Schools, provides twenty-one baccalaureate degree programs, six associate degree programs, and four certificate programs.

One of these degree programs is in education. Students can select a major in early childhood, kindergarten-primary, elementary education, special education, and secondary education (English, mathematics, or social studies). The WED program will also help men and women who have already earned a baccalau-

Figure 8.2   Intersection of Distance Learning and Teacher Education

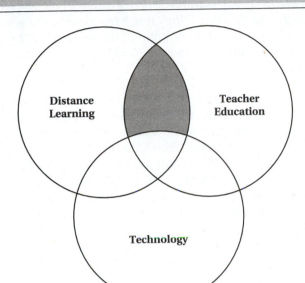

reate degree from an accredited institution seek teacher licensure. The only restriction to WED students seeking an education degree or licensure is that they must live within a 200-mile radius of the college to facilitate field experience, practica, and student teaching supervision by SMWC faculty.

The WED program consists of a series of five-month semesters. Each begins with an in-person appointment with instructors and WED advisers. Independent course work includes general studies courses, intensive subject matter preparation, and educational theory. While working on the courses during the twenty- to twenty-two-week semester, WED students communicate with their instructor by telephone, voicemail, e-mail and the postal service. As this book goes to press, no education courses are being delivered via technology.

The WED program is an excellent and enduring example that distance learning can work with teacher education. The WED students are successful in the achievement of their licensure and as teachers. The WED program heavily uses distance education, but also relies on periodic face-to-face contact with instructors and direct supervision of practica. As SMWC as a whole begins to use technology more frequently, the education program will evolve in that direction and provide WED students with a more integrated technology approach to their teacher education program.

Intersection of Technology and Distance Learning. Distance education, and on-line learning in particular, is not the strict domain of higher education and traditional teacher education programs. For-profit companies for a long time have offered training courses for corporate clients and learners with specialized needs (for example, Kaplan courses for the bar examination). Internet technologies have provided an explosion of business ventures that focus on distance education and learning opportunities (see Figure 8.3), and because of changing licensure requirements that may not specify degree or course requirements, teacher education is a viable market for these companies.

Figure 8.3 Intersection of Technology and Distance Learning

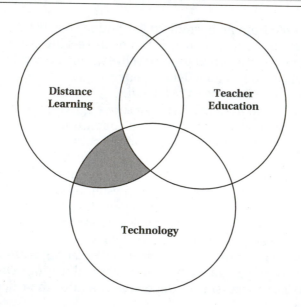

Although we will not debate whether an initial teacher preparation program should be offered solely over a distance, a number of programs are taking advantage of distance-learning technologies to reach new students. Examples of SCDEs that are involved in these activities are noted throughout the chapter. However, SCDEs are not the only ones that are considering using distance-learning technologies for the preparation of teachers. For-profit companies see a viable market in teacher preparation and professional development.

Sylvan Learning Systems is a familiar name to most educators. Its mission is to "be the world's leading provider of education services to families, schools, and industry" (Sylvan, 1998). Through one of its divisions, Canter, Sylvan provided degree and credit programs to thirty-five thousand teachers in 1998, all completed through distance learning. Another for-profit company with experience in the educational arena is Edison. Edison Schools Inc. is the nation's largest private manager of public schools. In order to ensure a steady supply of teachers for its schools, Edison announced in 2000 its plans to launch into teacher preparation (Walsh, 2000). Using existing connections with colleges and universities, company-owned campuses, and Internet courseware, the company already delivers professional development courses. This new venture will look to the possibility of offering both undergraduate and graduate degrees, with a guarantee of employment in Edison schools to students who meet certain graduation standards.

Finally, new companies are emerging that use distance technologies, in particular the Internet, to reach potential preservice and in-service teachers. One of them is Complete Teacher (**http://www.completeteacher.com**). Complete Teacher uses the Internet to reach students and provide them with an interface for enrolling in any of seven modules. The modules that are sent to the student are packaged in the form of computer-based training (CBT) and a handbook. Although Complete Teacher operates mostly in the realm of professional development at this time, it does promote its materials for preservice preparation.

The degree to which for-profit companies will ultimately affect SCDEs is still unknown and can stimulate lively discussion. It is unlikely that SCDEs nationwide will be eliminated due to this type of competition; however, it does demonstrate that teacher preparation is not the sole domain of the SCDE and that teacher preparation programs must consider what unique features these companies offer to in-service and preservice teachers. One of those key features might be the flexibility of distance-learning technologies.

Intersection of Technology and Distance Learning for Teacher Licensure. Teacher education encompasses many different types of programs. There are four-year and five-year undergraduate programs, five-year master's programs, and master's or licensure programs for students who have already earned an undergraduate degree. Although this last segment does not necessarily exist wholly outside teacher education, as Figure 8.1 would suggest, because the entire undergraduate requirements are not a factor, we are placing it outside the three-way intersection of technology, distance learning, and teacher education. We present two programs as examples of how distance learning and technology can be used to prepare students who already hold an undergraduate degree.

The Alliance for Catholic Education (ACE) at the University of Notre Dame in Indiana endeavors to develop a corps of highly motivated and committed young educators to meet the educational needs of underresourced Catholic school systems throughout the southern United States. ACE combines the efforts of the Institute for Educational Initiatives (IEI) at the University of Notre Dame, the National Catholic Education Association (NCEA), and the Departments of Education at the United States Catholic Conference (USCC) and the University of Portland. ACE recruits, educates, and places college graduates as K–12 teachers.

ACE targets graduates from a broad variety of undergraduate disciplines; these preservice teachers represent a diverse set of ethnic and cultural backgrounds. ACE participants include recent graduates from the University of Notre Dame and Saint Mary's College, as well as a number of other select colleges and universities. These graduates teach in approximately ninety parochial schools throughout the urban and rural southern United States.

ACE guides these teachers-in-training through a two-year immersion experience. The aim is to provide excellence in education and maximize opportunities for personal and professional growth for program participants. Students accepted into ACE and the master's in education program are provided with the opportunity for a high-quality master's degree experience, which builds on their solid undergraduate academic backgrounds in their disciplinary majors. The program leads to a master's in education, two years of experience as an instructor of record in a school system, and an initial teaching license.

The two-year program integrates graduate-level course work with an immersion experience in teaching. Over the first two summers after admission to the program, ACE teachers live and study together at the University of Notre Dame. At the end of the first summer, they travel to needy parochial schools in the South and Southeast to serve as full-time teachers during the regular school year. In addition to the support of mentor teachers in the parochial schools where they teach, all ACE teachers are brought together twice during the school year in a retreat setting to deepen and enhance their commitment to becoming professional educators. Upon completion of two years in the ACE program, participants have fulfilled the requirements for a master of education degree and have provided an urgently needed presence in the lives of our nation's neediest schoolchildren.

ACE has also initiated an effort to enhance and further integrate the role of technology in its year-round teacher training. In addition to their summer course work, ACE teachers installed in the various dioceses assume additional course work throughout the academic year via distributed learning. On-line courseware (WebCT), listservs, and e-mail are used as primary or supportive technologies. Two educational technology consultants provide support for faculty and explore avenues for integrating technology into the curriculum, including the intensive summer pedagogical experience.

Southeastern Louisiana University (SLU) has created a similar program as part of the State of Louisiana Alternative Post Baccalaureate Certification Program (information is available at **http://www.selu.edu/Academics/Education/distlearning.htm**). This program provides opportunities for individuals with non-education degrees to become certified teachers. The program strives to meet the needs of working adults who are currently teaching on nonstandard teaching certificates in secondary classrooms. To do so, the eighteen-hour sequence of professional education course work is offered via distance education. SLU uses web courseware and compressed video for distance-learning technologies. These courses allow preservice teachers to achieve professional course requirements for certification with limited class meetings on the SLU main campus.

A Vision of Distance Learning, Technology, and Teacher Education: The Three-Way Intersection

Given that there is not an example of a SCDE that extensively integrates distance technologies into the initial preparation of teachers, we paint a series of pictures of what a SCDE can do with distance-learning technologies to enhance the learning of its preservice teachers. These different strategies work to fulfill the three-way intersection shown in Figure 8.4.

Figure 8.4   Intersection of Distance Learning, Technology, and Teacher Education

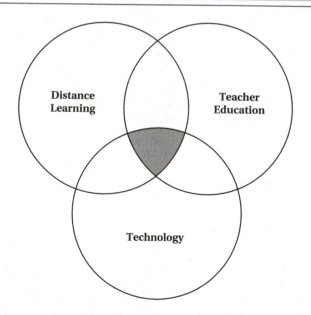

Distance Technologies to Reach Different Students. Much like the WED program at Saint Mary-of-the-Woods, distance education can be an effective tool to reach students who are not generally able to participate in higher education. Distance-learning technologies can extend the reach of the SCDE into new student territories. For example, in some parts of the country, rural areas have problems recruiting teachers for vacant positions. However, there may be an eligible pool of potential teachers in the community who are unable to drive the distance to a college but would like to be a teacher. Distance-learning technologies (e.g., computer-assisted instruction, web-based instruction, interactive television) can be used to deliver the courses and supervise fieldwork (e.g., web-based conferencing, interactive television).

There are obstacles to be overcome. The teacher education students who participate in such a distance-learning program must have access to the level of technology that will allow them to participate in computer-assisted instruction or web-based instruction. The school where teacher education students are placed for fieldwork must also have access to the same technologies and, ideally, to an interactive television setup that will allow for good field supervision. Computer technologies are becoming more prevalent in the schools and in the home. However, there remain pockets of the population who do not have these technologies at hand, and therefore the potential pool of teacher education students is reduced.

Distance Technologies to Reach into K–12 Schools. Faculty in academia can be somewhat self-centered, and when a proposal is given to reach into the K–12 school, it might be assumed that the goal would be to have the faculty deliver instruction to K–12 teachers and students in the field. Certainly this is a good practice and a practical application of distance-learning technologies, and it will be discussed later in this chapter in terms of professional development. However, distance technologies can put teacher education students into field experiences they might not otherwise be able to have.

For example, preservice teachers can use distance technologies to teach some specialty courses that are not available to a particular school. Consider this situation: a music student is expert in African drum music, students in a distant site have not been exposed to this type of music instruction, and no one in the school system has the necessary knowledge to deliver such a lesson. Through a variety of distance technologies, a preservice teacher could not only practice teaching with these technology tools, but also practice teaching her special interest area and provide a new experience for students in that school.

There are also other teaching opportunities that can be provided for teacher education students through distance-learning technologies. Local field placements may not provide preservice teachers with a diverse student body in terms of race, ethnicity, culture, educational background, and ability. Through distance-learning technologies, SCDEs can form partnerships with schools that will fill holes in the teaching experiences of preservice teachers and bring new experiences to schools that may not be located near a SCDE. Distance-learning technologies are available in most K–12 schools. Where they are not, a SCDE is likely to be able to find grant money for such an innovative program.

Teacher education students can also perform service-learning in the schools from a distance. Think of the number of essays that a high school English teacher might need to grade, or the volume of math homework problems a math teacher must review. With readily available technologies such as fax or e-mail attachments, teacher education students can work with in-service teachers to assist with the grading process. This is a learning process for the teacher education student and a definite service for the practicing teacher, and the K–12 students will enjoy the opportunity to receive feedback from college students.

Preservice teachers can also mentor distance K–12 students. Through e-mail, web conferencing, videoconferencing, and the telephone, teacher education students can tutor, counsel, and mentor students throughout the country. Finally, teacher education students can also work collaboratively with groups in the schools. For example, a teacher in the field may have her students in several small, cooperative learning groups. Each of these groups could be assigned to a preservice teacher who facilitates the group's work and learning process.

The options are limited only by the imagination. Many of these ideas can be performed face-to-face. However, the distance-learning technologies can bring teacher education students into different types of schools with a greater diversity of students than they might see if they are geographically limited.

Distance Technologies to Reach into SCDEs. SCDEs can add a different twist to the distance learning within teacher education. K–12 schools have a vast pool of resources that can be extremely beneficial to the development of teacher education students: the teachers. Think of when you might have seen a math teacher using manipulatives in new and clever ways. At that time, perhaps you thought to yourself, "Wow, this teacher could really teach our math education students quite a bit about teaching math." However, because this teacher lives eight hundred miles away, you knew there was no way to have her deliver a course at your university. Distance-learning technologies make this possible.

Using interactive television or web-based conferencing, the teacher in the field can become an adjunct instructor for the SCDE. Perhaps she is able to deliver a course three times a week during her planning period or immediately at the end of the school day, or she could be an occasional guest speaker. The SCDE is no longer limited to using teachers who are within easy driving distance of the university. With distance-learning technologies, the K–12 teachers who instruct in the SCDE could be located anywhere in the world.

Teachers are not the only ones in the K–12 school who can add information and content to SCDE courses. Superintendents, principals, counselors, and library media specialists all might be able to add to the dialogue and learning of teacher education students. Furthermore, the K–12 students themselves might be able to help the preservice teachers learn. Consider how powerful it would be to have several inner-city children describe the culture of their school to preservice teachers. Distance-learning technologies open a new realm of educational opportunities for preservice teacher development and learning.

We can reverse some of the ideas presented in the previous section. For example, a team of AP English students could assess the lesson plans created by a secondary language arts major. A group of kindergartners could provide feedback as to whether a series of activities is fun. Again, the options are endless.

Distance Technologies for K–12 Site Delivery of Teacher Education. A teacher education program that is delivered on site at the K–12 partner schools can provide students with important experiences and knowledge. Such a program can be an important laboratory experience that informs practice and helps preservice teachers determine their future direction. However, because a teacher education program involves more than just teacher education courses, it is difficult to keep students on-site (particularly a distant site) for long periods.

Not so surprising, distance-learning technologies provide another alternative. While on site in the K–12 school, a teacher education student can use distance technologies to take general education courses or other programmatic courses not offered on site. If a web-based educational development course is well designed and interactive, will it matter where the student takes the course? Perhaps it would be more relevant for the student to participate in that course from the school site where he can see child development in action. Therefore, while a preservice teacher is embedded in important field practica and courses taught by K–12 teachers in the schools, the student is also able to "attend" university-based courses. Distance technologies open new opportunities and solve many problems that may have faced SCDEs that are considering on-site delivery of teacher education.

PROFESSIONAL DEVELOPMENT, IN-SERVICE, AND DISTANCE EDUCATION

Up to this point, we have not spent much time discussing in-service training or professional development. SCDEs play an important role in the continued development of teaching professionals. In terms of distance education, whereas there are few distance education programs in traditional baccalaureate teacher preparation programs, there are numerous professional development opportunities available to in-service teachers through distance-learning technologies.

SCDEs use distance-learning technologies to offer master's degrees to practicing teachers. The list of graduate courses available at a distance is seemingly endless. Distance-learning technologies, and in particular Internet-based instruction, allow a teacher to take advantage of courses without the restriction of geography. Whereas fifteen years ago, a teacher would be able to choose from courses only at the most local SCDE, now a teacher can enroll at an accredited institution anywhere in the world.

SCDEs can also do more with distance-learning technologies and professional development. Teacher preparation programs are beginning to reach out to their graduates who are already teaching to provide support and advice to them during the critical early years of their teaching career (Basinger, 2000). Through these programs, SCDEs have advisers work with new teachers to provide advice and support and to assist with portfolio development. The current focus of these programs is the face-to-face contact between mentor teachers and the new teachers. Often the mentor teachers are released from their classrooms during this support period. Although this type of contact is important, it is also immensely labor intensive and expensive. There may be many new teachers who could benefit from contact and support from a mentor teacher that is conducted through distance-learning technologies. Furthermore, it could greatly enhance the role of the mentorship if the mentor teacher is in no way affiliated with the school system of the new teacher. A novice teacher may be more likely to disclose insecurities, fears, and problems if he understands that this information can in no way affect his future within that school system. The new teacher and the mentor can "meet" through e-mail, chat rooms, web conferencing, audioconferencing, or a host of other distance-learning technologies available in the schools.

In-service teachers can also seek professional development over a distance from a variety of sources outside the SCDE. Earlier in this chapter we discussed the for-profit training available for both preservice and in-service teachers. Companies like Sylvan, Edison, and Complete Teacher offer modules, courses, and even degrees to practicing teachers. There are also a number of not-for-profit organizations that seek to enhance the professional development of teachers and have found that distance-learning technologies are an effective vehicle.

The National Aeronautics and Space Administration provides numerous educational resources to K–12 teachers (**http://ebb2. gsfc.nasa.gov/edcats/2000/nep/programs/**). Some of these educational opportunities include distance-learning programs where teachers can challenge their own knowledge about math and science. Museums are partnering with on-line companies to offer on-line professional development experiences. For example, in 2000, the American Museum of Natural History partnered with Classroom Connect to offer on-line courses: "The Diversity of Fishes," "The Study of Spiders," and "Why Are There No More Woolly Mammoths?" (**http://cu.classroom. com/logon.asp**). The Global SchoolHouse (**http://www/ globalschoolhouse.org/**) has been an ever-present resource on the web for teachers. Through partnering with Lightspan.com, Global SchoolHouse provides a number of collaborative, on-line professional development modules. One advantage many of these organizations bring is that professional development experiences do not necessarily need to be within course work or be costly. There are numerous professional development tools and tutorials available on the Internet free of charge. Teachers who recognize they may need a tutorial to help them with a software package, for example, are likely to find numerous tutorials on the web for their use. Microsoft provides tutorials for all its software free of charge to teachers and students alike.

Ironically, distance-learning technologies themselves are assisting teachers to use technology. It has been shown that teachers learn how to use technology best by doing, not by merely watching (McKenzie, 1999). Distance-learning technologies bring a vast new pool of professional development and course work within easy reach of practicing teachers. However, in order to access those resources and new learning, the teachers must take advantage of the technology available to them. There are many stumbling blocks along the way, but teachers learn through their mistakes and in turn find the power of technology as a teaching and learning tool. For example, in 1996, I (Powers), decided that the students in my graduate course, "Accessing Information Through Technology," were not experiencing and understanding the full range of the Internet. Therefore, I began to offer the course over the web. In order to complete the course, students (the majority of whom are teachers) must successfully load the most current web browser, use e-mail, send attachments, participate in an electronic discussion group, participate in multiple chat sessions, lead a chat session, conduct web searches, and publish a web site. There are many other activities along the way to promote media literacy, but the use of those technologies is necessary to complete all other course tasks.

CONCLUSION

Distance-learning technologies provide SCDEs with the opportunity to reach preservice and in-service teachers in new and innovative ways. Programs and courses implemented at a distance for in-service teachers can provide a vision and direction for initial teacher preparation programs. Graduate courses offered at a distance can be used to inform practice and direct the efforts of undergraduate teacher preparation. Furthermore, distance-learning activities that are taking place in K–12 schools can provide additional guidance to SCDEs and a good reason to use distance-learning technology.

Distance-learning technologies also can enable SCDEs to meet several goals simultaneously:

- Reach new preservice and in-service teachers.
- Provide new teaching and learning opportunities for preservice and in-service teachers.
- Expand on the way the teacher education program is delivered in a cost-effective and time-effective manner.
- Demonstrate the use of technology for teaching and learning.
- "Force" preservice and in-service teachers to use technology to facilitate their teaching and learning.

An opinion piece in the *Chronicle of Higher Education* proposed that the process of learning about technology is Deweyian (Kuriloff, 2000). If experience is a foundation for education, then experience is necessary to be able to use technology effectively in education. This experience can come from a variety of sources; however, distance-learning technologies can readily supply that direct experience in the teacher education program.

■ REFERENCES ■

Basinger, J. (2000, May 5). Teacher education extends its reach. *Chronicle of Higher Education*, A18–19.

Business Wire. (1999, May 25). Online learning triumphs over the traditional classroom. *NewEdge*. Available at: http://www.newspage. com.

Kuriloff, P. (2000, April 28). Technology as a learning tool. *Chronicle of Higher Education*.

McKenzie, J. (1999). *How teachers learn technology best*. Bellingham, WA: FNO Press.

Moore, M., & Kearsley, G. (1996). *Distance education: A systems view*. Belmont, CA: Wadsworth.

Mory, E. H., Gambill, L. E., & Browning, J. B. (1998). Instruction on the web: The online student's perspective. In *Proceedings of the Ninth International Conference of Society for Information Technology and Teacher Education*, Washington, DC. (ERIC Document Reproduction Service. No. ED 421 090).

Olsen, F. (1996, August 6). "Virtual" institutions challenge accreditors to devise new ways of measuring quality. *Chronicle of Higher Education*. Available at: http://chronicle.com/free/v45/148/48a02901. htm.

Romiszowski, A. J. (1997). Web-based distance learning and teaching: Revolutionary invention or reaction to necessity? In B. H. Khan (Ed.), *Web-based instruction*. Englewood Cliffs, NJ: Educational Technology Publications.

Sylvan Learning Systems. (1998). *1998 Annual Report*. Available at: http://www.sylvan.net/annual_report.html.

Walsh, M. (2000, May 3). Edison to explore expansion into teacher preparation. *Chronicle of Higher Education*, 11.

9

Using Technology as a Catalyst for Change

The Final Report

In Chapter 1, we introduced you to eight higher education faculty and administrators who were charged with the responsibility for writing a brief report to the governor and commissioner of education regarding proposed legislation concerning the technology competence of beginning K–12 teachers, teachers already employed, and college faculty who prepare teachers. In subsequent chapters, we followed individual members of the group as they returned to their campuses and shared with others their impressions of the meeting with the governor and the commissioner of education. You will remember also that some of the eight, especially Bill and Lee, were quite annoyed by the meeting and the governor's request, while others were less hostile to proposed legislation.

Whatever individual feelings they may have had, they prepared a brief report for the governor and commissioner as requested. Following is their report.

Report of the Ad Hoc Committee on Technology and Teacher Education

Introduction

This report is our response to your October 17 request that teacher education institutions provide written advice regarding proposed legislation requiring technology competence of beginning K–12 teachers, teachers already employed in K–12 schools, and college faculty who prepare teachers for careers in K–12 schools. We want to express our gratitude for being invited to offer advice regarding the details of the legislation; we also wish to record our dismay about not being consulted prior to the decision to introduce such legislation. We think other approaches would have been better; the proposed legislation might have been unnecessary had we been consulted earlier.

We wish the governor, the commissioner of education, and members of the legislature to understand that we agree to the importance of technology in education today. Computers and other electronic tools are transforming every aspect of American society; it is surely true that technology will also change the way K–12 schools and teacher education institutions conduct their business. Our concerns are not with the goal but with the means for achieving technology use in schools and colleges.

We respect the state's right to establish new licensing requirements for K–12 teachers. However, it is nearly unprecedented for the state to withdraw licenses from teachers who already have them because they fail to meet requirements that were not in effect when they received their licenses. Existing teachers should be excused from the new requirement, but with many incentives to acquire technology competence. Furthermore, although the state certainly possesses accrediting authority over teacher education programs, we think it is a dangerous precedent for the state to attempt to influence the content of the teacher education curriculum and to decide who is and who is not qualified to prepare teachers. Having expressed our feelings about the overall effort, we now wish to offer specific ideas concerning the details of the proposed legislation.

Recommendations

1. We believe it will be a mistake to provide a single technology competence test for all teachers. Beyond command of basic computer processes, teachers need to be able to integrate technology effectively into the courses and grade levels that they teach. What is required of a high school chemistry teacher is very different from that required of a third-grade teacher. The tests should be variable according to grade level and subject matter concentration. The state should consult the teacher standards developed by the International Society for Technology Education.

2. The principal focus of the test should not be on a teacher's understanding of technology but on a teacher's capacity to use technology to enhance learning. Therefore, the fairest examination may be by performance, allowing teachers in their own classrooms, with the equipment available to them, to demonstrate how they use technology to support teaching and advance learning. The test could be performed live or be recorded by videotape for later review by examiners.

3. We also recommend that each test be divided into segments: for example, basic computer skills, using the Web. A teacher should be able to pass segments of the test without mastering all segments initially. Teachers should be allowed to re-take segments of the test as many times as necessary until they have achieved a passing score.

4. The goal of this legislation is to promote technology use in K–12 schools with the expectation that technology will encourage changes in the way schools conduct their work. If this is true, then the legislation should not be limited to classroom teachers; it should also include key administrators, counselors, and librarian/media specialists. Their roles are also affected by technology. Changes in schools require systemic efforts and cannot be accomplished by K–12 classroom teachers alone.

5. Regarding judgments about the technology requirements of college faculty, we believe it would be a mistake to include all faculty members who have prospective teachers in their classes. SCDEs encourage teachers to take courses outside of the SCDE. Although we agree that it would be desirable for all

college faculty to become confident in their use of technology, the short-term results of the legislation would lead to faculty denial of teacher education candidates to enroll in many of the courses in their subject majors because the faculty member does not employ technology. The rule concerning college faculty should apply only to faculty who teach courses that enroll 50 percent or more students preparing to teach.

6. It is also important to remember that college faculty have very diverse interests and abilities. The technologies employed by a physics professor, a business administration professor, and a music professor are very different. The law should expect that faculty demonstrate through their teaching the technology appropriate to their discipline, and nothing more.

7. Passage of the proposed legislation may have some unintended effects. For example, the legislation may require a reexamination of teacher education accreditation procedures. Currently, individual institutions are accredited on the basis of the programs they provide. Suppose an institution is no longer able to provide a course necessary for teacher licensure because it has no professor who meets the technology requirement. The SCDE might find the course in another institution and make it available as a distance-learning course. The proposed legislation may have the unintended effect of encouraging the sharing of students and courses among institutions, resulting in better programs and less cost, but only if accreditation procedures and rules allow it.

8. If the legislation is approved, there will be financial costs to SCDEs and K–12 schools, and the state must be ready to bear a substantial portion of these costs. For example, SCDEs are not typically the best-equipped units on a campus. Traditionally, other schools and colleges are given priority over SCDEs when it is time to purchase hardware and software. For SCDEs to model the use of technology, they will need a large infusion of funds to purchase equipment, build networks, and provide technical support. Second, there will be a great need for professional development in both K–12 schools and in SCDEs. It will be unfair to impose new requirements on K–12 teachers and college faculty and then deny them the resources required to meet the new requirements. And, third, about one-fourth of the teacher

education program occurs within K–12 schools where pre-service teachers observe classes and engage in student teaching. The state must provide a low-cost, high-bandwidth network that enables K–12 schools to work closely with the colleges that are preparing teachers. This may be one of the most beneficial ways to use technology for teacher education, but it will be used only if it is available and affordable.

These suggestions may make it possible for the proposed legislation to be acceptable to K–12 teachers and teacher educators. We are prepared to provide further elaboration, if invited to do so.

PROBLEMS OF CHANGE IN ■ ■ HIGHER EDUCATION ■ ■ ■

The scenario we have followed throughout this book is completely hypothetical, but it is by no means fanciful. A few states have passed such legislation, and there are governors and commissioners of education who would favor such legislation if they could successfully pass it through the legislature without causing a huge controversy. A substantial number of state and national officials believe that SCDEs are not doing a good job in preparing teachers to use technology, and they would like to change the situation to make it better if they knew how to do so. And therein lies the rub: How does one change a SCDE?

Producing change in any organization is difficult, and the process seems especially complex in colleges and universities, not only for people outside the system but for insiders as well. Colleges and universities seem best at preserving institutional traditions rather than changing them. The most radical-minded professor, willing to change every other institution in society, trembles at the thought of changing even the time when and place where he is accustomed to teaching his course.

SCDE Culture

Each SCDE has a culture that to a great extent is influenced by the institution of which it is a part. Institutional size is one factor. The culture of a four-member education department in a small liberal arts university will differ substantially from a one-hundred-member faculty of a school of education in a research university. Small SCDEs in liberal arts colleges differ among themselves, as will one school of education in a research university differ substantially from its peers in other research universities. Each has its own traditions, history, resources, and styles of leadership. Each has a culture that supports its work.

Shein (1992) defines culture as "a pattern of shared basic assumptions that the group learned as it solved its problems of external adaptation and internal integration, that has worked well enough to be considered valid and, therefore, to be taught to new members as the correct way to perceive, think, and feel in relation to these problems."

These "shared assumptions" include the language that is employed and judged appropriate by members of the culture. One way to gain a quick impression of a particular SCDE's culture is to observe how the members address one another. Do they use first names, or do they employ the term "doctor" or "professor" and use only last names when referring to one another? We have been in situations when the dean of the school was referred to by staff in the third person, for example, as "the dean" or as "Dean Smith," even when he was present! For example, the secretary might address Dean Smith directly by asking if "the dean is ready for his next appointment." How faculty and staff address one another and how students are addressed provide clues to the formality or informality of the culture.

The culture also provides rules for getting along in the SCDE, what will be rewarded, and what will be undervalued. Some SCDEs have adopted fairly strict rules for what can be included in promotion and tenure dossiers as evidence of solid performance. Even within a SCDE, some departments have adopted rules regarding the publications that count and those that have little merit. Thus, one department requires anyone considered for promotion to associate professor and tenure to have written a book; to be granted the title of full professor requires writing a second book. In another department, little value is placed on books; greater value is assigned to articles in refereed journals.

Some SCDEs favor service to the SCDE and to the college or university; others prefer service to K–12 schools, and still others give greater credit to service within national professional organizations. A few give credit for service to churches and charitable organizations within the community, whereas in other SCDEs, such service would be considered of no professional value.

In some SCDEs, teaching loads are relatively light—perhaps two courses or six credit hours each semester. Faculty members with external funds or a major research project may be excused from most or all instruction for a semester or more. In another SCDE, the teaching load may be relatively heavy: perhaps four courses or twelve credit hours each semester with no time allowed for research. In the first example, it is predictable that publishing research and obtaining grants have priority over teaching. In the latter example, lip-service may be given to the importance of research, but faculty are more likely to be consumers rather than producers of scholarship. In a research university, teaching graduate students and directing doctoral research typically carry much greater status than teaching undergraduates, a job often assigned to part-time faculty or graduate assistants.

SCDE faculty have their own notions of time and space. Work is done by semesters or quarters in some institutions. If a committee task cannot be easily completed within a semester or academic year, it will wait until the next academic year. No one is expected to do serious work for the institution between May and September. Faculty also have strongly held opinions about when is the best time to teach (say, Tuesdays and Thursdays at 11:15). They preserve time for personal study; a student who wishes to talk to a faculty member outside class often must make an appointment or catch the faculty member during scheduled office hours, which may be only two hours a week. Space is typically allocated according to seniority and rank, with the best offices going to those who have the highest status. Some classrooms or laboratories are preferred to others, and the people with the highest rank and seniority have first choice.

SCDEs have many rituals. Rituals and special dress accompany opening ceremonies, graduation exercises, and special assemblies such as those bestowing academic honors. There are rituals associated with recruiting faculty, reviewing faculty for promotion and tenure, and conducting examinations. The expression of these rituals varies from one SCDE to another, but the existence of rituals is held in common.

Governance practices are deeply rooted in each SCDE. Some decisions are reserved for administrators, others for faculty, and some are shared. Quarrels develop when the faculty believe the administration is encroaching on its territory. Determining the calendar, setting student admission and graduation requirements, and establishing the curriculum are typical faculty responsibilities, and administrators are wary about intruding into these domains.

The relationship between faculty and administrators is also ritualized. Unlike other sectors of society, promotion to higher levels of authority typically follows outstanding service at lower ranks. People become heads of marketing departments when they have shown success in sales or advertising. This is not generally the case in higher education. People do not become deans or department chairs by first being recognized as the best teachers or researchers, although they sometimes have that reputation. Becoming a dean or department chair is not accepted as recognition of outstanding faculty performance; rather, the candidate is judged to have some administrative skills and the desire to "bear the burden" of administration on behalf of his colleagues. The academic canon is that the best job is being a professor; deans and department chairs exist to serve the interests of the faculty. Leadership can be found within the faculty; the job of the dean or department chair is to discover the faculty's goals and mobilize efforts to accomplish them. Of course, there are many strong department chairs and deans who exert leadership despite the myths, but the wise ones are likely to pretend they are merely carrying out the will of the faculty. And when they retire from their administrative posts, they are expected to say that they are returning to their first love—teaching and research—regardless of the satisfaction and reward they may have gained from administration and however bored they are by teaching.

Perhaps the aspect of SCDE culture that contributes most to institutional inertia and the reluctance to change is the role performed by faculty. Faculty are employed as experts in special areas of knowledge. As holders of doctoral degrees and frequently authors of articles, monographs, and textbooks, they become the living authorities on whatever it is that they teach. For example, within a SCDE, there will be specialists on adolescent psychology, history of education, and elementary school science, among other fields. Each individual is likely to be very well educated; however, none will presume to tell others what they should teach in their fields of study. It all adds up to a kind of academic feudalism in which professors defend their territory and avoid encroaching on the academic turf of colleagues. Even the dean or department chair is unlikely to advise a faculty member on what and how they should teach. Note how different this is from K–12 schools in which teachers are treated as more interchangeable, and supervisors and principals are expected to oversee instruction.

This attitude of respect and deference to a faculty member continues throughout the faculty member's career, regardless of how out-of-date, stupid, vain, and arrogant he may appear to his students and colleagues. A faculty member with tenure can be replaced only if he commits a crime or breaks some university rule. Being judged a poor teacher is not grounds for dismissal.

Paradigm Shifts in SCDE Culture

SCDE culture is slow to change, but events can occur that produce change. Technology can be the stimulus to provoke radical change.

In recent years, it has become popular to write about paradigms and paradigm shifts. A *paradigm* is a set of rules and regulations that does two things: (1) establishes or defines boundaries and (2) informs people how to behave within the boundaries to be successful. The aspects of higher education culture we have described are major elements of the current SCDE paradigm. A *paradigm shift* takes place when the rules change and new regulations, procedures, and expectations follow. The result would be a new SCDE culture.

To understand why technology would contribute to a paradigm shift, we will look at some of the topics we have already described: time, space, academic titles, publications, and the relationship between students and faculty. How does a professor's concept of time change when instruction can be provided in an asynchronous mode and delivered anytime, anyplace? What happens to the importance of office space when a professor can teach from her office, her home, or a hotel room anywhere in the world? Of what value are titles when everyone in a chat room is recognized on a first-name basis, when it is difficult to distinguish the students from the faculty, and when value is placed on the merit of the idea rather than on the academic credentials of the source? What happens when professors publish electronically rather than in traditional journals? What value will be placed on such publications? What happens to the faculty role when the course is published electronically and made available to students throughout the world? Who owns the course: the professor or the institution that pays his salary? And what of students? Will they continue to be patient to enroll in semester-length courses on campus, when they have access to the best scholars in the field and can study the course at a pace appropriate to their lives and level of energy?

It is too soon to predict the ways that SCDEs will change as a result of technology, but they will change or be left behind. Nor is it surprising that there is tremendous resistance to technology among many SCDE faculty. We would be surprised if there were *not* resistance. Those who have enjoyed and profited from the existing higher education system must resist these changes; it is in their short-term interest to do so.

Throughout this book, we have provided examples of SCDE faculty and administrators who have embraced technology and are using it to reshape their instruction and even their institutions, but these are the pioneers. Behind them are many faculty who fear the effects of technology on their professional lives. Some judge technology to be a conspiracy by business to take over education; others judge technology to be a threat to academic jobs (if not their own jobs, then surely those of others); still others are threatened by the public exposure of their lack of technology competence; a few undoubtedly believe it to be an ineffective substitute to traditional instruction, while others claim it will add to their work load while making education impersonal. These are not hysterical responses. Any one and all of these fears could be realized if technology were not used properly.

SEVEN LESSONS FROM RESEARCH ON CHANGE

During the past four decades, there has been substantial research on school change and why school reforms often fail and only rarely succeed. Much less research has been done on the topic of change in higher education. Perhaps some of the research findings on change in K–12 schools will provide insights regarding change in SCDEs.

Michael Fullan, dean of the Faculty of Education at the University of Toronto, and Matthew B. Miles, senior research associate with the Center for Policy Research, are two of the most respected scholars on this topic. In 1992, they published an article, "Getting Reform Right: What Works and What Doesn't," in which they offered seven propositions for success. Presumably those who wish for SCDEs to change the ways they prepare teachers, using technology, will be more successful if they adhere to these research findings.

Lesson 1: Change Is Learning— Loaded with Uncertainty

The introduction of technology into a SCDE creates anxiety and uncertainty. To expect everyone immediately to change practices that have been successful in the past is unrealistic. The Apple Classrooms of Tomorrow (ACOT) studies of technology assimilation in K–12 schools found that it required at least two years before teachers began to feel comfortable and relatively proficient with computers. We should expect no less time from SCDE faculty. Indeed, some researchers have found that the absence of anxiety or difficulty in adopting a reform is probably evidence that nothing is happening.

Lesson 2: Change Is a Journey, Not a Blueprint

Certainly it is important to have a technology plan in hand when implementing technology, but no plan can account for all of the situations that will arise. The key terms are patience and flexibility. In this book we offer suggestions for processes that may be used, and we have provided many examples of exemplary practices. But there are no certain blueprints for adopting technology successfully. The situations vary enormously among SCDEs and within a SCDE over time.

Lesson 3: Problems Are Our Friends

Despite everyone's best intentions, problems will arise naturally from the demands of the change process itself, the people involved, and the culture of the institution. Problems should be treated as friends, because it is only through solving complex problems that institutional change can occur. Imagine that a few faculty are resisting the use of technology in their courses. One response is to ignore them, thereby avoiding the problem; another response is to be critical of them for their resistance. A better response is to understand why they resist as they do and attempt to overcome the obstacle they present.

Lesson 4: Change Is Resource Hungry

It may be that someday technology will result in cost savings for SCDE, but this will not occur in the beginning. A SCDE can expect to invest not only in hardware and software but also in technical support and professional development. There are ways to avoid wasting money (for example, not giving a new computer to a faculty member who has shown no evidence that he intends to use it), but the cost of change is always substantial and technology makes it more so. It is not likely that the SCDE will see much savings in personnel or supplies in the beginning. What is more likely is that the SCDE will begin to offer services and act more efficiently than it was able to do without the technology.

Lesson 5: Change Requires the Power to Manage It

Change does not manage itself. There must be someone or, even better, a group who monitors the implementation, keeps everyone informed, identifies problems, and tries to solve them. Research has shown that the leadership process works best when there is a responsible group that bears overall responsibility. In higher education, the group is likely to consist of faculty, staff, students, and administrators. One person may be charged with handling day-to-day routine matters, but policy issues and big questions need to be brought before a group charged with responsibility for the implementation of technology within the SCDE.

Lesson 6: Change Is Systemic

SCDEs have many opportunities to obtain funds for special projects that relate to technology. The usual way of responding is to allow those involved in the project to do whatever they like for the tenure of the project. When project funds expire, the system returns to its prior-to-project status. Projects often have no more lasting effect on an institution than does a blow by a fist into a piece of foam rubber. It is not that project funds should be rejected, but they must be employed to sustain the systemic initiative. Systemic reform means also that technology should be employed to change all aspects of the SCDE—from classroom instruction, through communication to faculty, staff, students, and alumni, to students obtaining grants and loans and graduates jobs. Every aspect of the SCDE should seek to use technology to modernize its practices.

Lesson 7: All Large-Scale Change Is Implemented Locally.

This is the lesson the governor and commissioner of education in the scenario need to understand. Change cannot be accomplished from afar. It can be done successfully only by the people who must live with the results. Only they know the local circumstances in sufficient detail to know how best to proceed in their situation.

■ ■ ■ CEO FORUM REVISITED ■ ■ ■

In Chapter 2 we introduced the CEO Forum STaR Chart for implementation of technology. The chart used eight different categories for SCDEs to use in measuring their progress toward achieving "Target Tech": Campus Leadership, Campus

Infrastructure, SCDE Leadership, SCDE Infrastructure, SCDE Curriculum, Faculty Competence and Use, Student Competence and Use, and Alumni Connections. The STaR Chart provides useful benchmarks for determining a SCDE's status and where progress is needed, but the chart is not very helpful in deciding how to introduce and employ technology successfully.

The seven lessons from research also serve as powerful reminders of how one should approach the prospect of introducing change into a system. What is needed now are some specific steps that SCDEs can take that will move them forward on the CEO Forum STaR Chart, while recognizing the lessons learned from research on system change.

NINE STEPS FOR SUCCESSFUL TECHNOLOGY IMPLEMENTATION

Following are nine steps we believe to be important for the successful implementation of technology within SCDEs. We believe these steps are relevant to SCDEs that wish to introduce change, even if they have no interest in technology. However, we believe that information technology is a powerful force in society today and will have an even greater influence in the future. Thus, we cannot imagine a SCDE planning its future without considering the role technology will play.

It is the future that we are considering in this section. From our own experience, we have found that people vary in their conceptions of the future. Some see it as largely a continuation of the present, just more of it. Some people adopt a fatalistic view: The future takes care of itself, and there is little we can do about it. Still others (and we are members of this group) think the future does not exist; it must be created. And although there are important constraints, people can create the future they want.

Step 1: Develop a Vision Statement

It may be useful to distinguish between predictions and vision. Predictions are based on trends. Weathermen are in the business of predicting the weather based on certain indicators such as air pressure and wind direction. Their ability to predict weather is very good so long as the future is a short one—a few hours or a day. They are unable to predict weather months or years into the future.

A vision is a statement about a desirable future. Our vision of good weather is at least as good as that of a weatherman, even if we are not capable of predicting the weather. SCDEs may or may not be good at predicting the future of teacher education, but they can all create visions of a desirable future for SCDEs and work hard to make their visions come true.

For reasons of institutional culture, it is difficult for an entire SCDE to develop a vision of its future. While professors have visions about their careers and departments may reach informal consensus about where they hope to go, it is hard to produce a shared vision for a large school or college of education.

One approach that has proved helpful is to ask faculty and administrators—and possibly staff and students also—to complete a survey concerning their beliefs about the future—both their predictions and their vision. Administering the survey during a faculty retreat can stimulate small group discussion, which can lead to reports from small groups and ultimately group consensus.

Figure 9.1 is not a complete survey instrument but is illustrative of what could be done.

Step 2: Prepare a Mission Statement

Vision statements tell others of the kind of world we want to build. Mission statements tell others the business we are in.

Superficially, it would appear that all SCDEs are in the same business: teacher education. But that is only partially true. In some cases, the main purpose of the college or university is to provide a sound liberal arts education for undergraduates; the job of the SCDE is to provide whatever courses or experiences are necessary for an interested fraction of the undergraduates to obtain teaching jobs, if they want them. In other higher education institutions, especially large research universities, the mission is primarily to teach graduate students and conduct research. Most of the instruction of preservice teachers is done by

Figure 9.1 Statements About the Future of Teacher Education

Predictions		Following are some statements about the future of teacher education. In the left-hand columns, you are asked to agree or disagree as to whether you think the statements are accurate predictions of what teacher education will be. In the right-hand columns, indicate whether the statements would fit your vision of ideal teacher education programs in the future.	Visions	
Agree	Disagree		Favor	Oppose
		1. Because of the cost of providing high-quality teacher education, the number of colleges and universities offering teacher education has declined to less than one-third the number in 2000.		
		2. Teacher education has become a competency-based profession. It is no longer necessary for a student to graduate from an accredited teacher education program in order to obtain a teacher's license. All that is necessary is to be a college graduate, pass written and performance teacher examinations mandated by each state, and perform three years of supervised apprenticeship in order to obtain a teacher's license.		
		3. The average entry age of beginning teachers is 25, and one-third of all new teachers have completed most, if not all, of their course work through distance learning and have never enrolled in a course offered on a campus.		
		4. Professional development schools, popular in the 1990s, have given way to virtual professional development schools; these involve close collaboration between the SCDE and K–12 schools electronically.		

Figure 9.1 *(cont.)*

Agree	Disagree		Favor	Oppose
		5. Some SCDEs offer year-round teacher education programs. Students are admitted in cohort groups, with a new group beginning each month. Faculty take their vacations when it is most convenient to them, rather than according to a rigid academic calendar. Many remain in touch with their students electronically even when they are not present on campus.		
		6. As computers have become increasingly more powerful and less expensive, they have also become ubiquitous. Every teacher education student owns at least one computer; faculty typically have two or three—at least one at the office, one at the home office, and a portable computer when traveling.		
		7. New teachers who are able to direct computer activities in schools are paid an average of 20 percent more than teachers who lack computer competencies.		
		8. Some SCDEs have established professional development programs to aid teachers in teaching more effectively with computers. This has become the most profitable part of the teacher education program.		

part-time teachers from local schools and by full-time graduate students who pay for their graduate studies through providing undergraduate instruction.

In order for a SCDE to create a vision and develop a realistic plan for achieving that vision, it must have a clear-headed understanding of its mission. If we limited our gaze to traditional missions of SCDEs and how these missions relate to technology, we might conclude that some institutions should have faculty conducting research and development relating to the use of technology for instruction and should be preparing the next generation of teacher education faculty who are competent in the use of technology. In other SCDEs, where the teaching load is too heavy to allow for much R&D and there are no graduate students, the faculty may be focused on their responsibility to ensure computer competence for their students by either providing it themselves or seeking outside resources that will offer what their students need.

These descriptions fit what one might expect SCDEs to do with technology within their traditional missions. However, technology allows SCDEs to undertake new activities that could move them in unpredictable directions and lead to new missions. For example, the web allows individuals and organizations to wield influence worldwide with relatively little investment. It has allowed a few colleges and universities that are not known as research universities to launch electronic professional journals. Technology can make a SCDE a world source of information about a particular educational topic, for example, student safety and discipline. The interest of K–12 schools in technology opens up new professional service opportunities for SCDEs: on-line courses, technology self-assessment instruments, and chat lines are only three examples. In these and other ways, SCDEs may choose to take advantage of technology to accept new and additional missions.

Step 3: Provide Leadership for Technology

The CEO Forum STaR Chart refers to both campus and SCDE leadership because both are important. The president, chancellor, or provost can establish technology as a campus priority and make resources available to assist school deans as they help implement campus priorities.

For example, in 1997, Brian P. Copenhaver, provost of the College of Letters and Sciences at UCLA, decided that every undergraduate student should have his or her own web page and every undergraduate course should have its own web site. The goal was to "personalize the University, to make students comfortable in a complex institution." Today, as soon as students have applied and been accepted for admission as undergraduates, they are assigned a password and can begin to build their own web pages. In the past, students had to depend on such print sources as course catalogues and schedules of classes. Now students have access to this and other information electronically. They can see when classes will be taught, check admission requirements (if any) for each class, and register for their classes electronically. Students regularly receive e-mail messages and notices from the university about upcoming events.

Copenhaver also insisted that all undergraduate courses have their own web sites. Professors may or may not develop their course sites; if they are uninterested or unwilling to do so, web site development is handled by staff. The result is that each student can look at class topics and examine reading and other assignments before registering for a course.

It is not necessary in situations of this kind that a provost insist that the SCDE adopt the same practice, although there is likely to be some pressure to do so. What is important is that at UCLA, for example, the direction has been established, students and faculty expectations are affected, and resources are available if the SCDE elects to participate.

Nevertheless, whatever help and support are provided by campus leadership, there is no substitute for the leadership that can and should be provided by the SCDE dean or department chair. While it is often the case that one or more individual faculty members may be more respected than the dean and have shown leadership skill, it is the dean or department chair where authority is vested. Unless he or she exercises leadership or delegates some portion of authority to another who will provide it, it is likely that little will happen.

The dean's job is not an easy one; attempting to change the culture, shift the paradigm, or introduce reform only makes it more difficult. In some institutions, leadership in a SCDE is short term and is passed around among members of the senior faculty. In such cases, SCDE administration is often judged to be a chore that should be shared rather than left to a single person to perform over many years. In these situations, the dean or department chair is very likely to see the job as one of maintenance rather than promoting change. By the time they have learned the job, their tenure—often only three years—expires.

A SCDE dean or department chair has many constituencies. She first of all is positioned between the campus administration who appointed her and the faculty who believe she represents them to the administration. The dean must be attentive to the concerns of students, interests that are generally different from those of the faculty and may run counter to the faculty's interests. SCDE staff are another constituency; they cannot be ignored because they usually run the SCDE on a daily basis, regardless of what the faculty may believe. Alumni, school teachers and administrators, state department of education officials, and deans of other colleges within the university have interests that they will bring to a dean's attention. Just attending to day-to-day business can be a full-time job.

Yet many SCDE deans or department chairs accept their appointments because they want to make a difference. They have ideas about how SCDEs can improve and have an even greater impact on the profession. Such leaders would soon be bored if maintaining existing customs and practices was all the job entailed. They want the challenge of attempting to leave the SCDE better than they inherited it, better at serving students, a better place for faculty and staff to work, a place better positioned to compete in the future.

It is precisely for this reason that some deans use technology as the focus of their reform agenda. One does not have to be a genius to recognize the role technology plays in American society and how technology is helping to transform every aspect of how we live and work. A dean need only to point to technology efforts underway in K–12 schools to make it clear that SCDEs have no choice in the matter. SCDEs will either change to reflect the influence of technology or be left behind. Even when a dean has another agenda important to her, such as promoting diversity or abandoning a subject-driven curriculum and replacing it with a case-based curriculum, technology can serve as the catalyst and the rationale for the other changes. For example, with regard to the theme of diversity, the dean or department chair can argue that the SCDE needs to attract more minority students into teacher education and it needs to provide those preparing to teach with experience in schools serving students with diverse backgrounds and needs. Technology may be the principal way to meet this objective.

There is no formula for becoming a successful SCDE dean or department chair. Successful ones have come in all shapes, sizes, ages, genders, and background experiences. The way in which leadership is provided will depend heavily on the personality of the leader and the nature of the SCDE. And what works in a major eastern city may not work at all in a small midwestern town. However, there are some general propositions that will likely fit most circumstances. Here are a few of the "rules" that other deans have followed to help them to make a difference:

1. Identify two or three issues or topics, and make those the priorities of your tenure. These need not be new topics, but if they have been advanced in the past, you need to give them new interpretation and new energy. If the priorities change every year or so, faculty lose track of what is truly important, and thus nothing is especially important. Let us assume that the integration of technology across all aspects of the SCDE is the top priority. The dean or department chair must give focus to the topic, explain it, and link it to other SCDE activities. He or she has the job of articulating and justifying the priorities.

2. Be persistent—even stubborn. There will be many opportunities to become discouraged and abandon the reform. Leaders must be single-minded and above discouragement, regardless of how they may feel at times. The idea will be attacked by some members of the faculty, including those counted as friends. The leader must not take personal offense by these attacks and indeed should expect them.

3. Recruit faculty who understand technology and will become allies. Among the most important decisions that deans and department chairs make is the recruitment, retention, and promotion of faculty. Without maintaining vigilance about who is being hired, it is possible that they will add faculty who will sabotage the agenda rather than advance it.

4. Create incentives to influence the way faculty and staff use their energies. Providing travel funds to attend technology conferences or to visit other SCDEs doing a good job with technology is but one incentive available to the dean. Providing summer grants to redesign courses so as to employ technology and funding professional development are other ways.

5. Raise funds to pay for technology and the accompanying support. This often requires personal attention by the dean; it may also include funding faculty to write grant proposals to support their work.

6. Be the principal cheerleader for faculty and staff who are providing technology leadership in the unit. Celebrations, public notices, and other devices help bring attention to those who are pioneers in the integration of technology. While being a cheerleader for success, it is also necessary for the dean or department chair to encourage risk taking. Some of the efforts will fail. The dean needs to provide the kind of encouragement that makes a failure accepted as part of the process of change.

Certainly leadership can be shared, and no dean or department chair can go far without the support of faculty and staff. Moreover, the faculty and staff must buy into the reform and provide leadership at various levels within the unit. All of this is true, but nothing is likely to happen if the dean or department chair fails to throw his or her authority behind the effort to integrate technology into the school.

Step 4: Prepare a Technology Plan

One of the dean's or department chair's tasks is to oversee technology planning. It is not necessary, and perhaps it is even undesirable, for the dean and his staff to prepare the plan. The plan ought to be developed by a broad constituency representing faculty, staff, and students. However, it is the dean's job to establish some criteria that the plan must address, set a time line for its completion, appoint a committee, and arrange for an appropriate review by faculty and staff.

Our opinion is that a technology plan is very important to the success of an effort to integrate technology within a SCDE. However, the plan should be fluid, capable of revision as conditions change within the school and as new technology becomes available. A plan provides a general blueprint for what the SCDE wants to accomplish with technology, but it should not become a straitjacket. The plan should be reviewed annually. The planning process is nearly as important as the plan itself. Engaging in planning allows the faculty, staff, and students to have a voice in how technology and which technology will be used in the SCDE.

Technology plans have sometimes been limited to setting forth a schedule for the purchase, allocation, and amortization of equipment and have been written mainly by those responsible for providing maintenance and support of technology in the SCDE. We do not discount the importance of including ideas about equipment purchase, allocation, and amortization in the plan, but these may be the least important segments. A good technology plan is an educational plan. It states the vision and mission of the SCDE and indicates how the vision will be accomplished through technology. Therefore, the plan should indicate how the curriculum will be affected, how faculty will gain needed competencies, and what requirements are expected of students. By means of such a plan, the SCDE is able to confront a number of issues facing the school while deciding on the role of technology.

There are many ways such plans can be developed. The checklist below may prove useful as a SCDE moves forward in the development of its plan.

TECHNOLOGY PLANNING CHECKLIST

A. Organizing for Planning

1. ☐ Choose a planning committee.
   - ☐ Include faculty, staff, and students.
   - ☐ Include skeptics.

2. ☐ Choose a chairperson.
   - ☐ Choose one who is widely respected in SCDE.
   - ☐ Choose someone friendly to technology but not a "techie."
   - ☐ Provide time and resources.

3. ☐ Prepare a committee charge.
   - ☐ Refer to the SCDE mission.
   - ☐ Offer an example of a vision statement.
   - ☐ Suggest the report scope and sample goals and objectives.

4. ☐ Establish a time line.
   - ☐ Set benchmarks for work, the preliminary report, and the final report.

5. ☐ Communicate the existence and mission of the committee.

☐ Make certain that all SCDE personnel know of the committee's existence and importance.
☐ Provide interim reports of the committee's work; give it high visibility.

B. Creating a Vision

1. ☐ Create an environment for visioning.

☐ The committee should encourage creativity and imagination.
☐ Do not seek early closure.

2. ☐ Undertake activities designed to stimulate vision.

☐ Employ consultants.
☐ Visit other SCDEs.
☐ Send committee members to conferences.
☐ Conduct brainstorming sessions.

3. ☐ Develop a vision for the use of technology in teacher education.

☐ Make certain the focus is on the preparation of teachers.
☐ Prepare scenarios of the future.

4. ☐ Communicate the vision to others.

☐ Hold a public hearing in which the committee shares its vision of the future with others in SCDE.

C. Conducting an External Scan

1. ☐ What are the forces that support the vision?

☐ Look at social and educational trends outside of the college or university.
☐ Look at trends within the college or university but outside of SCDE.
☐ What kinds of technology are likely to be available to education soon?
☐ What positions toward technology have professional associations adopted?
☐ What types of technology are private and government foundations supporting?

2. ☐ What are the obstacles blocking achievement of the vision?

- ☐ How are K–12 schools using technology?
- ☐ What negative factors exist outside the college or university?
- ☐ What negative factors exist within the institution but outside the SCDE?
- ☐ Will the technology needed be affordable?

D. Conducting an Internal Scan

1. ☐ Determine what should be assessed.

- ☐ What type and amount of technology are currently available?
- ☐ What are the attitudes of students, staff, and faculty toward technology?
- ☐ What exemplary practices currently exist within the SCDE?
- ☐ What level of technology integration exists currently?

2. ☐ Develop assessment instruments.

- ☐ Develop one or more survey instruments.
- ☐ Devise an observation instrument.
- ☐ Develop an interview process.

3. ☐ Develop an assessment method and process.

- ☐ Who will conduct the assessment?
- ☐ Who will be the subjects?
- ☐ How long will it take?

4. ☐ Gather and analyze data.

- ☐ Use technology to measure results to the degree possible.

5. ☐ Communicate and publicize the results.

- ☐ Do not be judgmental; simply report the data.

E. Setting Goals and Objectives

1. ☐ Develop a concise statement of learning philosophy.

- ☐ Link the statement to mission and vision.
- ☐ State what you believe about learning.

2. ☐ State educational goals as they relate to technology.

☐ Refer to existing SCDE and campus documents.
☐ Link the goals to vision and philosophy.
☐ Make it clear that technology goals are instrumental to educational goals.
☐ Provide goals that relate to faculty, staff, and students.

3. ☐ Establish priorities among goals.

☐ Determine the priority in which goals must be accomplished (e.g., first, second).
☐ Identify goals that can be accomplished quickly and others that can be pursued over time.
☐ Structure the goals according to function (e.g., professional development, curriculum).

4. ☐ Develop specific objectives for each goal.

☐ State objectives in terms of specific tasks.
☐ Link objectives closely to goals.

5. ☐ Publicize goals and objectives.

☐ Provide faculty and staff with the opportunity to react to goals and objectives.

F. Creating a Plan

1. ☐ Identify human resources.

☐ Determine who will be affected by the plan.
☐ Determine who will manage activities and be accountable for the achievement of goals and objectives.
☐ Develop faculty, staff, and student competencies; use ISTE standards as a guide.
☐ Describe a training program for faculty and staff.

2. ☐ Develop a time line.

☐ Decide who will do each task by a designated time.

3. ☐ Identify funding sources.

☐ Identify both internal and external funds.

4. ☐ Develop a budget.

☐ Note budget requirements for hardware, software, training, and technical support.

5. ☐ Develop a clear planning guide.

☐ Summarize all of the goals, objectives, and tasks in a published document.

6. ☐ Develop an evaluation plan.

☐ Indicate how the plan will be assessed and revised as needed.

7. ☐ Publicize the plan.

☐ Provide copies of the plan to all SCDE faculty and staff and other members of the college or university community.

G. Implementing the Plan

1. ☐ Get final approval of the plan.

☐ Get endorsement from SCDE faculty and administration; build support with the campus administration.

2. ☐ Secure the funding sources for budget.

☐ Gain sign-off on all budget items.

3. ☐ Purchase the equipment and software.

☐ Develop bid or quote specifications.

4. ☐ Follow the time line.

☐ Make sure the time line is followed and that responsibility for each goal, objective, or task has been accepted.

5. ☐ Focus on professional development.

☐ Put the program into operation.

6. ☐ Publicize the implementation.

☐ Arrange for press releases.
☐ Hold open houses.

H. Evaluating and Revising Goals, Objectives, and Plans

1. ☐ Determine the appropriate evaluation focus.

☐ Identify all of the tasks that should be evaluated.
☐ Measure results of professional development.
☐ Measure satisfaction with technology support.
☐ Measure the level of technology integration.

	☐ Measure attitude and behavioral change on the part of faculty and staff.
	☐ Measure student satisfaction and achievement.
2. ☐ Determine appropriate evaluation methods.	☐ Use attitudinal surveys.
	☐ Use performance measures.
	☐ Conduct observations.
3. ☐ Develop evaluation instruments and gather data.	☐ Pilot-test the instruments.
	☐ Revise instruments based on pilot tests.
4. ☐ Analyze data and prepare reports.	☐ Summarize data for both internal and external use.
	☐ Determine the factors that led to successful and unsuccessful results.
5. ☐ Decide how the plan should be revised.	☐ Modify processes and procedures that are not working.
6. ☐ Provide recognition of those who are performing well.	☐ Prepare press releases.
	☐ Hold recognition events.
7. ☐ Publish a status report.	☐ Make the report available to SCDE staff and faculty and others outside of the SCDE.

Source: This checklist was prompted by a similar worksheet created by B. J. Eib, Tom Bauer, and Lee Wiggam for use in K–12 schools.

Step 5: Create an Adequate Infrastructure

It is difficult to advise SCDEs what should be done with infrastructure in a field that changes so rapidly. The simplest rule is to build what you need to do your work that provides the greatest flexibility and opportunity to grow, at the least possible cost. This is a sound rule, but the broad guidelines are practically useless in helping to make immediate decisions.

For example, until recently, it was necessary to provide expensive cabling throughout the building in order to provide modern communications to desktops and classrooms. In the future, wireless capacity may be sufficient that one can avoid cabling. Until recently, voice, data, and video were provided separately and maintained by different vendors. Current trends are to integrate these functions and negotiate services with single vendors.

Increased use of simulations and virtual experiences require specialized equipment and more powerful servers than SCDEs usually employ. If SCDEs begin to employ simulations, they will need equipment that is currently unnecessary for their work. As each state builds **fiber backbones** and connects K–12 schools to each other and to higher education institutions, the opportunity to build closer links with schools, including conducting **virtual early experiences** in K–12 classrooms, will become available. Such opportunities will be exploited only if the SCDE has appropriate equipment and the will to modify instruction so as to take advantage of it.

Currently the purchase and licensing of software is an important item in a SCDE budget. In the future, the principal source of software for colleges and universities may be **application service providers** (ASPs). ASPs will function like a utility, and SCDEs will pay for software as they use it. The result may be greater opportunity to employ the most recent software as well as software intended for limited use.

Computers continue to shrink in size and price and grow in power. Today, few, if any, SCDEs require that preservice teacher education students own laptop and desktop computers as a condition of admission to the teacher education program. It is likely, however, that in the near future, all teacher education candidates will own a computer. No longer will SCDEs be required to provide ubiquitous access to computers; access to networks will become more important.

These are but a few of the factors that make clear rules regarding infrastructure difficult to develop. SCDEs need to employ individuals whose skill and responsibility is to keep the dean or department chair informed of the opportunities that technology provides, to appoint a technology advisory committee that can provide guidance for selection among the opportunities, and to set aside funds in the budget to keep the SCDE abreast of rapid changes in the technology industry as these changes affect teacher education.

Step 6: Revise the Teacher Education Curriculum

Whether the technology integrated into a SCDE has a major or minor impact will depend principally on how it is incorporated into the curriculum. Frequently technology is added without any consideration of the curriculum or patterns of instruction. Other SCDEs have used the occasion to invest in technology to reconsider how instruction is provided students; the technology serves as a catalyst for instructional reform. Clearly we favor the latter approach.

Technology is neutral; it can be used to support the status quo or to stimulate change. Modern information technology contains the power and capacity to perform tasks that are not easily done if one is limited to printed texts and face-to-face instruction. Few SCDEs are yet employing the full power of the technology they have purchased.

Throughout this book, we have provided examples of faculty who have restructured their courses to employ technology. They have restructured their courses to make them project based, requiring students to work on authentic tasks; they have used distance-learning technology to enable teachers-in-training to experience greater diversity among K–12 classrooms; they have used web sites and on-line instruction to encourage collaborative learning; and they have caused their students to develop electronic portfolios in order to save and to present their work to others. These are but a few of the ways that some SCDE faculty are transforming the ways they teach because of the opportunities technology affords them. We both predict and envision that during the next decade, we will see many more such changes that will eventually lead to a complete transformation of the teacher education curriculum.

Step 7: Provide for Professional Development

In earlier chapters, we have set out examples of SCDEs that are providing professional development experiences for their faculties and staffs. In the past, SCDEs had little need to offer professional development for their own employees, especially the faculty. Whatever faculty training was required was so individualized that each faculty member was expected to provide his or her own experiences. The institution contributed by making sabbatical leaves available in order that a faculty member could have the time to obtain such training.

The introduction of technology has changed the picture significantly. Many of the technology competencies the faculty need are generic and generalizable and can be provided to groups. The institution suffers when faculty are not competent in the use of technology; thus, the SCDE has an interest in promoting and supporting technology competence. And, finally, technology needs change rapidly. Being adequately prepared five years ago is not sufficient to help a professor and the SCDE stay on the cutting edge.

SCDEs have invested in various kinds of professional development. Providing funds for faculty to work on revising courses during the summer months, sending faculty to conferences and to visit other institutions, providing group classes through a full-time professional staff, and providing mentors to faculty by assigning skilled students to work with faculty are four of the most common forms of professional development. Surely there are other approaches in use that can be equally effective.

What is most important is that the SCDE attend to the issue of professional development and set aside funds in the budget to pay for it. An investment in the best, most up-to-date equipment available will be wasted unless the faculty and staff have the knowledge and skills to use it well.

Step 8: Secure Funds for Technology

The cost of becoming a technology-competent SCDE is not trivial, but the long-term cost of not doing so is even greater. Some portion of the funds necessary to support technology must be found within the operating budget. Some SCDEs have found that at least 10 percent of the budget is now used to purchase equipment and software, provide maintenance, and offer technical support. These costs do not include money for professional development. Depending on the funding principles employed by a college or university, a SCDE may expect to obtain some special, as well as ongoing, funds from the campus.

Technology and education are currently a high priority among federal and state governments and some private foundations. In fiscal year 1999, the U.S. Congress appropriated $75 million to help SCDEs become proficient in technology. Many of the corporations producing hardware and software have been willing to provide grants of equipment, software, and sometimes cash to assist both K–12 schools and teacher training institutions. And a few private foundations have been willing to invest in model programs, especially in cases where technology was used as a catalyst for teacher education reform generally. Funding priorities of government, corporations, and private foundations change frequently; thus, there is no assurance that proposals that were fundable in 2000 will remain hot topics. What is important is that SCDEs be aware that some of the costs of technology can be borne by external funds.

Step 9: Measure and Report the Impact of Technology on the SCDE

Higher education institutions, and SCDEs in particular, are not customarily held strictly accountable for their actions. Student enrollments may be affected if it is widely recognized that an institution is improving, declining, or retaining its current quality. SCDEs are generally accountable to state and national accrediting bodies, but accreditation visits happen infrequently and a SCDE can usually prepare well in advance to satisfy the accreditation standards. The vast amount of money that has been invested in technology, however, is leading to requests for information about how SCDEs are spending their money on technology and what they are getting in return. We expect this trend to continue. The example that follows is a report prepared by the College of Education of the University of Florida in summer 2000.

UNIVERSITY OF FLORIDA COLLEGE OF EDUCATION INFORMATION TECHNOLOGY INITIATIVE

The University of Florida College of Education began a multi-level technology initiative during 1999–2000 that included renovation of laboratory and classroom facilities, upgrades of all faculty and departmental computers, and a training program for college faculty.

In summer 2000 the College of Education reported on the progress it had made in using technology during the 1999–2000 academic year (University of Florida, 2000). The report not only records what was accomplished in the past but provides a baseline for what can be expected. Advances in technology continue as a college priority.

The College of Education employs approximately one hundred faculty, forty staff, and over one hundred graduate assistants. The information technology staff has one system programmer, two senior computer support specialists who are assisted by staff, and student assistants. The college's computer platform includes services for administrative and academic support, services and network for academic support, and in-house services, including web servers, **DHCP,** a mail server, **QuickTime server,** Macintosh- and Windows-based stand-alone PCs, Macintosh- and Windows-based laptop computers, and wireless networking.

Technology for Labs and Classroom

A large-scale upgrade of technology hardware and software in the Educational Technology Lab was one of the first steps in the college technology initiative. Among the initial upgrades were the technology training classroom, with hardware and software upgrades as well as installation of video and audio editing tools and digital image processing. A Collaborative Teaching Lab was created using **White Board,** Internet, and **Internet2** technology, providing access to real-time shared teaching opportunities with the University of Virginia and the University of South Florida. Additional technology upgrades for the media and science labs were completed.

In collaboration with the university's Office of Instructional Resources (OIR), all College of Education classrooms have been equipped with ethernet access, have new screens installed to accommodate multimedia presentations, and have been evaluated for lighting and sound quality. Five large classrooms have been equipped for multimedia presentations. Wireless Internet ports have been installed throughout the complex in anticipation of multiaccessibility in classrooms and labs.

Computer Upgrades for Faculty and Staff

During the 1999–2000 academic year, departments and the college shared the cost of a comprehensive program to upgrade all faculty and departmental office computers to the level of Macintosh G3 or equivalent. These upgrades paved the way for compatibility with OS 9 and OS 10 operating systems. Departmental conference rooms were provided with Internet access, and the college conference room was equipped for multimedia presentations.

Faculty Training Program

With the assistance of OIR and the Center for Instructional Technology and Training, the college initiated a technology training program for the faculty. This program began with a survey of faculty needs related to technology training and open forums for discussing course sequencing and formats for training. Faculty members were provided with a schedule of courses developed for and delivered in the Educational Technology Lab, as well as schedules for other campus-based courses. Also available to faculty were opportunities for working with consultants and developing independent training projects. Faculty electing to complete sixteen hours of training to strengthen their technology skills were issued laptop computers for instruction and research purposes.

During the first six months of 2000, 75 percent of the college faculty participated in the program, with 63 percent completing at least sixteen hours. In all, sixty-five faculty enrolled in over nine hundred hours of training during this period; fifty-four of them received laptop computers.

Classes developed specifically for the College of Education included design introduction, hands-on design, web standards, a two-part PowerPoint course, Netscape composer, web graphics, and a three-part WebCT course. Other classes were available on Excel, Access, MS Word, Forms, QSR Nud*ist 4, and Photoshop. Consultation and interest groups focused on WebCT, Photoshop, Eudora, and PowerPoint. Special independent projects included work with Claris Home Page, Adobe Page Mill, Final Cut Pro, iMovie, QuickTime Pro, Media Cleaner Pro, Adobe Photoshop, Adobe Premier, Dreamweaver, Fireworks, Inspiration, videoconferencing, and collaborative education systems.

Faculty completed evaluations of individual courses as well as final evaluations of the training experience. Course evaluations were used to modify subsequent training sections and to guide further course development. Final evaluations were reviewed to inform technology training goals for the subsequent year. Follow-up evaluations were planned for six months after training.

An overview of faculty self-reports indicated that approximately half of the participants enrolled in classes only, one-third chose a combination of classes and consultation, and the remainder chose to work independently or with a consultant only. Reported applications to course work included development of the following:

Web pages
WebCT for courses
Databases
Training CDs
Videos
PowerPoint presentations
Cyberspace group supervision and a course supporting student and instructor collaboration across four university campuses.
Enhanced on-line resources, including accessing Internet resources in the classroom and building web links into syllabi

Faculty also reported greater mastery over technology, including the following:

More confidence and more positive attitudes toward technology
Greater knowledge, skills, and language related to technology
Increased interest in and planning related to technology
Improved presentation skills
Greater professional satisfaction exhibiting work through web sites
More effective collaboration among faculty
Enhanced skills for grant writing and management
Strengthened organizational skills

Faculty reported that the laptops were beneficial as an incentive or catalyst for training, as a means of allowing more time for research, and as an aide in maintaining communication with colleagues.

Development of Cooperative Programs

During 1999–2000, the College of Education joined the Partnership in Global Learning (PGL), a cooperative venture including the University of Florida Center for Latin American Studies, OIR, the Lucent Foundation, Bell Labs, the Instituto Tecnológico de Estudios Superiores de Monterrey (Mexico), Pontificia Universidade Catolica do Rio de Janeiro (Brazil), Fundacâo Getulio Vargas (Brazil), and the Universidade Estadual de Campinas (Brazil). PGL is an international initiative designed to produce technologically enhanced and distributed learning on a global scale, working collaboratively to design and deliver state-of-the-art curricula in science and business fields in web-based formats.

In addition, the college is participating in the Opportunity Alliance Program with partner schools Raines and Ribault High Schools (Jacksonville) and Miami Senior High. Goals include shared technology training and development of training links among the partners.

■■ CONCLUSION ■ ■■

I (Howard) have framed a quotation of the English philosopher John Stuart Mill and have it standing on my desk in my home study. Whenever I go to my desk, this quotation faces me:

> History shows that great economic forces flow like a tide over communities only half conscious of that which is befalling them. Wise statesmen foresee what time is thus bringing, and try to shape institutions and mold men's thoughts and purposes in accordance with the change that is silently coming on. The unwise are those who bring nothing constructive to the process, and who greatly imperil the future of mankind by leaving great questions to be fought out between ignorant change on one hand, and ignorant opposition to change on the other.

Those words, written approximately 150 years ago, are equally relevant today. Modern technology is transforming every aspect of how we live and relate to others. It will also change the way we educate our children and prepare our educators. These changes will occur; there is no way we can build walls or fences to insulate education from the impact of technology.

The issue is what kind of changes technology will promote and whether education will be better or worse because of the power of technology. The answer to these questions is unknown, but they are in our power to shape. It is foolish for SCDEs to resist technology or attempt to ignore it. They might as well pretend that ocean tides do not exist. The technology exists to transform the way we educate our students. As professionals, we must decide how these technologies will be employed.

Paraphrasing John Stuart Mill, will SCDEs prove to be "wise statesmen or unwise statesmen"? Will they provide leadership or allow the struggle to be settled by "ignorant change" on the one hand and "ignorant opposition to change on the other"?

We have written this book to alert SCDEs to the opportunities that technology provides and to offer examples of faculty and administrators in a wide variety of institutions who are responding to the challenges posed by technology. We trust that this book contributes to the conversation on reasoned change through technology.

REFERENCES

University of Florida, College of Education. (2000). *College of Education information technology initiative*. Unpublished manuscript.

Fullan, M. G., & Miles, M. B. (1992, June). Getting reform right: What works and what doesn't. *Phi Delta Kappa*, 745–752.

Shein, E. H. (1992). *Organizational culture and leadership* (2nd ed.). San Francisco: Jossey-Bass.

Glossary

Abilene An advanced backbone network that supports the development and deployment of the new applications being developed within the Internet2 community. Abilene connects regional network aggregation points, called gigaPoPs, to support the work of **Internet2** universities as they develop advanced Internet applications. Abilene complements other high-performance research networks. *See also* Internet2.

Adaptive equipment *See* assistive technology device.

Alternative keyboards Specially designed keyboards that individuals with disabilities may use in place of standard keyboards to access computers; they provide flexibility in size, layout, and complexity.

Application software Software that is typically loaded onto a computer to perform a particular task, such as word processing e-mail, data processing, etc.

Application source provider (ASP) A new category of information technology (IT) outsourcing. ASPs deliver the same benefits of a complete IT infrastructure management, with a range of applications from Windows office productivity applications to financial and other functional applications. An ASP can connect multiple sites across remote geographies to a comprehensive, high-performance computing and application capability via the Internet or a private network.

Assistive listening devices Assistive devices that individuals with hearing impairments use in small or large group settings.

Assistive technology Devices or services that restore, maintain, or replace lost bodily functions through the use of technology.

Assistive technology device Any item, piece of equipment, or product system, whether acquired commercially off the shelf, modified, or customized, that is used to maintain, increase, or improve the functional capabilities of a person with a disability.

Assistive technology service Any service that directly assists a person with a disability in the selection, acquisition, or use of an assistive technology device.

Assistive technology specialist Specially trained professional who assesses assistive technology, selects devices, and provides training and assistive technology services.

Asynchronous Two-way communication that occurs with a time delay, allowing participants to respond at their own convenience (e.g., e-mail).

Asynchronous communication tools Communication in which interaction between instructor and student does not take place simultaneously using electronic tools (e.g., e-mail, discussion boards).

ATM (Asynchronous Transfer Mode) An information transfer mode of sending data in irregular time intervals that grew out of a need for international standards. ATM allows for the simultaneous transmission of data, voice, and video.

Attention deficit/hyperactivity disorder (ADHD) Diagnostic category of the American Psychiatric Association for a condition in which a child exhibits developmentally inappropriate inattention, hyperactivity, or impulsivity.

Augmentative and alternative communication Communication techniques and devices to assist individuals who are unable to meet their communication needs through speech; includes sign language, symbol systems, communication boards, and synthetic speech devices.

Authoring tools Software tools used in authoring—the process of creating hypermedia applications and computer-assisted instruction. Examples are digital imaging software, authoring programs (web editors, Hyperstudio, etc.), and animation software.

Backbone Network Service (vBNS) A nationwide network that supports high-performance, high-bandwidth applications. (**http://www.vbns.net/**)

Blackboard's CourseInfo A software course management system with course management tools that enable instructors to provide students with course materials, discussion boards, virtual chat, on-line assessments, and a dedicated academic resource center on the web. (**http://www.blackboard.com**)

Boolean web searches An Internet search refined by using logical operators, sometimes called Boolean operators. Boolean operators (the words OR, AND, and NOT) are used to combine search concepts in a more precise way than is possible with keyword searching.

Braille embosser Device that prints raised Braille dots on special paper.

Braille translation Conversion of print text files to Braille and vice versa.

Braillewriter Typewriter-like device with six-key chordic keyboard used to emboss Braille on special paper.

Constructivist An educator who follows a constructivist teaching philosophy, founded on the premise that we construct our own understanding of the world we live in by reflecting on our experiences. Learning therefore is the process of adjusting our mental models to accommodate new experiences.

Course accounts Computer files and folders set up on a local server, accessed through a password system, that provide a place for students and faculty to place and receive documents and carry on electronic class discussions.

Decision support systems A system that provides the tools and capabilities to process and present data in a way that assists decision making.

DHCP Dynamic Host Configuration Protocol—a system by which Internet protocol (IP) addresses and other low-level network configuration information can be dynamically assigned each time the system loads.

Didactic instruction Instruction in which the teacher seeks to inform the learner directly of the information the learner is expected to retain; often associated with lectures and guided discussion. It is the opposite of discovery or inquiry learning.

Digital video Video that is saved in digital formats (1's and 0's) instead of traditional analog and is compressed.

Discover:Switch Adapted switch that provides on-screen keyboard and mouse functions to enable a user to operate software programs by scanning characters on the screen, manufactured by Don Johnston, Inc.

Discrete speech recognition program A software program that allows user to enter commands and text to a computer by speaking instead of typing; in contrast to continuous speech recognition programs, it requires the user to speak individual words one at a time with a brief pause between each word.

Distance education Typically refers to distributed learning resources in academic settings. Can be used synonymously with *distance learning. See* distance learning.

Distance learning A system and a process that connects learners with distributed learning resources. Although it takes a wide variety of forms, all distance learning has the following characteristics: (1) separation of place and/or time between instructor and learner, among learners, and/or between learners and learning resources, and (2) interaction between the learner and the instructor, among learners, and/or between learners and learning resources conducted through one or more media. Use of electronic media is not necessarily required.

Distance-learning technologies Technologies used to deliver and enhance distance learning, such as video, electronic discussion boards, and web courseware.

DVD players Digital versatile disk—a high-density mass storage medium similar to CD-ROM, but capable of storing much larger amounts of information due to improvements in recording density and use of multiple layers per side. A DVD player is able to play DVDs.

Electronic discussion groups A group organized around a particular topic or subject of interest that shares information with each other and engages in conversations using electronic communication.

Electronic grade book A grade book that is kept on the computer and adds such functionality as e-mail reports, electronic seating charts with student pictures, customized attendance and behavior codes, interface with administrative grading functions, multiple automatic grading scales, and generation of student reports.

Electronic keyboard Resembles a small, lightweight laptop without a display but with a small screen that displays several lines of text; the machines can save approximately sixty-four pages of plain, unformatted text that can later be downloaded onto any other computer.

Emotional or behavioral disorder Chronic condition characterized by behavioral or emotional responses that differ from age, cultural, or ethnic norms to such a degree that educational performance is adversely affected.

Environmental control Ability to control one's physical environment; refers to such capabilities as opening and closing doors, turning on and off appliances, using the telephone, and regulating temperature controls, lights, and sound.

Ethernet The most widely used local area network technology. Uses coaxial cable or twisted pair and transmits up to 10 megabytes per second.

Fiber backbone A network made of bundles of glass threads that transmit data with light waves.

File transfer A method of serving and obtaining files over the Internet; can be as simple as sending an e-mail attachment or downloading a file from a server.

Filter A program through which data are passed and only data that match the specifications are allowed to pass through the filter.

Functional skills Skills that are immediately useful to a student, frequently required in school and nonschool environments, and enable a student to participate in less restrictive environments; examples are dressing, eating, riding a bus, making a purchase, and recognizing sight words.

Graphic slides Computer-generated presentation slides that use images; examples are digital photos and clip art.

Head-controlled mouse A computer mouse that is controlled by head movements.

Headpointer Rod with a rubber tip attached to a band worn around the top of the head; used by individuals who lack functional movement of arms and hands to access a keyboard or perform other manipulation tasks by moving the head and neck.

High-end data video projector Video projectors that will project not only high-end computer displays, but also high-definition TV and a variety of video formats.

HTML HyperText Markup Language—the programming language used to create web pages. HyperText is a document marked up (programmed) to allow a user to select words or pictures within the document, click on them, and connect to further information.

Hyperstack An information presentation that contains multiple forms of media such as video, text, graphics, and audio; the user can link from one page or element of content in a nonlinear fashion. Hyperstack is used mostly in conjunction with authoring programs such as HyperCard™, or HyperStudio™.

Inclusive education Special education service delivery model in which students with disabilities remain in their neighborhood schools with their age-appropriate peers in general education classrooms; special education services are provided in the general education setting.

Interactive Video Network A network dedicated to delivering two-way video and two-way audio.

Internet2 A testing ground network for universities to develop advanced Internet technologies. Uses the Abilene network backbone. *See also* Abilene.

International Society for Technology in Education (ISTE) International Society for Technology in Education—a nonprofit professional organization with a worldwide membership of leaders and potential leaders in educational technology. Dedicated to promoting appropriate uses of information technology to support and improve learning, teaching, and administration in K–12 education and teacher education. (**http://www.iste.org**)

Intranet A private network using standard Internet protocols but with limited or no connectivity to the public Internet.

Learning disability Disorder in one or more of the basic psychological processes involved in understanding or in using language, spoken or written, that may manifest itself in an imperfect ability to listen, think, speak, read, write, spell, or do mathematical calculations.

Low vision Visual impairment severe enough to warrant special educational services; a child with low vision is able to learn through the visual channel and generally learns to read print; may require use of large print or magnification.

Low-tech assistive devices Inexpensive, simple-to-make, easy-to-obtain, nonelectronic assistive devices, such as headpointers, reachers, mouthsticks, and modified eating utensils.

Media literacy The ability to access, analyze, evaluate, and produce communication in a variety of forms.

Mental retardation Substantial limitations in functioning; characterized by significantly subaverage intellectual functioning, existing concurrently with related limitations in two or more adaptive skill areas, and manifest before age eighteen.

Multimedia computer A computer configured with the necessary hardware to be able to use multimedia software that combines text, sound, video, and animation.

On-screen keyboard Keyboard that appears on a computer monitor; the user clicks a mouse to select keys or uses a switch to scan keys.

Orthotic device Device that assists or augments a body function, such as a brace or crutch.

Paraeducator Trained classroom aide who assists the teacher with instruction or other classroom duties; often works with students with disabilities under the direction of a special education teacher.

Partial participation Teaching approach that encourages students with severe disabilities to participate as fully as possible in activities and tasks, even though they may not be able to perform all of the steps independently.

Pirating The unauthorized copying of software.

Portal A web site or service that provides many resources and services, including e-mail, discussion forums, search engines, and specialized databases.

Programmed Learning A learning process characterized by controlled conditions. Information may be presented in small, controlled steps in order to manage human behavior and learning. Characterized by positive reinforcement.

Prosthetic device Device used to replace a missing or impaired body part or function, such as an artificial limb.

Pull-out program Special education service delivery model in which students with disabilities are removed from the general education classroom to receive special education and related services in another setting, such as a self-contained special education classroom or a resource room.

QuickTime Server A web server that offers streaming video and audio. *See* Streaming video and audio.

Related services Developmental, corrective, or other supportive services required for a student with disabilities to benefit from special education.

Residential facilities Facilities where individuals with disabilities may live, for example, institutions, group homes, foster homes, and apartments.

Resource room Classroom in which students with disabilities spend part of the school day and receive individualized special education services provided by a special education teacher.

Self-contained special education classroom Separate classroom for students with disabilities taught by a special education teacher; may be housed in regular schools or in separate facilities.

Slate and stylus Metal slate placed over thick Braille paper and pointed stylus that persons with visual impairments use to punch Braille dots on paper.

Special school Day school organized within a school system for students with disabilities.

Streaming video and audio A technique for delivering video and audio such that it is a continuous, steady flow of data. With streaming, the user can begin viewing a file before it is fully downloaded.

Switch control Method of controlling a computer or other electronic device by activating a switch, such as a pneumatic, button, air cushion, or tread switch.

Synchronous A type of two-way communication that occurs with virtually no time delay, allowing participants to respond in real time. Also, a system in which regularly occurring events in timed intervals are kept in step using some form of electronic clocking mechanism. *See also* Asynchronous.

System architecture The framework that describes how system components (e.g., servers, desktop machines, nodes) interact and work together to achieve total system goals.

T-1 line A leased circuit, usually provided by a telecommunications company, that provides fast data transmission rates of up to 1.5 megabytes per second.

Technical infrastructure The equipment that makes up the local or wide area network (e.g., the routers, servers, cabling, hubs, switches) and is necessary for basic operation.

Technology rich An environment that is using technology to enhance teaching, learning, and assessment. Does not necessarily imply a school filled with many computers.

Touchscreen Clear, flat panel placed over a computer monitor that allows users to make selections by gently touching; alternative to typing on a standard keyboard.

TouchWindow A touch screen designed specifically for young children and individuals with disabilities that can be used on the monitor or placed flat and used as a switch. Manufactured by EdMark.

TransPac Provides high-performance Internet service connecting the Asia Pacific Advanced Network to global networks for the purpose of international collaborations in research and education.

Two-way interactive video and two-way audio Two sites interact with audio and video as if they were co-located.

UNIX A popular multiuser operating system. The name is a play on an even older system, MULTICS.

User interfaces A set of commands or menus through which a user communicates with a computer program. Determines how easy the program is to use.

Videoconferencing Conducting a conference between two or more sites using the computer to transmit video and audio data. The data are carried over the network.

Virtual Items with no direct corresponding physical equivalent—for example:

Virtual early experiences "Visits" by teacher education students to field sites using distance-learning technologies.

Virtual libraries An on-line database that is organized similarly to a conventional library but uses web links and web resources.

Virtual reality applications The software that creates artificial environments and provides input to users on at least three of the five senses to make users feel as though they are really in the environment.

Visualization technologies Graphics software technology that allows for large-scale, three-dimensional modeling.

Visualizer A software tool that allows for three-dimensional rendering, modeling, and animation.

Web-based training (WBT) A form of computer-based training in which the training material resides on web pages. Typical media elements used are text and graphics. Sometimes referred to as *on-line courses* and *web-based instruction.*

WebCT On-line course management software that provides instructors with tools to create a course web site that includes discussion forums, assessment, and other related course documents. (**http://www.webct.com**)

WhiteBoard An area on a display screen where multiple users can write and draw. Used frequently in on-line conferencing.

WinMini Small, alternative keyboard with sensitive membrane keys for people who have limited range of motion in their hands, manufactured by Tash, Inc.

Wireless communication A communication network that uses high-frequency radio waves rather than wires to communicate between nodes.

Word prediction software Software program that speeds up typing by allowing the user to select words from a menu of choices instead of typing letter by letter; word choices change as the user types more letters.

Resources

WEB SITES

ABLEDATA   (http://www.abledata.com)

A searchable database of more than 25,000 assistive technology products.

Assistive Technology On-Line   (http://www.asel.udel.edu/at-online/assistive.html)

An on-line database on assistive technology organized by the Applied Science and Engineering Laboratories at the University of Delaware.

CATALISE—Consortium for the Application of Technology and Learning in Schools of Education   (http://www.catalise.org/index.html)

A developing resource for technology in teacher education that also posts reports and webcasts of related events, such as the NCATE 2000 Technology Expectations.

CEO Forum on Education and Technology   (http://www.ceoforum.org/)

The home of the CEO Forum STaR Chart. Documents produced by the organization are available on-line here, as well as the interactive assessment tool for SCDEs.

Closing the Gap Resource Directory   (http://www.closingthegap.com/rd)

An annual directory of more than 2,000 computer-related products for children and adults with special needs.

Distance Education Resources for Faculty and Developers
(http://cuda.teleeducation.nb.ca/distanceed/)

A highly useful site for faculty members who are considering the development of on-line distance education. There are links to tutorials, tips, on-line discussions, instructional design basics, course delivery information, and other materials. This is a very rich, robust resource.

Faculty Trends, Templates   (http://www.utexas.edu/cc/cit/
facweb/templ.html)

Templates for on-line syllabi and vitas that are especially helpful for faculty who are getting started with integrating technology.

International Society for Technology in Education
(http://www.iste.org)

On-line copies of NETS for Teacher and Students is available through this site, under the heading of "Standards Project."

MERLOT—Multimedia Education Resource for Learning
and Online Teaching.   (http://www.merlot.org)

A rich resource for teacher education faculty who wish to integrate technology using on-line resources. Composed of peer-reviewed, on-line teaching resources, this site can be used to find a large variety of teaching ideas, resources, and instructional tips related to web sites posted by other educators.

Microsoft Education Web Site   (http://microsoft.com/education/)

An educational web site with marvelous resources available. Through the link to Instructional Resources, for example, you can access tutorials for key Microsoft software (designed from a teacher's point of view). There are also lesson plan ideas on how to integrate technology in the classroom.

Milken Exchange on Education Technology
(http://www.mff.org/publications/publications.taf)

The Milken Family Foundation has been a leader in the discussion of using technology in the classroom to enhance teaching and learning. The web link presented here provides access to a number of valuable documents published by the foundation, for example:

Technology in American Schools: Seven Dimensions for Gauging Progress

Will New Teachers Be Prepared to Teach in a Digital Age? A National Survey on Information Technology in Teacher Education (co-authored with the International Society for Technology in Education)

Transforming Learning Through Technology

A Continuum for Professional Development: Gauging Professional Competency for Technology-Supported Learning

National Center to Improve Practice in Special Education Through Technology, Media, and Materials (http://www.edc.org/FSC/NCIP)

Information about the effective use of technology for students with disabilities.

Trace Research and Development Center   (http://trace.wisc.edu)

A research, development, and resource center on disability access and universal design at the University of Wisconsin-Madison.

Webquest   (http://edweb.sdsu.edu/webquest/webquest.html)

The official webquest web site, although webquests are now found all over the Internet. This site provides background information and excellent examples of webquests.

BOOKS

Ackermann, E., & Hartman, K. (2000). *Searching and researching on the Internet and the World Wide Web.* Wilsonville, OR: Franklin, Beedle & Associates.

This book can be useful as a textbook for classes that will use the Internet as a research and reference tool. It is also very useful for faculty members who may need more confidence on personally conducting effective, efficient web searches, and how to guide students to find information effectively on the Internet. The book comes with a student data disk that contains summary web pages for each chapter with exercises, terms, and summaries. This disk can be an effective tool for demonstrating the multiple uses of technology.

American Association of Colleges for Teacher Education. (2000). *Log on or lose out: Technology in 21st century teacher education.* **Washington, D.C.: Author.**

Consists of papers prepared for a conference, "The Future of Schools, Colleges, and Departments of Education in the Age of Technology." More than fifty participants contributed their ideas. The book also contains recommendations for action that grew from the conference discussions.

Bailey, G. D., & Bailey, G. L. (1994). *101 activities for creating effective technology staff development programs.* **New York: Scholastic.**

Sets out exercises that provide a light-hearted but informative look at how to understand the changing role of technology.

Bloom, J. W., & Walz, G. R. (Eds.). (2000). *Cybercounseling and cyberlearning: Strategies and resources for the millennium.* **Alexandria, VA: American Counseling Association and CAPS.**

Consists of twenty-seven chapters that examine technology and its implications for counselors and counselor education. Special attention is given to issues associated with cybercounseling.

Bozeman, W. C. (1999). *Educational technology: Best practices from America's schools* **(2nd ed.). Larchmont, NY: Eye on Education.**

Contains a valuable section that profiles K–12 schools that are using technology in innovative, exciting ways. These profiles can provide teacher educators with rich examples to use in the classroom.

Dede, C. (Ed.). (1998). *Learning with technology: 1998 ASCD yearbook.* **Alexandria, VA: Association for Supervision and Curriculum Development.**

Describes schools that are using technology successfully today and predicts how technology will be used even better in the future.

Fisher, C., Dwyer, D. C., & Yocam, K. (Eds.). (1996). *Education and technology: Reflections on computing in classrooms.* **San Francisco: Jossey-Bass.**

Much of what we know today about the use of computer technologies in the classroom is based on research that emerged from the Apple Classrooms of Tomorrow (ACOT) project. This book was written in recognition of the tenth anniversary of the project and provides reflections and research of those involved with the use of technology in the classroom. This book contains good foundational information about educational computing

George Lucas Foundation. (1997). *Learn and live.* **San Rafael, CA: Author.**

Provides rich, detailed examples of classrooms where technology is being used to enhance teaching, learning, assessment, and the whole educational environment, plus contact information about how to learn more. Comes with a video.

Grabe, M., & Grabe, C. (2001). *Integrating technology for meaningful learning* **(3rd ed.). Boston: Houghton Mifflin.**

Puts together neatly in one package a number of elements useful to teacher educators. Technology standards for K–12 teachers and students are covered, as well as examples from classrooms. This can be a useful textbook for a stand-alone technology class or used on a continuous basis in an integrated technology approach. The book provides teacher education students with topics, valuable definitions, and technology tips.

International Society for Technology in Education. (2000). *National Educational Technology Standards for Students: Connecting Curriculum and Technology.* **Eugene, OR: Author.**

A rich resource that describes not only the student technology standards but also curriculum integration plans for different grade levels and subject areas. The curriculum integration plans are further tied to content standards. This book is a wonderful resource for teacher education students who could build on the ideas presented. ISTE's web site (**http://www/iste.org**) looks at student technology standards.

Johnson, D. L., Maddux, C. D., & Liu, L. (Eds.). (1997). *Using technology in the classroom.* **New York: Haworth Press.**

Looks at technology in K–12 classrooms and is particularly useful to readers who are unfamiliar with the ways technology is currently used in schools.

Jonassen, D. H. (Ed.). (1996). *Handbook of research for educational communications and technology.* **New York: Simon & Schuster.**

Consists of forty-two research summaries of topics that relate to educational communications and technology, including one on distance education. The handbook is useful for those who wish to learn more about the research relating to technology and instruction.

Kearsley, G. (2000). *Online education: Learning and teaching in cyberspace.* **Belmont, CA: Wadsworth.**

An excellent primer for teacher educators who have little or no familiarity with the background, definitions, and reasons for teaching on-line. In a straightforward manner, the book describes on-line education, defines terms, and provides numerous examples from all levels of education, including K–12. Other resources may give more specifics for creating learning environments, but this one provides information and resources to get started on creating on-line education.

Kerr, S. H. (Ed.). (1996). *Technology and the future of schooling: Ninety-fifth yearbook of the National Society for the Study of Education.* **Chicago: National Society for the Study of Education.**

Each year, NSSE publishes two-volume yearbooks that deal with important issues. This one offers thoughtful views relating to the role of technology in education.

Mantyla, K. (1999). *Interactive distance learning exercises that really work!* **Alexandria, VA: American Society for Training and Development.**

Explores how best to translate exercises that have worked successfully in face-to-face classrooms into a variety of distance-learning formats with a variety of distance-learning technologies.

National Association for the Accreditation of Teacher Education. (1997). *Technology and the new professional teacher: Preparing for the 21st century classroom.* **Washington, D.C.: Author.**

This report, prepared by NCATE's Task Force on Technology and Teacher Education, was designed to guide the development and implementation of technology in accredited SCDEs and to guide NCATE's use of technology in the accreditation process. It also served notice to NCATE institutions that standards relating to technology were in the offing. Also available at **http://www. ncate.org/pubs/m_pubs.htm#tech_prof_teach.**

Palloff, R. M., & Pratt, K. (1999). *Building learning communities in cyberspace: Effective strategies for the online classroom.* **San Francisco: Jossey-Bass.**

Examines strategies to help create an active, supportive learning environment. The second part of the book, which defines and elaborates on different instructional strategies, is highly useful.

Schlechty, P. C. (1997). *Inventing better schools: An action plan for educational reform.* **San Francisco: Jossey-Bass.**

This book, written by one of the foremost leaders in education reform, describes how modern technology has transformed the way schools conduct their business.

Sikula, J. (Ed.). (1996). *Handbook of research on teacher education* **(2nd ed.). New York: Simon & Schuster.**

Summarizes research on teacher education around forty-eight topics, including "Information Technology and Teacher Education" by Jerry W. Willis and Howard D. Mehlinger. Their chapter summarizes research on technology and teacher education primarily for the decade preceding the 1996 publication date of the handbook.

Technology and learning. (2000). San Francisco: Jossey-Bass.

A reader that has compiled a number of resources discussed and referenced in our chapters. Contains national reports on technology utilization and technology standards for teachers and covers social issues (equity, access, literacy) and learning issues through seminal works in the field. This book brings together in one place a number of important documents for educators who are serious about using technology in teaching, learning, and assessment.

U.S. Congress, Office of Technology Assessment. (1995). *Teacher and technology: Making the connection.* Washington, D.C.: U.S. Government Printing Office.

The most comprehensive report of its time relating to the capability of K–12 teachers to use technology well. Chapter 5, "Technology and the Preparation of New Teachers," pointed to the deficiencies in teacher education programs that affected the ability of new teachers to employ technology effectively.

CDs

Captured Wisdom, by North Central Regional Educational Laboratory   (http://www.ncrel.org/cw/)

Available on both CD-ROM and video (there is also a limited web version). The CD-ROM version is an interactive series of stories of how teachers are using technology to effect change in the classroom. There are video examples, lesson plans, goals, learning issues, and other components, all designed to help users better understand how technology can help shape curriculum and the learning process. Used in the CD-ROM version, it can be another tool for SCDEs to integrate technology while also teaching about technology and curriculum.

Inspiration, by Inspiration Software   (http://www.inspiration. com)

An easy-to-use, visual learning tool that inspires students to develop ideas and organize thinking. Through diagramming or outlining, students can create visual representations of information, such as concept maps, webs, and idea maps. *Inspiration* is a popular and powerful piece of software in the P–12 learning environment. SCDEs can use this software to acquaint students with its utilities and also as a learning tool to understand concepts in higher education. In terms of in-class integration, *Inspiration* can be used as a powerful brainstorming tool.

Learner Profile, by Sunburst Communications   (http://www.sunburst.com)

A technology tool that can be used for assessment and can be modeled by the SCDE faculty member. *Learner Profile* provides electronic tools to assess presentations, performances, and portfolios; collect anecdotal records; and report to parents. *Learner Profile to Go* is an additional tool that allows faculty members to collect assessment information directly onto a PalmPilot, to be downloaded later into the regular software for full reporting. Another good tool to model how technology can enhance teaching, learning, and assessment.

Principal Connections, by Appalachia Regional Educational Laboratory   (http://www.ael.org/pnp/browse/pc2000.htm)

SCDEs that prepare educational administrators will find this CD-ROM and companion web site helpful when training administrators to recognize, evaluate, and promote effective technology use. The self-paced program helps to examine roles of technology leaders, identify barriers to integrating technology into schools, and learn strategies to help teachers become more accepting of technology.

JOURNALS

Journal of Technology and Teacher Education

The official journal of the Society for Information Technology and Teacher Education. Topics include in-service and preservice teacher education, as well as faculty development. Articles cover a broad range of topics on technology in teacher education from all different types of SCDEs. This journal is a good place for information on how other institutions are working with technology.

Learning and Leading with Technology

This journal is published by the International Society for Technology in Education. The articles are designed to help teachers use technology in the classroom. For SCDEs, this journal can be used in the teacher education program to provide curricular exemplars on the use of integrated technology in P–12.

Special Education Technology Practice   (http://www.setp.net)

This journal, published by Knowledge by Design, focuses on assistive and instructional technology that has a practical focus for professionals working in special education and highlights applications of technology that enhance teaching, learning, and performance.

PROFESSIONAL ORGANIZATIONS

Closing the Gap   (http://www.closingthegap.com)

This organization publishes a comprehensive annual directory of assistive technology hardware and software and a bimonthly newsletter, *Closing the Gap: Computer Technology in Special Education and Rehabilitation.* It also hosts one of the nation's premier conferences on assistive technology each year in Minneapolis, Minnesota.

International Society for Technology in Education (ISTE) (http://www.iste.org)

ISTE is a nonprofit organization that works to promote the appropriate and effective use of technology to support learning, teaching, and administraton in K–12 education and teacher education. We have cited this organization and its publications frequently throughout this book. A yearly standard membership in this international organization is around $60, and members receive a discount on all publications, as well as a subscription to either *Learning and Leading with Technology* or *Journal of Research on Computing in Education*. A more inclusive membership is also available that comes with journals and membership in a number of special interest groups. ISTE is one of several organizations that provides leadership to the National Educational Computing Association, which sponsors that annual National Educational Computing Conference each year.

Rehabilitation Engineering and Assistive Technology Society of North America (RESNA)   (http://www.resna.org)

RESNA manages a credentialing program in assistive technology. It also maintains a special interest group for special educators, hosts an annual conference, and publishes *Assistive Technology, RESNA News,* and *RESNA Press.* RESNA members, including individuals with disabilities, researchers, engineers, therapists, and educators, maintain a particular focus on assistive technology research and advocacy efforts.

Society for Information Technology and Teacher Education (SITE) (http://www.aace.org/site/default.htm)

A division of the Association for the Advancement of Computing in Education (AACE), SITE is an international organization of teacher educators and affiliated organizations that work to create and disseminate scholarship regarding the use of information technologies in teacher education. A membership in SITE provides an annual subscription to the *Journal of Technology in Teacher Education* and *Educational Review.* A one-year membership in AACE with the two journals is about $80.

Technology and Media (TAM) Division of the Council for Exceptional Children (CEC)   (http://www.tamcec.org)

Membership in TAM is open to all CEC members who are interested in the use of technology in special education. TAM sponsors an annual special education technology conference and offers several publications, including the *Journal of Special Education Technology, TAM Connector,* and the *TAM/CASE Series on Assistive Technology Policy and Practices.* In addition, TAM is a leader in advocating for federal and state assistive technology legislation.

Index